THE 1969 SEATTLE PILOTS

THE 1969 SEATTLE PILOTS

*Major League Baseball's
One-Year Team*

Kenneth Hogan

McFarland & Company, Inc., Publishers
Jefferson, North Carolina, and London

LIBRARY OF CONGRESS CATALOGUING-IN-PUBLICATION DATA

Hogan, Kenneth B., 1965–
    The 1969 Seattle pilots : major league baseball's one-year team / Kenneth Hogan.
       p.   cm.
    Includes bibliographical references and index.

    ISBN-13: 978-0-7864-2786-4
    softcover : 50# alkaline paper ∞

    1. Seattle Pilots (Baseball team)—History. I. Title.
GV875.S433H64   2007
796.357'6409797772—dc22   2006033190

British Library cataloguing data are available

©2007 Kenneth Hogan. All rights reserved

No part of this book may be reproduced or transmitted in any form or by any means, electronic or mechanical, including photocopying or recording, or by any information storage and retrieval system, without permission in writing from the publisher.

On the cover: *(top)* The 1969 team assembled on the field at Sick's Stadium *(photograph by Bob Stearns); (bottom)* Sick's Stadium after its demolition in 1979 *(Rainier Valley Historical Society)*

Manufactured in the United States of America

McFarland & Company, Inc., Publishers
   Box 611, Jefferson, North Carolina 28640
      www.mcfarlandpub.com

Contents

Preface	1
1. Early Seattle Baseball	3
2. Emil Sick and the PCL	7
3. A New Beginning	14
4. Building a Team	16
5. Getting Ready	22
6. Birth of a Team	27
7. The Season's First Half	32
8. The Season Continues	89
9. The Failure	124
10. The End	132
Appendix A: Pilots Interviews	145
Appendix B: By the Numbers	179
Notes	191
Bibliography	193
Index	195

Preface

On April 8, 1969, there was a buzz around Seattle. This old, yet up-and-coming town had never been considered one of America's big or great cities. No, it was not New York, or Washington, or Boston. It was not on the level of Cleveland, Baltimore, Detroit, or Minneapolis either. Even Los Angeles and Oakland were considered to be superior by those on the West Coast. But things would change today.

Twelve hundred miles away, with a first-inning pitch from the Angels' Jim McGlothlin to Tommy Harper, Seattle would join the big leagues. Any hint of an inferiority complex would be gone: Seattle was major league. Nobody or nothing could take that away, or could they?

Three days later, on April 11, Major League Baseball would finally be played in Seattle. Thousands of fans would meet their team at the airport and then later cheer them on at Sick's Stadium. Enthusiasm was high for this team that none of the locals had ever seen but who they now heartily embraced. What no one could have known was that their beloved team of rejects, retreads, rookies, and the rehabbing would be gone in less than a year, turned into a footnote in baseball history. How could a dream that took so long to materialize come completely crashing down so quickly?

As a boy growing up in America I was like most other young boys of the '60s and '70s. Baseball was never far from my mind. Along with playing it, watching it and talking (arguing) about it, I possessed thousands of baseball cards. Along with the Yankees, the All-Stars, and the "In Action" cards were a multitude more of less importance to me. Among those, however, were a few cards that caught my attention and interest. I knew every team, every stadium, every uniform and variation, or so I thought. Who were these mysterious "Pilots"? What was a Pilot? But there is no team in Seattle. And what were these strange uniforms about? So began my interest in the Pilots, though I was a Brooklyn kid who had never even left New York.

The biggest obstacle in writing about the Pilots is researching them. Although 1969 is not that long ago in relative history there is not a wealth of information out there. They were in a small market, in last place, and were gone in a year. There wasn't much media coverage in that era to begin with. Much of what had been written and photographed is gone. Statistical information can be found on just about anything and so, too, the Pilots. But a story about a team needs more than numbers. A face needs to be put on the team, the reader needs to know what it felt like to be there and why things happened. For that information I went right to the source. Sixteen gentlemen helped me with this project with their recollections, information, and opinions. The fourteen players and two staff members who I spoke to turned reference material and stats into a fascinating story, a journey through a long, tough season until they all were forced to move on.

This book will take you through that season starting from the earliest attempts to bring baseball to the Pacific Northwest to the ultimate achievement of joining the major leagues. You will experience what the players experienced from spring training 1969 to spring training 1970. It will then lead you to all of the attempts to save the franchise to the ultimate move and lingering effects.

Chapter 1
Early Seattle Baseball

The history of the Seattle Pilots does not start in 1969. The seed was planted years prior. No story about the Pilots would be complete without first describing Seattle's rich baseball past. For baseball was not new to Seattle and the Northwest in 1969.

The national pastime was brought west at least as early as the Civil War. Seattle of the late 1800s was a bustling port city filled with laborers, wide-eyed opportunists, tough characters, and transients. Miners, fishermen, prospectors, and shop owners made up Seattle's very first local baseball teams. The city was growing by leaps and bounds but the workers of Seattle needed some form of recreational activity other than saloons and burlesque theaters. As with most early frontier towns the development of baseball was strongly tied to industry. Many of these amateur and semi-professional teams were sponsored by local businesses. These companies employed enough workers to field a team or two. Other teams were organized by churches, trade associations, and social organizations. Matches, as they were originally called, were played primarily on Sundays and an occasional Saturday. There were no laws preventing Sunday play in this rugged outpost town. Actually, there probably weren't many laws at all. Although professional leagues would capture the hearts (and wallets) of local fans, these industry teams would continue to play on into the 20th century before mostly dying out prior to World War II.

Professional baseball came to Seattle on May 24, 1890. Approximately 1,200 spectators watched the Seattles beat the Spokanes 11 to 8.[1] The city was hooked and became part of the professional circuit the following month when their own team joined the National Association of Baseball Clubs. The Reds, as Seattle's first professional team was known, played in the Pacific Northwest League. They were so named due to their scarlet caps and baseball socks. The league consisted of just three other teams, Tacoma, Spokane, and Portland. Seattle did not have to wait long to win its first professional championship: The team captured the crown in 1892 (we're still waiting for the Mariners). Unfortunately, the league quickly became financially unstable and folded after that season. Seattleites would have to settle for their amateurs again until 1898.

Daniel (D.E.) Dugdale was a former Major League ballplayer, manager, and general manager. The portly catcher was passing through Seattle on his way to Alaska where he had a business endeavor, he was looking to strike it rich in the Klondike Gold Rush. He never made it beyond Seattle. Dugdale was taken by the natural beauty of the Puget Sound area and the opportunities that abounded in the city. There was no need to travel to Alaska; he would stake his claim here. Once he had settled, D.E., as he was known, was surprised to learn of the lack of a professional baseball team and the fate of the Pacific Northwest League. The shrewd business side of Dugdale saw an even greater opportunity in doing something that he loved. He set about to establish another professional league for the area. With financial assistance from friends back in Detroit, Dugdale formed the Northwestern League in 1898. The Seattle team would once again compete against teams from across the Northwest. The city of Seattle is named after an Indian chief, Sealth; with this in mind Dugdale named his first team the Braves. After five successful seasons the still-fresh league would face its first major challenge. The Pacific Coast League was expanding and saw a big profit to be made in Seattle, Dugdale's territory. Dugdale and his backers refused to budge as they would not sell their team. Why should they? They had done all the work establishing Seattle as a professional ball town and the PCL was an outlaw league anyway. Because the PCL had refused to join the National Association of Baseball Clubs it was viewed as inferior and illegal by the rest of the official leagues. This did not seem to bother the PCL, who promptly ran the Northwestern League right out of business. For one lone season, 1903, Seattle had two professional baseball teams. Dugdale and his partners tried to convince the local fans that his team was the true Seattle team and better entertainment. This was a tough sell even with local sentiment on his side. The PCL had more money than the NWL and raided their best players. As the season wore on, attendance became more lopsided until it was evident that the city could not support two teams and that the Braves would lose out to the PCL's Siwashes. During the off-season of 1903–04 some visiting teams of the NWL informed Dugdale that they would not be making the trip to Seattle next season due to the lack of fans.[2] (Even back then visiting teams got a portion of the receipts in every town they played in.) This sealed his team's fate and Dugdale sold the Braves to the PCL's Siwashes. Although the Siwashes did not need to purchase the Braves it made sense for them to do it just to elim-

1. Early Seattle Baseball 5

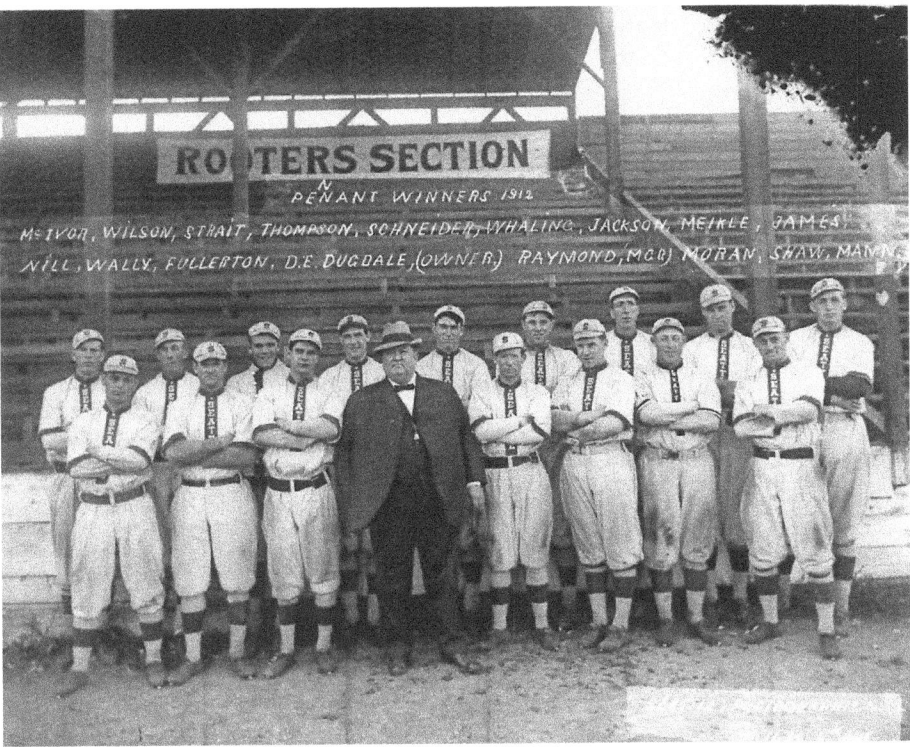

D.E. Dugdale (center) and his 1912 Seattle Giants. The city had many teams in many leagues over the sport's early years, but Dugdale's would be the one that would last (Museum of History & Industry, Seattle).

inate the competition. As for Dugdale himself, he would stay involved in Seattle baseball as a player, manager, official, and owner for the next 30 years. Indeed, he is considered to be the father of Seattle baseball.

Dugdale's success was only mildly better than that of all of the city's early teams. These included the Chinooks, Clam Diggers, Purple Sox, Turks, Giants, Tillikums, and Indians. Obviously, there was a big native–American influence in the region. The leagues too came and went with the Pacific Coast League outlasting the Northwestern League and the Pacific Northwest League. Dugdale remained in Seattle and engaged in other business interests during his brief absence from the game.

Prior to the 1907 season the Siwashes left the PCL to join the new Northwestern League. The owners were savvy enough to bring back Dugdale as the team president. After renaming the team the Giants he set about to build a new ballpark; old, small Athletic Park was no longer up to the challenge. In 1912 he opened 15,000 (some say less) seat Dugdale Park.[3] The wooden structure was Seattle's first double-decked park. During their relatively short time (12 years) in the Northwestern League, Dugdale's team won five pennants. These were Dugdale's most successful years. He had taken an idea and built it into a championship professional baseball team with a brand-new stadium; further, he enjoyed popularity and status among his fellow residents. In 1919 the team switched leagues once more and returned to the Pacific Coast League for the last time. There would be no more switching leagues, at least until 1969. With the new league came another new name, this time the Rainiers. After a few seasons this too was changed to the Indians. In 1924 the Indians captured the PCL pennant for the first time. Things went along nicely for the remainder of the 1920s as Seattle participated in the roaring '20s with the rest of the nation.

In the mid–1930s Seattle's baseball prospects had become pretty bleak. After Dugdale's death in 1934, attendance for the PCL's Indians began to decline. On July 5, 1932, the team's 20-year-old ballpark, Dugdale Park, had burnt to the ground. The team's home games were transferred to Civic Field, which was a general sports field intended for high school events. It was said to have an exceptionally poor playing surface and some visiting teams refused to play here. Some players described it as like playing on concrete.[4] The outfield wall was a wooden rickety structure that looked as if it were about to collapse at any moment.[5] In their final four seasons at Civic Field the Indians lost 119, 102, 93, and 96 games. This drove attendance, and revenues, down even further.

By the end of the 1937 season, players were all owed one month back pay. The State of Washington now sent tax collectors to pay the team a visit, as they were owed as well.[6] Unfortunately they were just a few among many collectors calling in notes. It appeared the end of baseball in Seattle was at hand. (Strangely, this exact story would repeat itself 33 years later.)

Almost out of nowhere a savior appeared in the form of Emil Sick.

Chapter 2
Emil Sick and the PCL

Emil Sick was born in Tacoma, Washington, in 1894 and spent his life in the brewery business, never showing any interest in baseball. Working his way up in the industry under his father, Emil eventually became president of Sick's Rainier Brewery and Sick's Century Brewery in Seattle.

Sick was friends with another lifelong brewer, Col. Jacob Ruppert. Ruppert's second profession was being owner of the New York Yankees. At a brewers' convention in New York City, Ruppert advised Sick to buy the Pacific Coast League's failing Seattle team, that it would be a good investment.[1] There had been several earlier attempts to purchase the team but each prospective team of buyers backed out once they learned of the franchise's mounting debts. Sick was different, though: He had enough money to do this himself, there was no association to fall apart, there were no partners to back out. On December 17, 1937, Sick did indeed purchase the team; at the time he had no idea that it would become one of his most profitable investments.

Sick paid $100,000 for the team, additionally he assumed all of its debts. However, the previous owner, Bill Klepper, did not reveal all of the team's debt to Sick. After buying the franchise he found himself owing $150,000 more when leagues, banks, and other institutions called in their loans. Sick had little choice but to pay as the PCL would not allow the team to operate until its finances had been straightened out and all debts paid.

The new owner realized that in order to be successful he had to put a good product on the field and make fans comfortable. He went to work in earnest, completely revamping the team. First, he hired long-time baseball man Roscoe Torrance to be his general manager. Sick gave the team's new vice president $25,000 to spend on new talent. One impact move that GM Torchy Torrance made right away was hiring the very well respected and successful manager Jack Lelivelt. Lelivelt had been at the helm of the 1934 Los Angeles Angels that had a record of 137–50, a minor-league record. Next, the team's name was changed from the generic Indians to the Rainiers. This was not done to remind fans of the majestic Rainier Mountains as much as it was to remind them of Rainier beer! And finally, and most importantly, construction was begun on a long-overdue new stadium.

Construction on Sick's Stadium began shortly after January 1, 1938, on the site of old Dugdale Park. A contractor from Canada was hired to build the park. This contractor, like Sick, was not a baseball man, and although the ballpark came out fine there were some shortcomings. The plans called for two-thirds of the seating to be covered grandstands, but when completed the stadium had one-half covered seating and one-half uncovered bleachers. This would cut into the team's profits only slightly back then but would come back to haunt the city 30 years later when trying to procure a major-league franchise. The water pressure in the park was never great either; this too would mean little until 1969.

Due to construction the team actually opened the 1938 season in woeful Civic Field, but on June 15 the first game ever was held at Sick's Stadium. Built at the cost of $350,000, Sick's was the finest field in the Pacific Coast League.[2] Indeed, this steel and concrete structure was actually better than some major-league ballparks.[3] It opened to much fanfare and was very well received by the citizens of Seattle. Relaxing in their new park, the fans seemed not to mind the 3–1 loss to rival Portland. Emil Sick had become an instant hero in Seattle and he was given a resounding ovation that day.[4]

From the time the stadium opened in 1938 through 1952 the Seattle Rainiers were the number one minor-league team in attendance in the country. If not actually winning the pennant, Seattle was at least in the race every year. In their first four years at Sick's Stadium the team really got things turned around, winning 100, 101, 112, and 104 games. After just missing taking it all in '38, the Rainiers won three consecutive PCL championships from 1939 to 1941. In that first season Seattle fans were entertained by pitching phenom Fred Hutchinson, who racked up 25 wins and garnered Minor League Player of the Year. Unfortunately, as is the ritual in minor-league towns, their hero was gone right after the season to the Detroit Tigers, where he would have an All-Star career and win 18 games in '47. Seattle was always a top level minor-league team regardless of classification. Therefore, a benefit to the fans was that they got to see a lot of Major League ballplayers either on the way up, or on the way down. A drawback, though, was that a player usually never stayed in town very long. This phenomenon increased as time went on when the team established working relationships with Major League clubs.

In 1940 Washington native and future Hall of Famer Earl Averill finished his playing career in the Rainiers' outfield. He had been released from his

Local hero Fred Hutchinson pitching at Sick's Stadium for the Rainiers in 1938. Note the farm just beyond the left field wall. It was a fixture for many years until replaced by housing (*Seattle Post-Intelligencer* Coll., Museum of History & Industry, Seattle).

contract with the Tigers during the season and finished his Major League career with over 2000 hits and a .318 average. As the war in Europe and the Pacific raged, the PCL games at Sick's continued with mostly replacement players. Spring training for the team was even held in Seattle as unnecessary travel was eliminated. On July 17, 1944, an All-Star charity event, held at Sick's Stadium to help the war effort, was attended by baseball's greatest hitter, Ty Cobb.[5]

In 1948 the Rainiers signed their first formal agreement with a Major League franchise. They aligned themselves with the Detroit Tigers, with whom they had done a good deal of business already. For one lone season, 1951, the Rainiers were managed by Hall of Famer Rogers Hornsby. The great second baseman would be offered another Major League job after the season and moved on to manage the Browns. Finally, in 1952 the color line was broken in Seattle. Art Wilson (Inf) and Bob Boyd (1b) are the first black players to play for the Rainiers.[6] Wilson had actually played 19 games for the New

Emil Sick in 1938. He is credited as the man who saved baseball in Seattle (Museum of History & Industry, Seattle).

York Giants the previous year, his only ML experience. Boyd went up to the White Sox and Orioles, where he hit .318 in '57 and .309 in '58.

In 1957 the team was managed by another colorful baseball character, Lefty O'Doul. Like Hornsby, he stayed just one season before retiring after managing 24 years in the PCL. O'Doul is probably the most noted PCL player/manager in history and one of San Francisco's baseball icons. After beginning his career as a pitcher he injured his arm after just 34 games in the Majors and a 1–1 record. He continued to pitch in the PCL, hoping his arm would get better, but it did not. He was washed up at 26. Lefty, whose love for the game was limitless, then staged the mother of all comebacks. He switched to playing the outfield and made his way back through the PCL to the National League. In 1929 he batted .398 with 254 hits for the Phillies. In 1933 he was a member of the first NL All-Star team. He hung up his spikes after 11 seasons and a .349 average. The following season Seattle fans enjoyed watching future Major League All-Stars Vada Pinson (.343) and Claude Osteen play for their team. Up until 1952 the Pacific Coast League had AAA classification by minor-league standards. It was at this time that the league was given open classification, which meant that it was independent of major league teams. They were no longer minor-league franchises of major-league teams.

The PCL had been thought of for years as the third major league by many fans and players alike. Now it appeared that their real chance for that designation had arrived. There were no major-league teams west of St. Louis and so the push began to make the major-league system three-tiered by adding the West Coast's PCL. Its supporters' hopes were dashed when in 1958 the National League transferred franchises from Brooklyn and New York to Los Angeles and San Francisco, respectively. The PCL even had to relocate two teams out of LA and Frisco in order to make way for the majors. Simultaneously, the PCL's open classification collapsed and they reverted back to AAA status. Their dominance over the west had evaporated overnight and the remaining PCL teams established working relationships with major-league teams.

Although they would have liked to have done otherwise, the Seattle Rainiers began a relationship with the Cincinnati Reds at this time (1958). They had little choice, since there were financial and security benefits to being hooked up with a Major League club. After four years, in 1961, Emil Sick, who saved baseball in Seattle, sold his team to the Boston Red Sox. The Bosox, more than the Reds and Tigers before them, used the club frequently for replacement players and to rehab their own players. Several times when the Rainiers were in a pennant race at the end of the season Boston would call up their 2 or 3 best pitchers for their own pennant chase.[7] Adding to Seattle fans' frustrations was the fact that these pitchers would usually just sit on Boston's bench for a month. The parent team would continue to use the Rainier name for their top farm club, a name that Sick had bestowed on them back in '38. The Seattle community was saddened in 1964 with the passing of Mr. Sick, who had provided them with a fine baseball team and venue for 25 years. For the '64 season Earl Averill Jr. played for the Rainiers after his Major League career had concluded, just as his father did 23 seasons before. Also during the Red Sox's last year of ownership they showcased Wilber Wood and Rico Petrocelli for the local fans.

More changes were now inevitable for the franchise. First, the City of

Seattle purchased Sick's Stadium from Emil Sick's heirs for $1.1 million. After the 1964 season the Red Sox sold the team to the California Angels and the new owners promptly changed the longstanding name Rainiers to the Seattle Angels. This somewhat disenfranchised local fans.[8] The California Angels' four-year run in Seattle, 1965–1968, could not be thought of as successful as attendance continued to drop off. This was not entirely the fault of the Angels, however, as they were working against some forces over which they had no control. Seattle fans had now been long disappointed at not being a major-league city. They thought they were going to become one through the back door when the PCL became the third major league. This was never to happen. Seattle had two other close calls with Major League Baseball. In 1964, Indians owner William Daley was looking to move his team. Although he liked Seattle his problems with Cleveland officials were resolved and he opted to stay put. He did tell his Seattle hosts that Sick's Stadium was unacceptable, especially in light of a flurry of new major-league stadium construction.[9] However, while the Angels resided in Seattle, local fans did continue to see former and future Major Leaguers such as Jay Johnstone, Rick Reichardt, John Olerud Sr., Chuck Cottier, Tom Burgmeier, Hector Torres, Jim Bouton, Steve Hovley and Earl Averill Jr. (son of the Hall of Famer who had just

The 1968 Seattle Angels, the city's last PCL team. In this photograph are future Pilots Gus Gil, Steve Hovley, Jim Bouton, and Curt Rayer (trainer) (PCL Archives).

played eight years in the Majors himself). In 1966 the PCL's Angels won Seattle's last Championship under the guidance of their skipper Bob Lemon.

It was also very frustrating watching two former PCL rivals, Los Angeles and San Francisco, enjoy yearly success on the major-league level. Another factor was television, which most households had by now. Major League Baseball could be watched several times a week, eliminating the need to pay to see minor-league games. Seattle baseball was in a downward spiral. Could anyone pull them out of it?

In 1967, Charlie O. Finley, the colorful and controversial owner of the Kansas City A's, visited Seattle in his cross-country quest to find a new home for his club. His always contentious relationship with Kansas City leaders was at an all-time low and he was looking for any way out of town. This was a golden opportunity for Seattle but again they failed to capitalize on it. Finley was in town for Sea-Fair weekend and was said to have been impressed with Seattle. He saw a lot of promise for the region and thought the majors would do well here. However, he agreed with his fellow owner Daley in his disappointment with Sick's Stadium. Upon leaving the ballpark he was said to remark, "It's aptly named."[10] He shortly transferred his team to Oakland, where they had just built a new stadium. The opinions of both Daley and Finley would wind up being prophetic.

Chapter 3

A New Beginning

In 1938 Emil Sick hired a former PCL player and local boy, Dewey Soriano, to be his general manager. Soriano basically engineered the Rainiers' rise to glory in the 1940s and '50s. As a one-time Rainier himself he was very aware of what Seattle fans wanted and he set out to accomplish just that.

By the mid–1960s there were well over 500,000 residents of Seattle, making it the 18th largest metropolitan area in the country.[1] Additionally, there were 1.5 million people within a few miles' driving distance.[2] The city had already hosted a World's Fair (1962) and beginning in 1966 had a professional sports team when the Supersonics were one of eight new expansion teams in the NBA. They moved into a ready-made court, the Coliseum, which was left over from the World's Fair. So why not professional baseball?

Dewey Soriano, who was now the president of the PCL, formed the Pacific Northwest Sports Inc. with his brothers Milton and Max. Max had served as legal counsel to the Pacific Coast League. Together they made the first coordinated, strong push to obtain a Major League Baseball team for Seattle. Although Dewey was a lifelong baseball man he was a relative unknown to MLB executives and owners. In a shrewd move, the Sorianos hired William Daley to be the team's chairman of the board. Daley, who was 75, had owned the Cleveland Indians from 1955 to 1966. He would be a key factor in helping run the business end of the ballclub. The fact that he was financially wealthy did not hurt either; he would wind up owning 47 percent of the Pilots, compared to the Sorianos' 34 percent.[3]

The American League's annual meeting in 1967 was held in Chicago on October 16–18. There the owners would approve the move of the Kansas City A's to Oakland and discuss the possibility of expansion for the 1971 season. It was contentious from the start. Charlie Finley, the A's owner, was, to say the least, not a well-liked man among his fellow baseball owners. Additionally, when his move to Oakland looked as if it was going to be approved, representatives from Kansas City, who were there to prevent that, became furious. This should not have affected the league's decision except for one fact: One of the members of the Kansas City delegation was Senator Stuart Symington. Symington was not happy that his city was losing its team and threatened lawsuits to hold the move up.[4] The league, in order to make all of the problems go away, tied Finley's move out of Kansas City to the expansion of the AL by 2 teams, to a total of 12. One of the new teams, of course, was granted to Kansas City. The question remaining was where would the second team go?

Seattle's delegation to the 1967 AL meetings consisted of the Soriano brothers, Daley, King County officials, and U.S. senator Warren G. Magnuson. Senator Magnuson was chairman of the Senate Commerce Commission, which held sway over baseball's anti-trust exemption. Basically, the players had no rights, the owners liked it that way, and Magnuson could change this. Was it any surprise, then, when Seattle was awarded the second expansion franchise with Pacific Northwest Sports being the owner? The Sorianos and the rest of delegation were ecstatic. Major League Baseball was on its way to Seattle!

For the moment everybody seemed happy but this was not the reality. Someone with no connection with Seattle would upset the apple cart in such a way as to have far-reaching negative effects in Seattle. Missouri senator Symington was very angry that the two expansion teams would have to wait until the 1971 season to begin play; that was 3½ years away.[5] Kansas City was about to start building a new stadium and he did not want the city to be without a baseball team for three seasons (1968–1970). AL president Joe Cronin pulled the owners back in for an 11th-hour amendment to the agreement. The expansion teams would begin play in 1969 instead. Not only did this satisfy Symington and the Kansas City delegation but it also made the Sorianos, Daley, and the citizens of Seattle happy as well, as they would realize their dream of Major League Baseball that much sooner. Little did they know the seeds of failure had now been planted.

There were also some conditions put on both the owners of the new club and Seattle officials. First, the enlargement of Sick's Stadium from 11,000 seats to 30,000 by opening day. Second, the passage of a $40 million bond issue for a new domed stadium by the voters of Seattle. Third, that the construction of the domed stadium begin by December 31, 1970. The league insisted on a domed stadium due to the region's inclement weather. The owners were made to understand that if construction did not begin by this date or any additional conditions imposed by the league were not accepted the league then had the right to move the team. To the Sorianos and Daley all of these requirements seemed well within reach. It wouldn't take long for things to go wrong.

Chapter 4
Building a Team

Dewey Soriano wasted no time in returning to Seattle and getting down to business. First was the job of convincing voters to pass the stadium referendum. Without that there would be no major-league team in Seattle, as the awarding of a team was contingent on the building of a new stadium. Dewey brought in noted athletes and baseball players to barnstorm the town, convincing voters of the merits of spending to obtain a major-league team. Mickey Mantle, Carl Yastrzemski, Ron Santo, Joe DiMaggio, and Y.A. Tittle spent weeks attending banquets and rallies in the buildup to the February 6, 1968, vote. On election day 62.3 percent of Seattle voters pulled the YES lever for the stadium referendum.[1] The final hurdle had been passed and the city was now assured of the membership in the big leagues.

Upon learning of the successful vote the Sorianos began the process of forming the organization. Dewey Soriano first had to resign his position as the president of the PCL. Next, he and Max hired Marvin Milkes as the team's general manger. Milkes had been a member of the California Angels' front office and had worked his way up from GM of their AAA club, the Seattle Angels. Gabe Paul Jr., a respected, career baseball man, was hired as the traveling secretary. Baseball people who were exposed to the Pilots during their one season generally agreed that Milkes was the weak link in the chain.

The front office had to concentrate on three main areas: (1) Establishing a team identity. This included a name, home and away uniforms, a logo, a saying or jingle, souvenirs, bumper stickers, etc. (2) Obtaining players. (3) Ensuring the expansion of Sick's Stadium. Of course, as with any expansion team, there were many more duties for the front office to attend to. These included establishing relationships with a TV station, a radio network and hotels in every American League city; obtaining suppliers for stadium food, consumables, and souvenirs; printing tickets, selling season tickets, advertising, procuring insurance, and hiring stadium workers.

4. Building a Team

In the summer of 1968, Pacific Northwest Sports, Inc. ran a contest to name the town's new team. The name Pilots was chosen over Green Sox, Kings, Rainiers, and ironically, Mariners. It was felt that the name represented both the area's nautical and aviation industry.

Besides being known for being Major League Baseball's only one-year team in the past 100 years, the Pilots are also remembered for their uniforms, which may have been the most unusual in baseball history. It didn't start out that way though. At first the uniform was very nondescript: white for home and gray for away, with a blue PILOTS spelled out in an arc across the chest. The cap was equally bland, blue with a yellow S. These uniforms are often seen in photos taken during the 1969 spring training. Some baseball cards even carried photos of the Pilots in these uniforms that were never worn during the season, since they were gone by then. Stuart Modrem, an artist for the *Seattle Post-Intelligencer*, created a uniform based on that of an actual pilot, both maritime and aviation.[2] The home uniform stayed white while the away set became light blue. The team's logo was created too—a ship's wheel surrounding a baseball from which gold wings extended—and was affixed to the chest of both uniforms as a pilot's wings would be. But what really made them stand out was the cap (and helmet). In what could only be described as a bizarre design, a gold braid was added under the S and gold leaves, or "scrambled eggs" as they are known in the military, were added directly onto the bill. The only thing that even rivaled this was the California Angels' halo hat that had a white ring stitched around the top of it during the late '60s.

Reactions were mixed and wide-ranging. From bold to gaudy, innovative to embarrassing. Pilots pitcher Jim Bouton, never one to keep his thoughts to himself, said the uniforms "made us look like goddamn clowns."[3] Apparently, there was a good deal of complaining about them in the team locker room and they even took a hit in the local press (and in all of the other American League cities papers when the Pilots were visiting). However, the players interviewed for this book generally seemed to like them. Maybe distance has made the heart grow fonder. Regardless of the opinions the uniforms were here to stay.

The next order of business was actually obtaining players and staff that would form the team, a job that would fall mainly to Milkes. The first player to become a member of the Seattle Pilots organization was minor-league infielder Marv Staehle when Milkes purchased him from the Portland Beavers on April 1, 1968. He would, however, never play for the Pilots, instead remaining in the minors. In accordance with the rules of Major League Baseball an expansion draft is held every time new teams are added. All established Major League teams are allowed to protect a certain number of their players from the draft. The expansion teams alternatively pick unprotected players from the pool for $175,000 each until both teams have 30 players. After that the draft is concluded. Since the NL was also expanding by 2 teams in 1969 (San Diego Padres and Montreal Expos), the Pilots and Royals were limited to picking from AL teams.

The draft was to be held on October 15, 1968. But Milkes and Dewey Soriano, along with director of scouting Ray Swallow, would not sit idle until then. Just after the 1968 World Series between the Tigers and the Cardinals concluded in early October, St. Louis third base coach Joe Schultz was named the Pilots' very first manager. Schultz was a plain-talking baseball lifer who had paid his dues while working toward his first major-league managerial job. He had a 10-year major-league playing career (1939–1948) as a seldom-used catcher and pinch-hitter. Immediately after that he coached for the old St. Louis Browns before moving into managing in the minors. After bouncing around the minors in the '50s and '60s it was back to St. Louis, where he took the third base coaching job for the Cardinals in 1963. Schultz was elated to finally be managing in the majors, but it was with a heavy heart. He had played and coached in St. Louis for years and was just coming off two World Series appearances with the Cards (1967 and 1968).

Joe Schultz, the Pilots' new "pilot," at spring training in 1969. He was elated at finally becoming a big-league manager and was full of optimism for the team and his own baseball future (Photo File).

In the weeks leading up to the draft Milkes purchased several players from other clubs. Most notable was Yankees pitcher Jim Bouton who was a former 20-game winner for their championship teams of the early '60s. He had hurt his arm in 1965 and never fully recovered. Jim was in the minors in 1968 playing for the Seattle Angels under GM Marvin Milkes. He was working on becoming a knuckle-ball pitcher, but the Yankees were not impressed. They sold Bouton to the Pilots for $20,000. Milkes was also able to get the Yanks to pay $8,000 of his $22,000 1969 salary. Also purchased from New York was a decent first baseman/outfielder named Mike Hegan, who was a highly touted minor-leaguer but who had not impressed in several call-ups.

Next it was off to Boston for the day all of Seattle had anxiously been waiting for. October 15, 1968, began with much hope and anticipation for everyone involved; by the end of the day the Pilots would finally have a team. The process actually began the previous day when Dewey Soriano won a coin toss against the Royals' owner, Ewing Kaufman. With AL President Joe Cronin present it was now official, the Pilots would have the first pick.

The Pilots' front office strategy was to draft a team of veteran players that could take the field and immediately compete.[4] Unprotected veterans usually had flaws, injuries, or were on their way out; therefore, it was very unlikely the team would compete for the pennant but third place was not unrealistic. Milkes felt that the fans in Seattle had waited long enough for a major-league team and would not stand for a long building and nurturing process. The Royals, on the other hand, planned to build for the future by picking prospects and younger players.

When the draft started the Pilots chose first baseman Don Mincher from the California Angels with their first pick. Mincher, a ten-year veteran with the Senators, Twins, and Angels, was a member of the 1967 AL All-Star team and the only bona fide homerun hitter available. However, he never hit for a high average and received a severe beaning during the 1968 campaign. Returning to the line-up during the season, he suffered headaches and dizziness, which resulted in the Angels' giving up on him.[5]

For their second pick the Pilots chose former Reds All-Star outfielder Tommy Harper, who was now a member of the Indians. The fleet-footed leadoff man was coming off consecutive sub-par seasons. Their third pick was Tigers shortstop Ray Oyler; taking the sure-handed but light-hitting player would prove to be a dubious decision. White Sox catcher Gerry McNertney and Twins pitcher Buzz Stephens closed out the first round.

The Pilots finished out the draft by choosing both veterans and unproven players. Notable picks included former three-time All-Star pitcher Gary Bell and a versatile starter/reliever from the A's named Diego Segui. Jack Aker and Steve Barber were also pitchers of some note whose careers had tailed off. Aker was a relief specialist and Barber was a former 20-game winner and All-Star for the Orioles. The most polished player chosen was outfielder Tommy Davis. He was a former two-time NL Batting Champion (1962 and '63) for the Dodgers who also could hit for power. A severe ankle injury in 1965 almost ended his career. After rebounding slightly he bounced around with a few teams before winding up in the expansion draft. Davis himself later said that his ankle was never the same and that he came back after one year from the injury which was too soon.[6] Picked at the end of the draft was a minor-league pitcher from the Detroit organization named Mike Marshall. After a cup of coffee with the Tigers in '67 he came late to spring training in '68 due to college. Although he had a fine AAA season at Toledo, going 15–9, he was never able to crack the World Champion Tigers staff. Or intransigent manager Mayo Smith kept him down there as punishment, then irrationally exposed him in the expansion draft. The most notable pick, although they did not realize it back then, was a fiery outfielder with six major-league at-bats. Lou Piniella would eventually become a baseball favorite in Seattle although not with the Pilots and not as a player.

Once the team was in place the Pilot brass returned to Seattle to continue their work and start on a PR program. The coaching staff was chosen at this time too. Schultz was allowed to bring over Ron Plaza to serve as first base coach. This was against Milkes' position of not allowing a manager to choose his own staff and it would be the only pick afforded to Schultz. Milkes next chose Eddie O'Brien to be the bullpen coach. O'Brien, the athletic director at Seattle University, had not been in organized ball in years and had just four years' experience as a player in the '50s. Awarding him the job was more of a favor so he could attain his fifth year of major-league eligibility to qualify for the pension plan. His brother, another former ballplayer, was also an official in the City of Seattle government. This is definitely not a good reason to give someone a coaching job on an expansion team (or any other team for that matter) where there are many young players and essentially no one has played with each other before. The pick of O'Brien would be one of many examples of the shortsightedness of the Pilots hierarchy. The last two coaching positions were given to Sal Maglie (pitching) and Frank Crosetti (3rd base). The New York legends were hired to teach and for their name recognition with the fans. Again, both of these men were at the ends of their very long careers and may not have had the patience or interest to deal with all of the issues of a start-up team.

Meanwhile, back at Sick's Stadium... One of the main requirements to getting, and keeping, a team was the rehabilitation and expansion of their park. Whereas everything else appeared to be going as planned, this project suffered many frustrating setbacks. The Pilots essentially became a team at the end of 1967 during the AL's winter meeting; but work could not begin on Sick's Stadium until after the 1968 PCL season, one year later. The minor-league Seattle Angels had a lease through then. In December of '68 the bids for the work were opened and they all came in much higher than expected. In order to cut down on the price the original goal of 28,500 seats was reduced to 25,000, a decision that was only reluctantly agreed to by the AL. The Seattle government and the team, along with its backers, began to argue over who was responsible for what. Once things got straightened out, work finally began on Sick's Stadium; however, it was already after January 1, 1969. What happened next was just par for the course for the Pilots. The Northwest suffered its worst winter in decades and work on the ballpark virtually stopped. There were also squabbles among contractors and sub-contractors, further delaying the job. While spring training was about to start in Tempe, things were not going well in Seattle.

Chapter 5
Getting Ready

As spring training drew near, Seattle's baseball fans became ever more anxious to finally see their team on the field. But, as most things went for the Pilots, this too would be wrought with obstacles. Marvin Miller, head of the Major League Baseball Players Association, had been trying to renegotiate the pension fund with the owners since the middle of the 1968 season. The owners decided to delay the talks until after the '68 season; when they finally began, months went by with little progress. In early February the players decided to strike if there was no agreement in place by the start of spring training. This had never been done in Major League Baseball before and the owners called the players' bluff. When spring training opening day came, the teams opened camp without their established players, the strike was now official.

The Pilots' spring training complex was located in Tempe, Arizona. Newly built, 6000-seat Pilot Stadium was a beautiful minor-league complex that was located in the shadows of purple, rust, and brown rising hills. It may have been the most striking minor-league facility in baseball.

The manager surveying his young players at the Pilots' spring training facility, Feb. 1969 (AP/Wide World Photos).

Their clubhouse may not have been large but as the players would find out it was far and away better than the one they were headed to. One feature the players liked was a soda fountain machine.[1]

But when their inaugural camp opened, in strolled rookies and minor-leaguers, but no one else. Joe Schultz and his coaches opened camp and ran the young players through their paces. The owners, shocked that a strike was actually upon them, relieved Commissioner William Eckert and replaced him with Bowie Kuhn. On the morning of February 25th it was announced that the strike was over. Although only 10 days of spring training were lost, it hurt the four expansion teams the most. Remember, the manager and coaches did not really know what they had as far as talent was concerned, and could have used that lost time to conduct more evaluations. Furthermore, the players needed time to gel as a team; essentially none of them had ever played with each other before.

The Pilots finally opened their Cactus League season with an easy 19–3 win vs. the Indians, a victory made more impressive by the

Marvin Milkes, the Pilots' general manager, was serving in that capacity for the first time in the major leagues. Considering the Pilots were an expansion team, his choice as GM, along with rookie manager Schultz, may have been an unwise combination (Milwaukee Brewers).

fact that Mincher, Harper, and Davis, the team's three big hitters, had not yet arrived at camp. Greg Goossen was the designated pinch-hitter for the game as part of an experiment that the AL was conducting during the '69 spring training. Not knowing that it was the future, Goossen said at the time, "Are they trying to tell me something about my glove?"[2] After the game Schultz boldly predicted a third-place finish in the AL West for the Pilots in 1969.[3] He may have been wise to keep that thought to himself.

As spring training wore on the team's weaknesses became apparent. The team was winning, and losing, a lot of very high-scoring games. Reporters who were following them felt that many of the players, and most of the pitchers, were of AAA talent and that Schultz's prediction would fall miserably short.[4] Additionally, most of the established players had questionable medical histories and may wilt during the long, hot season. Steve Barber, who was supposed to be the anchor of the staff, was already in the trainer's room using the diathermy machine somewhat regularly. He would need it throughout the season. Bouton was still learning the knuckleball and while he was

Lou Piniella at Tempe, Arizona, in April 1969. His days with the team were numbered and he would never "officially" be a Pilot. It was said that Schultz took a disliking to him (Photo File).

doing fairly well with it he was still inconsistent. After he gave up a tremendous home run one day, outfielder Tommy Davis told him, "I was tracking it pretty good until I lost it in a cloud."[5] There were only four knuckle-ballers in the majors at the time and the Pilots coaching staff was very leery of it.

As it turned out the Pilots finished with a 12–16 record, respectable enough for a first-year team. However, moves were made to cover their shortcomings. Infielder Chico Salmon was traded to the Orioles for a big right-handed pitcher, Gene Brabender, who would be used as both a starter and in relief. The other significant move was made when Milkes traded Lou Piniella to the Royals for outfielder Steve Whitaker and pitcher John Gelnar on the final day of spring training. It was said that Schultz did not care for Piniella and was not impressed with his play.[6] It did not help his cause that he was one of the few young players that refused to report back in February due to the Players Association action. After just two weeks of spring training Piniella and Schultz got into a heated argument when Schultz told sportswriters that Lou would not make the team if his throwing did not improve; Piniella had already told his manager that his arm was tired by the end of last season and he wanted to go a

Lou Piniella's phantom Pilots card (Topps).

Tommy Davis at spring training at Tempe, Arizona, March 1969. The empty stands were a sign of things to come (AP/Wide World Photos).

little slow with it this spring.⁷ Dewey Soriano was out of town when the trade was made but was so angry when he got back he nearly fired Milkes. It was said of Milkes and Schultz that Piniella wasn't their style.⁸ Gelnar would go 3–10 for the Pilots while Whitaker would get less than 30 hits including just 9 extra base-hits. As for Piniella, he won the 1969 AL Rookie of the Year Award, and would follow it up with several All-Star and World Series appearances in a career that lasted until 1983 as a player and then as a Manager of the Year recipient.

Mike Hegan led the camp with a .375 average. He was followed by Ferraro .372, Gosger .358, Davis .349, Rollins .340, and McNertney .325. One long shot to make the team was 42-year-old Bill Henry. Perhaps because of the thin staff, the journeyman reliever, who had pitched in over 500 games since 1952, was the final man named to the bullpen. However, a couple of days later, just before the team broke camp, he walked into Joe Schultz's office and retired. He told his teammates that he thought he was holding a younger man down, preventing him from earning a living. Schultz accepted his decision and told the team he really respected him for doing that.⁹ He was replaced by John Morris.

After the final roster was set the team broke camp and headed for San Diego, where they would play a couple of exhibition games. From there it was on to Anaheim and the Major Leagues.

Chapter 6

Birth of a Team

Dateline: April 8, 1969. "The most significant event in Seattle baseball history takes place tonight at Anaheim Stadium. Seattle begins its first major league season, the climax, for fans in the area, of years of waiting," wrote Lenny Anderson of the *Seattle Post-Intelligencer*. The Pilots' inaugural season began amid an air of excitement, nervousness, and accomplishment.

Reporters swarmed the Pilots just as they did in three other cities, where the Padres, Expos, and Royals were also playing their first-ever games. The scribes looked for quotes, especially from Mincher and Pattin, who had been Angels the previous year and who both left disappointed. Mincher felt he had fully recovered from his beaning and was surprised to have not been protected by his club in the expansion draft.[1] Pattin, a starter by trade, was angry with having been used as a reliever in all but 4 of his 52 appearances in 1968, an opinion he openly voiced repeatedly to manager Bill Rigney.[2] But there would be no negative quotes, just good feelings about the game that was about to begin.

The Pilots' very first line-up was announced to the crowd: Tommy Harper (2B), Mike Hegan (RF), Tommy Davis (LF), Don Mincher (1B), Rich Rollins (3B), Jim Gosger (CF), Gerry McNertney (C), Ray Oyler (SS), Marty Pattin (P).

As Angels pitcher Jim McGlothlin strode to the mound the Pilot dugout was silent with anticipation. How many people back in Seattle were sitting on the edge of their seats or simply standing and pacing? Harper dug in at the plate while McGlothlin looked in and then went into his wind-up. Perhaps it was opening-day jitters but his first pitch sailed over Harper's head. Harper hit the next pitch down the left-field line for a double. Hegan came up next and worked McGlothlin to 3 and 2. He crushed the payoff pitch over the right-centerfield wall for a 2-run homerun and a 2–0 lead. Next, Davis singled and then Mincher was ironically hit by a pitch in his first at-bat as a

Joe Schultz receives a key to the city of Seattle at a downtown ceremony just before the first home game (AP/Wide World Photos).

Pilot. Rollins then grounded out to put runners on second and third, which was followed by Gosger striking out. Gerry McNertney, with two out, blooped a single to left, scoring Davis and Mincher. The weak-hitting Oyler ended the inning with the third out. The infant Pilots were up 4–0 after their first half-inning of play. They already had their first hit, home run, RBI, run scored, and rally. Maybe now would have been a good time to sell the team.

In the bottom of the second the Angels got back one run but Hegan, attempting to make a diving catch in right, hurt himself. The ball hung in his mitt for a second but he ran headlong into the wall, knocking the ball out of his glove. He lay motionless on the warning track but he eventually got up and left the game with a bruised hip and wrist and a cut lip.

Pilot starter Marty Pattin was lifted for Diego Segui in the sixth. After getting into trouble in the bottom of the ninth, Segui left with none out and runners on first and second, giving way to Jack Aker. Aker first faced Jim Fregosi, retiring him on a sacrifice. Next, Jay Johnstone grounded out to second, knocking in one run. The Pilots now led 4–3 with 2 outs in the bottom of the ninth with a man on third and the dangerous Rick Reichardt coming to the plate. Reichardt tapped a slow roller to third as the runner broke for home, and the race was on. Rollins fired to Mincher at first and the Pilots won their inaugural game. The team rushed from the dugout and surrounded Aker, who was credited with the save. When the players came back

6. Birth of a Team

Seattle Pilots opening day at Sick's Stadium, April 11, 1969 (Museum of History & Industry, Seattle).

into the dugout they were greeted by the sight of an excited Joe Schultz jumping up and down yelling, "Hurrah for our team!"[3] The jubilation continued in the clubhouse. Marty Pattin (1–0) was credited with the win for the first-place Pilots. It was a good day for expansion teams as the Royals, Padres, and Expos each won their own first games too. The *Seattle Post-Intelligencer* called the contest a cliff-hanger that had all the drama, excitement, and taut suspense of a seventh game showdown in the World Series.

The following night was overcast with a threat of rain and found Anaheim Stadium enveloped in mist. The game was played with the Pilots losing 7–3 and splitting the series. Brabender (0–1) picked up the loss in relief of Marshall. The team was relieved the season had finally started and that they were headed back to Seattle.

Back in Seattle it was a different story, however. The team arrived back in town on the morning of the 10th and was greeted by both press and fans at the airport. They then joined in a parade to downtown where a crowd of 500, including Senators Magnunson and Jackson, waited for them. Speeches were given by Seattle Mayor Floyd Miller, Milkes, Daley, and both Max and

Dewey Soriano. Finally, everyone returned to the Grand Ballroom of the Olympia Hotel, where the team was feted at a luncheon. Good feelings were running high as tomorrow would be Seattle's home opener at 1:00 PM.

However, over on Rainier Avenue these good feelings were non-existent. As the party went into the night, so did the work at Sick's Stadium. Things were so far behind, in fact, that while the players and fans were going to bed, the ballpark's scoreboard was being installed. Laborers had to work through the night in a vain attempt to complete their work. Dewey Soriano's worst nightmare was coming true; he had wanted all work completed by 11:00 AM, prior to fans arriving at the stadium, which he knew would be early. By the time the sun came up it was obvious they were not going to make it on time. Only 6000 additional seats were in place, bringing the total up to 17,000, a fact that greatly irritated the American League, since they had already capitulated on the seating once.[4]

It turned out to be a gorgeous, sunny day for the Northwest's first Major League Baseball game; but as fans started drifting in they did it to the sound of electricians and carpenters whizzing and banging away. It only got worse as the workers frantically continued their jobs as game-time drew dangerously closer. In fact, the one-o'clock start time came and went without them stopping. Seven hundred fans were kept outside and missed the first three innings; a full hour passed as carpenters finished installing their seats. For now the stadium would have just 17,000 seats and the right-field bleachers would not be installed until May. The new left-field fence had not been completed either, and there were gaping holes in the temporary fence, giving pedestrians a free view of the game. The Sick's fiasco, despite one million dollars in improvements, was an example of how what could go wrong did go wrong for the Pilots, and this was only their temporary ballpark.

Yet despite all of this, good feelings seemed to abound (with the possible exception of those

An extremely rare child's bank that was given out by Peoples National Bank in Seattle in 1969 to customers who opened new accounts. Today a bank in excellent condition can cost $200 to $250. This was one of the few examples of community and business support that would be afforded to the team.

700 fans). Pre-game ceremonies included Commissioner Kuhn, AL President Cronin, former Seattle Rainier baseball greats, and Manager Joe Schultz, who received a floral horseshoe and a crown. All those in attendance watched in amazement as their Pilots, dressed in immaculate white uniforms, ran onto the field to take their positions. Gary Bell, who had been warming up, now walked off the mound as the ball was thrown around the infield. Rollins, at third base, soft-tossed the ball back to Bell, who took the mound and looked in toward McNertney. The White Sox's Luis Aparicio stood firm in the batter's box and glared back out toward Bell, who wound up and threw a strike past him. A standing crowd of 17,850 cheered and pumped their fists; they had been waiting for this moment for years. Aparicio then grounded out weakly to Oyler at SS.

In the bottom of the 1st inning leadoff hitter Tommy Harper singled off White Sox starter Joel Horlen. The speedy Harper quickly stole second to the delight of the crowd. He would eventually come around to score on a Rollins single. The Pilots led 1–0 after one inning. They would go on to score six more runs including a Mincher 2-run home run and Gary Bell's own 2-run double. Bell was equally superb on the mound, giving up nine hits and recording the Pilots' first shutout in the 7–0 win. Despite the shortcomings of the ballpark the Pilots' season thus far was nothing short of a complete success. The fans, players, and management left the stadium feeling great and with nothing but high hopes for the future.

Chapter 7
The Season's First Half

On Saturday, April 12, the afternoon following the home opener, the Pilots again defeated the White Sox. This time it was by the score 5–1 as Segui (1–0), who looked sharp and struck out eight, picked up the win and Aker got his second save. That Saturday night, more than any other night, must have been a great time to be a Pilot fan. After years of trying you finally get your team and they look very strong opening the season with a 3–1 record. You also have your manager and GM guaranteeing a third-place finish for them.

Seattleites would not need to wait until the dog days of August to watch the wheels come off the cart. The Pilots' dog days would start right here in April. After jumping out to a fine start, the team would wind up with a 7–11 record for April. By May 7th, after the first 30 days of the season, the team would be 8–17. Third place would look more like a pipe dream by then.

April 13

The Pilots wrapped up their first home stand by getting bombed 12–7. Chicago's bats woke up, hammering five home runs (five different White Sox hitters) off a string of ineffective Pilot pitchers. Pattin could not repeat the success of the team's inaugural game and took the loss evening out at 1–1. In fact Pattin could only record one out in the game! He gave up back-to-back homeruns to Pete Ward and Bill Melton. Pattin also threw in a single and two walks in his one-third inning of work.

April 14

After a fine spring and having pitched less than 2 innings during the regular season, Milkes demoted Jim Bouton to AAA Vancouver. Promoted

On April 16, the Twins' Rod Carew retires Mincher on the front of a double play (*Seattle Times*).

in his spot was pitcher Bill Edgerton. He had played in a total of 13 innings for the 1966–67 A's. This would be the first of Milkes' many moves, some would say too many. This trade was a prime example of that as Bouton would be back soon and pitch in 57 games for the Pilots versus 4 for Edgerton.

That night the Royals came into Sick's Stadium for a one-game series that was billed as a battle between the expansion teams. The Royals won 2–1, tagging Marshall with the loss (0–1). Marshall actually pitched well enough to win but this would be the first of several losses that he was undeservedly credited with. Mike went all nine innings, giving up just two runs, one earned. There were a total of 12 hits in the game but both teams could push across just three runs total. The 3,611 attendance would indicate the Seattle-area fans did not really buy into this rivalry either.

April 16

Minnesota came to town for a single game today. Although Detroit was still strong as the defending World Champions, and the Athletics were a young and talented team on the verge of a dynasty, the Twins were heavily favored to win the American League pennant. The Pilots would wind up believing it before the season was over. The Twins jumped on Bell quickly for three runs in the first inning but the team got back one run in each of the fourth, fifth, and sixth innings. Bell had put the first three Twins on in the second, it was obvious that he didn't have it today and was lifted for Segui. Jim Gosger hit a solo home run to lead off the eighth and put his team ahead 4–3 (he also broke his own 0–17 slump). Edgerton and Morris both pitched very well in relief, holding the Twins in check. It was a rare good outing for both pitchers whose careers with the Pilots would be short. Jack Aker was brought into the game in the ninth to close out the Twins, but it didn't work that way. With one out Rod Carew doubled, which set up Tony Oliva for a game-tying RBI single. After a visit from Schultz, and a time out so the grounds crew could work on the muddy mound, Harmon Killebrew was intentionally walked. Greg Nettles advanced the runners and with two outs Rich Reese smacked a game-winning, 2-run double. The Pilot bats were silent in the bottom of the ninth and Aker (0–1) got hung with the 6–4 loss. Gosger went 3 for 4 with two doubles and a homer in his best game as a Pilot.

April 19

After playing five games at Sick's Stadium in front of excited local fans, the Pilots took it on the road and flew to Chicago to get a look at the White Sox and historic Comiskey Park. Marty Pattin (2–1) took the mound on Saturday night with temperatures hovering just above freezing. He pitched a fine game, giving up just one run, and picked up the win with the help of a 3-run Tommy Davis home run. Pattin took a 5–0 lead into the bottom of the ninth and retired the first two batters but just could not get the third out. He allowed three straight singles to load the bases. Even a grand slam now would still not tie it for the Chisox, so Schultz allowed Pattin one more batter and a chance for a shutout. He walked Bradford, which forced in a run. Reluctantly, Joe Schultz walked to the mound and got Marty. Segui came in and quickly got Hanson to pop out and got credit for his first save of the year.

On Sunday the team's fortunes turned quickly. The Pilots held even with the Chisox until the tenth inning of the first game of a double-header. Gary Bell righted himself from his previous terrible outing and went 8⅔ innings, giving up two runs. Segui (1–1) finished out the ninth fine but with one out in the tenth he gave up a walk-off home run to Bill Melton (him again). Young Wayne Comer hit his first home run of the year. The Pilots' record fell to 4–5 after this game; the team would never reach .500 again.

The defeat in the previous game may have taken some of the steam out of the team because they lost the second game 13–3. Barber started but could not make it out of the fourth inning, giving up five runs. Switching to the bullpen did not help as the relievers gave up another eight runs in the sixth inning. Josephson, Bradford, and Melton all homered in that frame for Chicago. The Pilots' staff had already given up a staggering ten home runs to the White Sox in this young season.

April 21–23

The Pilots now flew into Kansas City to continue the historic rivalry. The crowds were not good here either as the three-game series averaged below 10,000 per game. The Pilots won the first game but lost the second and third. In the first contest Mike Marshall (1–1) went 8⅔ innings before tiring. He gave up a run before yielding to Aker, who got Juan Rios to ground out for the last out with two men on. Marshall finally got his first win as a Pilot and helped his cause with two base hits. Tommy Harper stole his eighth base in just 11 games.

Maybe there was something to his rivalry after all, since in the second game there was a bench-clearing brawl. Royals catcher Ellie Rodriguez barreled hard into Harper at second base, which resulted in the two of them fighting. Both teams spilled out onto the infield and Oyler wound up fighting the Royals' other catcher, Jim Campanis. After about 20 minutes order was restored and the field was cleared. A quick meeting was held by the four umpires and both Rodriguez and Harper were ejected from the game. Gus Gil came in to replace Harper at second base. The Pilots wound up losing the game too. Segui (7 innings pitched, 6 hits, 2 runs) and Aker (scoreless 8th inning) were victims of no run support as their teammates managed just three hits against Mike Hedlund and Moe Drabowski. Segui dropped to 1–2 in the 2–1 loss.

The final game of the 3-game series was a heartbreaker for the Pilots. Pattin started and threw 2-hit ball through seven innings and opened the bottom of the eighth with a 3–1 lead. After a few hits and walks made it a 3–2 ballgame, Brabender came on with one out. He quickly recorded the last two outs and the game went to the ninth. The Pilots failed to score in the top of the inning and the Royals had one last chance, trailing by one. Brabender got the first out but then gave up a single and was replaced by Bill Edgerton. This experiment did not work as Edgerton gave up a double to the only batter he faced (Bob Taylor), putting men on second and third. Schultz took another walk to the mound and brought in Jack Aker. The experienced Aker walked Rios to load the bases, then Harrison lined a shot to centerfield that was scooped up by Jim Gosger, who fired home. With the tying run already across the plate, the ball just beat Royals pitcher Tom Burgmeier, who was pinch-running, but one-hopped in front of McNertney and bounced off his chest protector. Edgerton (0–1) got hung with the loss and Pattin's gem was wasted. This was just one of many very well-pitched games by the starters that would be blown by the relief corps.

However, as the Pilots' season wore on the roles would actually reverse: The starters would become worn out and much less effective, and additions to the relief staff would make the bullpen considerably better. This would be the general theme of the team, all of the parts never seemed to fire at the same time.

April 25–27

The Pilots' third straight loss came during the first game of a three-game series vs. the young and powerful A's. The team got crushed 14–2, dropping them to 5–9 on the season. Starter Gary Bell (1–1) took the loss after not getting out of the fourth inning. Reggie Jackson contributed two home runs and a single before being, not surprisingly, hit by a pitch in the ninth inning by Bill Edgerton. Although, maybe it wasn't on purpose. In just one inning of work Edgerton gave up six hits, including Green's HR, and allowed six runs to score. Jackson would have the last laugh when he came around to score on Dick Green's 3-run home run.

An angry Milkes promoted pitcher Charlie Bates from Vancouver after the game. Milkes and Schultz wanted to carry an extra pitcher due to the ineffectiveness of the staff so they demoted infielder Mike Ferraro. The only problem was that Ferraro was even angrier and refused to report, he felt he was being unfairly judged after just 4 at-bats.[1] He had batted .372 in spring training and although he was not happy riding the bench in Seattle, he did not want to go back down even more. The former Yankee prospect had batted .351 in spring training in 1968 with the Yankees and was voted the Outstanding Rookie in camp by the sports writers. He made the Yanks only to be sent down to AAA Syracuse after 11 games. He was not going to go through that again and dug his heels in. Milkes blinked and traded him to the Orioles for left-handed pitcher John O'Donoghue. The trade wound up being a blessing for the Pilots as O'Donoghue would pitch in 55 games and post an ERA under 3.00.

In the next game Steve Barber, pitching in what may be his best game of the season, shut down the A's on one hit through eight innings. Barber also had two singles and scored a run. Steve went out for the ninth but opened up the inning by issuing two walks. The next batter, Danny Cater, doubled in one run to ruin the shutout. After Barber walked the next batter to load the bases he was removed in favor of Segui. Segui allowed two more runs to cross the plate but was finally able to get out of the inning. Barber evened his record at 1–1 while Segui came in for a save (2) in the 6–3 victory.

The following night, however, the Pilots couldn't keep the momentum going. Pilot pitchers again got smacked around with their starter Mike Marshall picking up the loss (1–2) in his first bad outing. Sal Bando of the A's hit 2 home runs off Marshall and collected seven RBIs in the 13–5 laugher. Reliever Charlie Bates was equally bad in his very first appearance and was immediately sent back down to Vancouver after the game, never to be seen again. He put six men on and allowed five runs to score in 1⅔ innings. Showing their respect for Reggie Jackson, the Pilots staff pitched him cautiously and walked him four times. The strategy backfired as Jackson came around to score three of those times. Pitchers John Morris and Bill Edgerton were also sent

Steve Barber, a former All-Star and 20-game winner. He was injured for most of his stay in Seattle (Brace Photo).

A full size pennant and two mini-pennants. These were sold at Sick's Stadium and through the team. In nice condition today the full size pennant is worth $40 and the mini $10.

An unusual white variation of the Pilots pennant. This full size pennant was not sold at Sick's Stadium or through the team. It does have the MLB logo and may have been sold or given away by Major League Baseball Promotions. This variation is seen for sale from time to time for $60 to $75.

down after the game, replaced by Jim Bouton and Darrell Brandon. Whether these moves were necessary or not is debatable but they exemplified Milkes' habit of quick (or panic-driven) reactions. Either way, the Pilots were happy to see the A's leave town.

April 28–29

The Angels were next to come in but were rained out for the first game of a two-game series at Sick's Stadium. On the 29th, Marty Pattin, who had been hot so far this season, took the mound on a cool Tuesday night in front of not quite 2000 fans. He would be nothing less than spectacular, giving up no hits through seven innings and just two after nine. The Angels' Lynn Mc-Glothlin was pitching a fine game too; he gave up just six hits, but one was a solo homer to Larry Haney

On April 29th, Ray Oyler tags out Jim Fregosi at second to end Pattin's two-hit gem (*Seattle Times*).

As Oyler runs off the field, Fregosi argues that he was pushed off the bag, to no avail. These photographs also clearly show baseball's two most unusual hats ever (*Seattle Times*).

in the eighth that resulted in a 1–0 Pilot victory. Sadly, Pattin had pitched an 11-strikeout, 2-hit shutout (2 walks) in front of almost no one. The 1,954 paying customers would be the team's poorest attended game of the year. That ridiculous figure was shocking for any Major League Baseball game. This was a very telling problem for the team and should have been a major concern even as only the first month of the season came to a close.

April 30–May 1

The Pilots traveled to Metropolitan Stadium for the first time to play the Twins, who were heavily favored to win the AL West, Brabender started and did well through four, but in the fifth he allowed the

Pattin's gem on April 29 may have been the best-pitched Pilot game (**Topps**).

Sick's Stadium in 1969. In the background is Puget Sound and downtown Seattle. The Space Needle can be seen in the distance at right (C.P. Johnston Postcard Co.).

first four batters to reach and was relieved by Darrel Brandon. When Brandon took the mound he did so with the bases loaded; Carew on third, Oliva on second and Killebrew on first. As he looked in toward McNertney and started his wind-up. Carew broke for home plate. Brandon's throw to home pulled McNertney toward first base and Carew slid past his sweeping tag to complete a triple-steal. Brandon had just relieved Brabender and was making his first appearance as a Pilot. He had not even thrown a pitch when this happened. Brabender, who Milkes got to upgrade the staff, was now 0–2 and not having a good year. Twins starter Tom Hall (2–1) not only pitched a fine game (6 IP, 9K, 2BB, 3 earned runs) but helped his own cause with a single and double and two runs scored.

So April came to a close with the infant Pilots standing at 7–11. All things considered, this was not a disastrous record, although it didn't take too much evaluation to see that pitching was a problem.

In the second game of the two-game set, Gary Bell (1–2) started and got into a few jams. He left the bases loaded for Bouton in the fifth with one out. Jim got the hitter to tap a knuckleball back to the mound, allowing him to fire home to McNertney for the force out. The next hitter (Leo Cardenas) struck out to end the inning. Bouton pitched two more scoreless innings in his first game since being recalled, but it was not good enough as the Twins ended up holding on for a 4–1 victory. It was amazing that Minnesota only scored four times as Seattle's staff allowed them 13 hits and 7 walks in the game. The Pilots' bats were basically silent save for Comer's second home run of the year. The two-game sweep was a sign of things to come as the powerful Twins would repeatedly beat up on the Pilots.

May 2–4

The team flew into Oakland for their first visit to Oakland–Alameda County Stadium. The first game was another seesaw affair with the A's leading 4–0 and then 6–1 until the Pilots tied it at 6–6. The A's went ahead 8–6 in the sixth inning and hoped to hold the lead with Lindblad pitching fine relief. In the seventh Rollins doubled, knocking in Comer to make it a one-run ballgame (8–7 Oakland). Barber had drawn the start but put three men on in the first inning to load the bases without recording an out. Schultz and trainer Curt Rayor went out to the mound and then removed the obviously hurting pitcher, who even had trouble getting loose before the game. Steve was relieved by Darrell Brandon who promptly allowed four Oakland runners to cross the plate, assisted by his own and Oyler's errors. Bouton gave up two homers and Aker relieved him only to give up two more runs. In the top of the ninth Tommy Harper led off with a triple, bringing all of the Pilots to the dugout steps. Mike Hegan struck out, then Wayne Comer grounded out to third, preventing Harper from moving. With two outs Mincher walked and was replaced by a pinch-runner (John Kennedy). The Pilots' last hope was Rich Rollins, who popped out to left, completing the team's failure. Aker (0–2) got credit for the loss. The Pilots went through 6 pitchers and 19 players total in the contest.

In the second game of the series, Mike Marshall (1–3) was staked to a 2-run lead in the first and pitched all eight innings in a good, four-hit performance. But as the rest of the AL was finding out, two runs would not be enough against the emerging Athletics, as the final score was 3–2, despite the fact that the Pilots out-hit the A's 9 to 4. A's starter Chuck Dobson also threw a complete game and despite giving up 9 hits he had 10 timely strikeouts.

On Sunday afternoon the team split a double-header. Pattin was good in the opener, upping his record to 4–1 in a 6–4 win. O'Donoghue came in and pitched the ninth for his first save. Comer (3), Mincher (5), and Harper (1) all homered in their team's 12-hit attack. Rollie Fingers, who had not been converted to a reliever yet, was not sharp and took the loss (2–1).

Any hopes of getting out of Oakland with a split were quickly dashed when Brandon (0–1) got shelled in his first start, lasting just 1⅓ innings. It was also Brandon's last start and he would be gone after just eight games and an 8.40 ERA. Bouton, Aker, and Segui finished out the game. Despite being down 9–0 going into the 7th inning the Pilots did not give up. They scored four in the 7th and three in the 8th but could not overcome the hole that Brandon had put them in, finally losing 11–7.

May 6–7

The Pilots returned to their home turf after a discouraging 1–5 road trip to host Boston, Washington, and New York. None of these teams were considered to be playoff-bound and it was hoped the team could turn things around. Brabender started the first game of the homestand and lasted only four innings while throwing over 100 pitches. Gene allowed seven men to reach base and was relieved by the usually solid tandem of Segui and Aker. Both were equally brutal in allowing another ten base-runners in less than two innings of work. Brandon finished up the game by allowing a home run to O'Brien. It was a sloppily played game in the field, too, with four errors by Seattle: Mincher, Rollins, and Oyler (2). When it was over the Pilots had lost 12–2 with eight of Boston's runs being unearned. Worse, the Pilots used a total of five pitchers in a blowout, something teams try to avoid.

The following day a tiresome scenario played out again in this young season as Gary Bell could not hold a 3–0 lead or a 4–4 tie as Boston won 5–4. Although Bell wasn't bad, and did pitch into the seventh, he got credit for the loss, dropping to 1–3 on the season. The former All-Star was trying hard to turn it around but not finding any answers to his struggles. He was not helped by his team's silent bats that could only muster six singles against Sonny Siebert (2–3).

May 9–11

On Friday, May 9, the lowly Washington Senators, now managed by Ted Williams, came to town for a three-game series. The Senators hadn't had a winning season in over 10 years and the Pilots were hoping to stop a long slide, having just lost 7 of their last 8 games. On Friday Mike Marshall pitched one of Seattle's best games of the season, beating Joe Coleman 2–0 on a 2-hit shutout. Seattle won despite getting just three hits in the game against Coleman (7 innings) and Casey Cox (1 inning). In the bottom of the first, Tommy Harper led off with a single and wasted no time in stealing second. When Rich Rollins came up next and hit a single to center, the speedy Harper scored. It would be all the Pilots would need today as Joe Coleman settled down and pitched a great game the rest of the way. In the bottom of the fourth

7. The Season's First Half

Mike Marshall's season looked bright after his two-hit game on May 9. Although his 1969 season was disappointing, he would win the 1974 Cy Young Award with the Dodgers (Photo File).

Rich Rollins was a sure-handed former All-Star third-baseman, but his grand slam on May 10th was one of his few offensive highlights in 1969 (Photo File).

inning Mincher was hit by a pitch, then Steve Whitaker drove him in with a single for an insurance run. The pace changed the next day.

Both the Pilots' and Senators' bats would come alive on Saturday. Marty Pattin had started and was awful. He gave up five hits and five runs in the first inning and left the game. In the fifth inning Brandon was on the mound for Seattle and had the following

Dave Baldwin would lose to the Pilots on May 11 while still a member of the Senators. Acquired in the '69-'70 off-season, his 1970 Topps card shows him at the Tempe, Arizona, spring training complex. Despite having a Pilots card he never pitched for the team (Topps).

1969 Pilots yearbooks sold for $1 at Sick's Stadium. They cost more than $100 now.

line score: walk, balk, wild pitch, walk, single. Finally, Joe Schultz took that long, slow walk to the mound and replaced Brandon with John O'Donoghue. It was the fifth inning and the Pilots were down 10–3. In the top of the sixth Washington made it 11–3 on an error and a passed ball. At this point none of the 7360 fans could have thought they were watching a Pilot victory! In the bottom of the sixth the Pilots scored 8 times, including a Rich Rollins grand slam and a Mincher 2-run home run, and the score was tied 11–11. The game would seesaw with Washington taking a 13–12 lead until they allowed the Pilots to tack on three more in the bottom of the eighth for a 16–13 home team win. The Pilots had collected 12 hits and 12 walks. By the ninth inning Seattle had run out of pitchers and Gary Bell was summoned from the bullpen in the very unusual role of reliever. He allowed just one walk and recorded his first save. Mike Hegan had his best day as a Pilot, going 3 for 4 with a double, four RBIs, and two walks.

On Sunday afternoon the series wrapped up in no less cliffhanging a fashion. It was Bat Day and the 12,363 fans that showed up represented the highest attendance figure since Opening Day. Brabender started and was still trying to shake the rust off from his abbreviated spring training. He was showing signs of (very) slowly coming around. Today he pitched 4⅔ innings, giving up four hits and four walks. Gene was replaced by Segui, who had an off day and was not much better. The Senators struck first with 2 runs in the opening frame on Frank Howard's 12th home run. In the Pilots' half of the 1st inning Hannon was not sharp and allowed walks to Rollins and Mincher, then singles to Whitaker and Haney, which put the score at 2–2. The score was tied 5–5 going into the bottom of the ninth thanks to Frank Howard's 13th home run of the season. Howard, the Senators' only star and known affectionately as the Capital Punisher, had thrilled the crowd with his mammoth shots. However, with one out in the bottom of the ninth, pitcher Dave Baldwin quickly got two strikes on Mincher. He could not slip the third one by him as Mincher hit a solo, walk-off home run for a 6–5 win. The three-game victory would be the Pilots' only real series sweep of the season. (The Pilots beat the White Sox on Sept. 8th in both ends of a double-header during a quick two-game series.) Segui (3–2) picked up the win, his second in two days. The Pilots sat in their clubhouse after the game eating and drinking, they were elated but unwinding from an exhausting series. The next evening they would be playing the Yankees for the first time.

May 12–14

Pilots fans had a right to be excited again: Their team had just swept a series and the Yankees were coming to town for their initial visit. Granted, these were not the same Yankees that had won 15 pennants between 1947 and 1964. Also, Mickey Mantle, the team's last link to the '50s, had retired at the start of spring training a few months earlier. But they were still the Yankees. In an interesting side note, after hearing of Mantle's decision to retire, both the Pilots' and the Royals' front offices tried to convince Yankee brass to per-

Top: On May 12, at home against the Yankees, Bobby Murcer slides into Oyler hard at second base. *Bottom:* After Oyler is knocked to the ground he shoves Murcer into the dirt as well (both photographs: *Seattle Times*).

suade Mantle to return for 1969. They even unofficially offered to pay part of his salary; they surmised this would be offset by their respective attendance gains. Mantle declined.

On Monday the 12th the first game would have all the excitement as advertised. Bobby Murcer, who would become an All-Star center fielder for the Bronx Bombers, hit a 2-run home run in the top of the first. In the bottom of the first Seattle responded with seven runs of their own. New York starter Al Downing, who had a fine All-Star career, was wild and failed to record an out. He put four men on base, three by walks. Yankee manager Ralph Houk took a walk out to the mound and lifted Downing and called in Mike Kekich. Kekich did not have much time to warm up and it showed. Before he got out of the inning he gave up three more runs on three hits, including an RBI single by Marty Pattin. When Murcer came to bat in the top of the third the Pilots had already jumped out to a 7–3 lead. Marty Pattin threw a pitch directly over Murcer's head, causing Murcer to glare out at him and almost walk out to the mound. Home plate umpire Bill Kunkel gave Pattin a warning for the toss. Murcer then lined his next offering into right field but was called out trying to stretch it into a double. In doing so he knocked Oyler down at second base. Ray got up and jumped on Murcer's back and the melee was on.

Both benches emptied as players began swinging and grabbing around the area of second base. With the fight becoming more violent, police came onto the field, which sent Ralph Houk into a tirade.[2] Eventually order was restored but not for long. When Pattin came to bat in the bottom of the third, Yankee hurler Fred Talbot brushed him back with a pitch near his head, earning himself an ejection. Both managers were now warned by Kunkel.

In the fourth inning the tension reared its ugly head one last time. Yanks second baseman Horace Clarke came to bat with two outs and singled home Tom Tresh and Frank Fernandez, who had been on third and second. McNertney and Fernandez collided as the catcher took a throw from Comer and tagged the Yankee out. Both players wound up on the ground wrestling as the benches emptied yet again. The Pilots held on to an 8–4 victory as Pattin

Top: Oyler jumps on top of Murcer, causing both benches to empty. *Bottom:* Both players continue to struggle as their teammates rush toward them (both photographs: *Seattle Times*).

The game was interrupted for 20 minutes until order was restored (*Seattle Times*).

upped his record to an impressive 5–1. Marty had another fine game, going all nine innings and allowing just three earned runs. A disappointing crowd of 8763 witness the excitement.

The next night (Tuesday 5/13) 19,072 fans turned out to see Washington resident Mel Stottlemyre start for New York, or maybe they were afraid they would miss some of the action. This represented the Pilots' largest home attendance for the season. The Pilots won a 5–3 come-from-

Pilot catcher Gerry McNertney, a good-natured, easy-going player, wound up as one of the combatants during the May Yankee series. In the background of his 1970 Topps card is manager Joe Schultz (Topps).

Ray Oyler is the only Pilot to have his own fan club (National Baseball Hall of Fame Library, Cooperstown, N.Y.).

behind victory, extending their winning streak to five. This would also represent their longest win streak of the season. Gary Bell was actually better than Stottlemyre, who went 6⅓ innings and gave up 6 hits, 4 walks, and 5 runs. Bell, who picked up his second win (2–3), went 8 innings, giving up 6 hits, 4 walks and 3 runs. Segui closed out the 9th inning for his third save. Gerry McNertney hit his first home run of the year and collected three RBIs.

On Wednesday night a nice crowd of 12,273 turned out to see the conclusion of what had thus far been an exciting series. Mike Marshall started for Seattle and, in an all too familiar story, pitched well but lost. After retiring the Yankees in the top of the 1st, the Pilots scored two in their half on Whitaker's first home run and a couple of passed balls. The score stayed 2–0 until the 7th after Marshall, and New York starter Bill Burbach, settled in. In the top of the 7th Marshall tired and allowed consecutive walks and consecutive singles and two passed balls. That allowed the Yankees to take a 3–2 lead. A single by Murcer drove in the first two runs and tied the game. The young Yankee was becoming public enemy #1 in Seattle. Schultz hooked Marshall in favor of O'Donoghue, albeit too late. Marshall up until this

Comer wearing his 1969 preseason, spring training uniform. He showed much promise in '69 but his career tailed off after that (Topps).

point in the season had pitched very well and into the late innings of his games. He was a bull-type pitcher who rarely tired and this may have influenced the manager's bad decision of staying with him too long today.

However, the Pilots still had three innings to get one run to tie the game. This strategy was compromised when the Yankees led off their half of the 8th inning with a triple (Jimmie Hall) and a homer (Tom Tresh) off Jack Aker, putting the score at 5–2. The Pilots failed to score in the bottom of the inning and went to the 9th down three runs. In the last frame Don Mincher led off with a single and was followed by Comer, who also singled. The Seattle crowd was now on its feet and so were the players in the home dugout. A come-from-behind victory would give the young club a six-game winning streak and some invaluable confidence. Light-hitting infielder Gus Gil was due up next and Schultz elected to stay with him and let him bat. Gil responded with a double that drove in both runs, the players rushed out of the dugout to greet Mincher and Comer. All they needed now was one more hit to drive in Gil. Ralph Houk went to his bullpen again and brought in starter Stan Bahnsen. In this unusual role the Yankee hurler struck out McNertney, Rollins, and Gosger for his only save of the year. The crowd, and even some of the players, just stood and stared at the field in disbelief for a few moments.

May 16–18

After the exciting Yankee series the Pilots left town for their first East Coast trip. In Fenway Park on Friday night for their first time in Boston, the Pilots played a four-hour affair in front of a 33,709 sellout. Marty Pattin was not as sharp this time out but was able to match Sonny Siebert for six innings. The score was tied 4–4 going into the 11th inning thanks to Comer's 2-run home run and Pattin's own RBI single. Comer, Harper, and Kennedy all homered and Mincher added an RBI double before the top half of the inning was over. Ten Pilots came to the plate, Gosger led off the inning with a triple and came up again to make the third out. The Pilots had used so many players that Mike Marshall was used to pinch-run in the inning. Going into the bottom of the frame with a 10–4 lead, Aker relieved Bouton for what looked like Bouton's first win of the season. It wasn't that simple. Aker was awful and, after giving up a single, walk and home run (to Rico Petrocelli), had to be bailed out by O'Donoghue. The Red Sox scored 5 but came up short when Yastrzemski struck out to end it. O'Donoghue picked up his second save and Bouton was now 1–0 as Seattle barely held on for a 10–9 victory.

On Saturday Gary Bell started against his old team, whom he had represented at the All-Star game just one year ago. He didn't do too well and it appeared that he was not the same pitcher that he was in '68. After four innings he had given up six runs was relieved by Darrel Brandon. Brandon and Segui threw one-hit ball for four innings but Seattle was never able to get back in the game and lost 6–1 to Mike Nagy (2–0, complete game, 6 hits, 5 K, 1 BB).

The Pilots took the final game of the series on Sunday as Marshall (3–4) had another impressive performance and picked up the win. The team's bats came alive again today and collected 12 hits with Oyler (2), Haney (2), and Marshall (1) hitting round-trippers. In addition to his homer Marshall singled and had an RBI and two runs scored. The Pilots took a comfortable 9–1 lead into the bottom of the ninth, but Schultz made the same mistake he had made recently with Marshall and kept him in too long. Expecting Marshall to constantly throw complete games because the relievers were overworked due to the other starters' not going deep into ballgames was unfair to him. An obviously fatigued Marshall was actually able to record two outs after an inning-opening single.[3] At that point the floodgates opened. Joe Lahoud walked, Reggie Smith singled, Mike Andrews walked and Carl Yastrzemski homered. Just like that, five runs were in. Schultz had no choice at this point but to bring in a reliever. Diego Segui got the call and promptly gave up singles to Tony Conigliaro and Jones. The power-hitting George Scott came to the plate, representing the tying run in what had been a laugher 15 minutes earlier. Segui got Scott to ground out to John Kennedy at third for his fourth save. The Pilots were 7–2 in their last nine games. Attendance for the 3-game series was an impressive 80,006; for many of the young Pilots these were the largest crowds they had ever played in front of.

Jack Aker, a fine major league pitcher, started out great for the Pilots until a few bad games drove his ERA up to 7.54. With Milkes as GM his audition with Seattle was quickly over. He was shipped to New York on May 11 (Photo File).

May 19

At this point in the season the Pilots appeared to be getting their act together. They were actually playing exciting baseball and had their record up to 15–19 (it had been 8–17 as recently as May 7). Maybe they were getting to know each other and finally gelling as a team. That's why it came as a surprise when Milkes pulled the trigger on two trades with the Yankees. Struggling pitcher Jack Aker (0–2, 7.54) was swapped for another pitcher with a high ERA, Fred Talbot (0–0, 5.00). This was one more example of Milkes' impatience with the pitching staff. Aker was a far superior pitcher who had more years left than Talbot. In a less significant deal, outfielder Jose Vidal was swapped for journeyman outfielder Dick Simpson. The one somewhat uncomfortable aspect of these trades was the incident from a week earlier when Talbot threw at Marty Pattin's head. Fortunately, Pattin did not hold a grudge and the Pilots players even playfully fined Talbot upon his arrival to the clubhouse.[4]

May 20–22

The Pilots flew into Washington, D.C., to play at R.F.K. Stadium for the first time. Marty Pattin got the call for Tuesday night's game. After giving up two runs in the first he settled down until a controversial call in the bottom

A trade of little significance was consummated on May 19 when the Pilots sent outfielder Jose Vidal (top) to the Yankees for outfielder Dick Simpson (bottom) (National Baseball Hall of Fame Library, Cooperstown, N.Y.).

A 35-cent scorebook that was sold at Sick's Stadium. Many different versions of Pilots scorebooks exist. Today they sell for $35 to $45.

Merritt Ranew, who was also a member of the 1962 expansion Houston Colt .45s (Photo File).

of the fourth sunk him. In the Pilots' 3rd inning the team was able to take advantage of Washington pitcher Jim Hannan's wildness and draw three walks and a single. With one run already in Ray Oyler came up with the bases loaded and hit a long shot to right field just out of the reach of Stroud. Comer, McNertney, and Kennedy all crossed the plate as Oyler dove into third a second too late and was tagged out by Ken McMullen. But the Pilots had put four on the board. In the bottom of the 4th, Ken McMullen led off with a walk. Next, Bernie Allen smacked Pattin's first pitch down the first base line all the way to the wall and the 335 FT sign. The ball disappeared and the first base umpire (Cal Drummond) signed a home run. This sent Mincher (1B), Harper (2B), and Hegan (RF) into a fit and they all ran toward Drummond yelling. Schultz ran out to continue the argument, and along with Crosetti's help, got the players away from the ump. After a few seconds Schultz, who was unusually animated, took off his eye-glasses and handed them to Drummond.[5] This funny photo appeared in newspapers across the country the next day. It also earned Joe his first ejection of the season. The game continued, tied at 4–4 and Pattin still throwing. The Pilots went ahead in the 8th when they were able to push one run across on back-to-back singles by Comer and Kennedy. Pattin was still pitching in the bottom half of the inning and, in addition to tiring, pitched too carefully to Frank Howard and walked him. Long-ball hitter Mike Epstein stepped to the plate and crushed a ball over the centerfield fence for a 6–5 Senator victory. Pattin went 7+ innings and struck out eight but got hung for the loss (5–2). Once again, Schultz had left a pitcher in one inning too long.

Brabender got the call for Wednesday's game. Big Gene finally had a decent game by not giving up a run for the first 5⅓ innings. He got the win, his first of the season, against three losses. It was not a great game by any means (5 hits, 6 BB, 6K) but it was enough to get Milkes off Schultz's back

Catcher Jim Pagliaroni, with Wayne Comer behind him, practices at Comiskey Park. "Pags" was a player whose career was winding down, while Comer was a rookie (Brace Photo).

about Brabender. With the GM's tendency for trades it's surprising that Gene was still with the team. Although it was already the end of May, Brabender would wind up with the most wins on the staff. In the game Mincher hit his 8th home run and Hegan had an RBI triple. There was also an unusual amount of base running going on. Three Pilots had stolen bases, Davis (2), Harper (19), and Comer (6); while three were caught stealing, Harper, Mincher, and Davis. Segui pitched the 9th inning boosting his save total to five.

Bell started the final game of the series on Thursday and once again did not fare well. However, neither did the Senators' pitchers as the lead switched hands five times. Bell put 11 men on in 4⅔ innings and gave up four runs, including Mike Epstein's 11th home run. The Senators' starter, Pascual, was chased after just 2⅔ innings. Segui (4–2) came on and pitched another three scoreless innings for the win as the Pilots hung on to a slim 7–6 victory courtesy of a Wayne Comer 3-run homer in the 7th. This game highlighted a problem for both franchises, a crowd of only 4242 attended to watch two teams that were playing unexpected .500 ball.

May 23–25

After leaving Washington, the final stop on the team's road trip was Cleveland. Joe Schultz held a team meeting prior to the first game and told the players that they had enough ability on the team to win in the AL and that they should concentrate on fundamentals and in his words, use common sense.[6] Schultz also knew that Dewey Soriano, Max Soriano, Milkes, and

William Daley would be in the stands of Municipal Stadium watching. Mike Marshall started and was not as sharp as his last outing. The Pilots lost 7–1 to a terrible Indians team, dropping Marshall to 3–5. Marshall was simply hittable today and left after three innings in favor of Bouton. On the other side of the field Indians starter Dick Ellsworth (2–1) held Seattle batsmen to just four hits all day and got a complete game victory. Continuing a trend, an anemic 5633 fans attended this Friday night game at 80,000-seat Municipal Stadium (that's 74,367 empty seats!). It was a good thing the Pilots' hierarchy attended, the Indians needed the business. But seriously, this had to be noticeable and disappointing to them. Obviously they were more concerned with home attendance, but a team does collect a portion of the road gate receipts, and the Pilots were drawing poorly in most cities except Boston and New York. But in those cases it had less to do with the Pilots coming to town and more to do with the fact that the Yankees and Red Sox drew large crowds most of the time regardless of who they were playing. The American League should have realized that there was a problem in Washington, Seattle, and Cleveland and moved to do something about it. Two of these teams would not last long and the third (Cleveland) would continue to founder and almost be sold and moved several times over the next 20 years.

Segui's May is one of baseball's best months for a pitcher (Topps).

The following day, however, the Pilots' brass was treated to excellent pitching performances by Barber and Talbot (1–0), who was appearing in his first game for the team and picked up his first win of the season, beating Sudden Sam McDowell 8–2. Barber was doing well but his arm stiffened up on him and he came out after four innings. Talbot pitched scoreless ball for the remaining five innings. The Indians' All-Star starter could not even get out of the 2nd inning and was followed by a string of five relievers. Of the 21 hits in the game 19 were singles.

After splitting the first two games Pattin was sent to the mound on Sunday for the rubber game. Unable to hold the lead after pitching well, he gave way to Segui in the 7th inning. Diego (5–2) held the Indians in check and got credited with the win after a late Pilot rally. The winning run scored on a bases-loaded walk by Tommy Harper in the 8th that made it 3–2. In the game Harper stole three bases, upping his total to a league-leading 25. Gary Bell uncharacteristically closed the game out for his second save of the year.

If the season ended here, there would be no question who the Pilots' MVP was. During the team's last 14 games, starting May 10th, Diego Segui had picked up an amazing 4 wins and 3 saves! This fantastic run would make any pitcher jealous.

May 27–28

The Pilots returned home to Sick's Stadium and a day off after a successful 6–3 road trip. The home stand would not be as easy, however, as the mighty Orioles and World Champion Tigers were due in.

Opening vs. the O's on Tuesday, Gene Brabender (2–3) exacted some revenge on his former team by going the distance and beating them 8–1. Gene felt he had finally straightened himself out and was pitching in a groove, it was his first fine game of the year and it came against a quality team.[7] Helping him out was a 10-hit Seattle attack including home runs by Oyler (3), McNertney (2), and Hegan (3). Oyler's home run went about 305 feet, just clearing the outfield fence. The notoriously light-hitting infielder remarked at the time, "As soon as I hit it, I knew it was out." The Pilots record now stood at 20–21, and were 12–4 over their last 16 games. The players and Schultz were feeling good about their performance; however, it was as close as they would ever get to .500 again. After the game, pitcher Darrell Brandon (0–1) and his 8.40 ERA

By the middle of May, John O'Donoghue had stepped forward to become one of the team's most important pitchers, too (Photo File).

were sent down to Vancouver and replaced by John Gelnar. Milkes also purchased experienced catcher Jim Pagliaroni from the A's. The Pilots now had four catchers: McNertney, Pagliaroni, Ranew, and Haney. Milkes made the move with the knowledge that Haney was going to be called up by the military for two weeks and Schultz felt the team needed more than Ranew as a back-up. Ranew was reportedly very angry when the move was made and considered it to be a slap at him. Interestingly, Pagliaroni had a broken index finger and was immediately put on the disabled list. Milkes was aware of the injury but wanted the veteran catcher anyway.[8]

For the second game of the series 21,700 fans turned out to see Jim Palmer take the mound for the O's. Except he didn't. Palmer noticed stiffness in his back while warming up and could not shake it. Dave McNally was called on to replace him. Only on the Orioles could a pitcher of Palmer's statue be replaced by a pitcher of equal stature. Baltimore and McNally (7–0) easily handled the Pilots, besting them 9–5 and dropping an injured Marshall to 3–6. Marshall gave up homers to three different Orioles. On the Pilots' end Oyler stunned the O's by hitting a home run for the second straight day, giving him four this year. The only other bright spot for Seattle was Jim Bouton throwing one inning, striking out Frank Robinson and Boog Powell, and getting Brooks Robinson to pop up. Schultz also gave Earl Weaver an incorrectly filled out line-up card before the game at home plate. This resulted in Tommy Davis being called out for batting out of order after he had just hit a 2-run double in the 5th inning; the out killed a Pilot rally. The third game of the series was rained out.

On a good note the team would wrap up May with a 13–13 record for the month.

May 30–June 1

The people of Seattle finally got to see the World Champion Tigers when they came to town for a three-game weekend series. On Friday afternoon McNertney, Hegan, and Comer all homered. Comer enjoyed playing against his old team as he was the first Pilot to get four hits in a game. Unfortunately this was not enough as Pattin (5–3) did not pitch well in the 8–5 loss. Pattin was relieved by O'Donoghue in the 5th and John gave way to Segui after the 7th. Pilot pitchers gave up 12 hits and four walks to Detroit. And Gil committed two errors. You could not beat the 1969 Tigers playing this way, no matter how many runs you scored. The attendance of 12,084 was good for the Pilots but should have been much better considering who they were playing. Strangely, the American League had scheduled this as a day game on a Friday. A night game could have brought in another 10,000.

Tommy Harper and the Orioles' Frank Robinson fight for third base at Memorial Stadium in June. The Pilots couldn't draw crowds on the road either, as evidenced by this photograph (©Bettman/CORBIS).

Saturday afternoon's game was the first nationally televised Pilots game. It was shown coast-to-coast except for the Seattle area where it was blacked out. The blame for this could be laid squarely on the shoulders of the Sorianos, who overestimated the value of their games in the local market and wound up without a local TV contract. Prior to the season Milkes had stated that the Pilots would wind up with one of the best broadcast contracts in the country.[9] It must have been extremely frustrating for a Pilot fan in Seattle to know that somebody in Miami was watching his team while he could not.

The game started strangely when Tigers pitcher Joe Sparma could not find the plate in the first inning. Fortunately for him the Pilots refused to cooperate. Tommy Harper led off and walked on four straight pitches. Mike Hegan stepped to the plate and Sparma immediately threw two balls to him. Inexplicably, Harper tried to steal second with the opposing pitcher still having not thrown a strike and he was thrown out. Hegan took the next two pitches for balls and walked to first. Tommy Davis came up and took one ball and on the second pitch swung at a ball up at his shoulders. He tapped it to the third baseman for the second out. On the next pitch Hegan, for some reason, tried to steal third and was thrown out to end the inning. It was not one of the Pilots' proudest moments. Joe Schultz had wanted to stress fundamentals. Joe Sparma got out of the inning without ever throwing a strike: eleven balls!

Sparma wound up not just surviving the first inning but almost throwing a no-hitter. With one out in the bottom of the ninth Mincher hit a towering double to break it up. Up next was Comer, who grounded to Mickey Stanley at short. The usually sure-handed Stanley threw the ball away, allowing Comer to go to second and Mincher to cross the plate. The score now stood at 3–2, but Sparma got Rollins to ground out and Haney to fly out to end the game. Sparma's record went to 3–1 while Gary Bell's dropped to 2–5.

After being 1-hit the previous day, the Pilots roared back on Sunday and beat the Tigers 8–7 in a seesaw game with Segui (6–2) picking up his team leading sixth win. Comer (8), Mincher (9), Harper (4), and Whitaker (2) all homered in Seattle's 12-hit attack. The Pilots were losing 7–6 going to the bottom of the 7th when Comer hit his solo HR to tie it. In the bottom of the 8th Rich Rollins led off with a single and was lifted for a pinch-runner (Dick Simpson). After McNertney made the first out (Simpson to second), Merrit Ranew was due up. Due up after him was the pitcher Segui so the Tigers elected to walk him intentionally with first base open. This curious move became a dubious one. Tommy Davis hit for Segui and flied out to right field. The fact that the Tigers intentionally walked light-hitting Ranew when they knew Davis was available on the bench to hit for Segui is hard to justify. Detroit's manager Mayo Smith got away with that one, but with two out Tommy Harper singled to center, driving in Simpson with the winning run.

June 2–4

The Pilots, who were three games under .500, began a three-game homestand against the lowly Indians. Seattle was still in third place and the hope

Coach Frankie Crosetti at Tiger Stadium in June (photograph courtesy Rainier Valley Historical Society, Seattle, Washington).

was for a sweep. Barber started game 1 and pitched four good innings before getting into trouble in the fifth on walks. He managed to get out of the inning and was relieved by Bouton, who pitched the final four. Barber (2–1) pitched just long enough for the win while Bouton got credit for a long save (1). Hegan went 3 for 3 with two home runs (5 & 6) and Whitaker also got three hits and a stolen base in the 8–2 victory.

In the second game a struggling Tribe starter, Luis Tiant (2–7), put it together for a great game, besting Marty Pattin 3–1. Pattin actually pitched a good game too (7 IP, 5 H, 4 K, 0 BB, 3 R) but lost for the third straight time. Solo homeruns by Duke Sims and Lou Klimchock did him in. Ray Oyler, who suddenly was looking more like Killebrew and Jackson than a sub–.200 infielder, cracked his fifth homer.

The Indians ruined the Pilots' plans when fireballer Sam McDowell beat them in the third game 10–4 taking the series for Cleveland. Sudden Sam pitched a 4-hitter over seven innings and struck out 10. Mike Marshall's woes continued as he lasted just two innings. He was relieved by Talbot, Bouton, and O'Donoghue. The Pilots' pitching corps were ineffective and allowed 14 hits today, including three to McDowell. Marshall had been one of the Pilots' "Diamonds in the Rough" in the spring and had emerged as one of their two best starting pitchers. To watch him now there was obviously something wrong physically.

June 6–7

The Pilots were in the air again as they flew to Baltimore to start a fourteen-day eastern road trip that would also take them to Detroit, New York, Milwaukee, and Chicago. On Friday night (6/6) Gary Bell started against Dave McNally. Bell put ten men on base and never made it out of the fourth inning, the poor outing dropped his record to 2–6. After the game, a 5–1 loss, Schultz and Maglie met with Bell to tell him that he was being dropped from the rotation. If Gary was frustrated at being a Pilot, his frustration would not last long. The following day Milkes dealt him to the White Sox for reliever Bob Locker. This may have been Milkes' best trade as Bell, once a fine Major League pitcher and former 3-time All-Star, was essentially done, while Locker was durable and had a rubber arm. The way Schultz was using the bullpen he would need one. Bell's career would be over in a few months, as he could not turn things around in the Windy City. When he was traded, Mike Hegan said of the popular player, "Gary's the kind of guy who's good for a club even when he's not pitching well."[10] Fred Talbot threw three innings of 1-hit ball in relief of Bell but it was not enough. The Pilots could not solve McNally, who pitched his way to a 4-hit complete game win, extending his perfect record to 8–0. McNally would have shut out Seattle were it not for a 6th inning error and balk that allowed their lone run to score.

The Saturday's trade did not have an immediate effect on the team as they lost 10–0 that afternoon, getting shut out for the first time all season. It was a rude welcome home for Brabender, who started and walked seven and gave up three hits in 3⅔ innings. Gene was followed by the usual parade of relievers: Gelnar, Segui, Bouton, and O'Donoghue. They put a total of 16 Orioles on base, compared to the Pilots' own two hits. Palmer meanwhile was terrific. He went the distance and got credit for the shutout and improved his record to 7–2. The starting pitching staff of the late '60s and early '70s Orioles was one of

Steve Whitaker, in front of Comiskey Park's distinctive scoreboard, was a Washington State native who came out of the Yankee system with much promise (Brace Photo).

the best in Major League history. Right from opening day they were probably just too good for anybody to catch.

On Sunday afternoon the Pilots reluctantly took the field one more time in Baltimore. They would face Mike Cuellar, another 20-game winner and All-Star. The O's were a team that it did not matter who was pitching. Tommy Harper came to the plate to lead off the game in the top of the 1st and popped out. It was at this point that the game took a very unexpected turn. Dick Simpson walked, Tommy Davis singled, Comer reached on an error by Mark Belanger (he didn't make many), Kennedy singled, McNertney singled, and Oyler singled. At this point Earl Weaver had no choice but to pull Cuellar in what was his worst outing of his career. Jim Harden came on in relief and first faced Steve Barber, who greeted him with another single. By now five runs were in without the benefit of an extra base-hit, and 9000 fans were silently amazed. Harden worked his way out of the inning without further damage but Baltimore was never able to overcome this lead.

Because Barber came out of the game after just 4⅓ innings he could not get credit for the victory. The official scorer gave the W to John O'Donoghue (1–0), who went 3⅓ no-hit innings in relief. The Pilots showered and headed to the airport, where they thankfully took a flight out of Baltimore to Detroit, where they had a game the next night.

In addition to having to face the Orioles there were other reasons for not wanting to be in Baltimore. By 1969 the industrial city had become rundown and even dangerous. It was a city that lacked things to do in your off hours and had no very nice hotels by then. During the season the Pilots had to actually switch hotels in Baltimore due to player complaints. Baltimore would go through a renaissance twenty years later, but in 1969 it was one of four cities on the Major League circuit that had suffered heavily from urban blight, the others being Washington, Philadelphia, and Detroit. Making it worse was that the stadiums in these four cities were all in their downtown or inner-city areas. In Washington there were still good hotels and lots of things to do and see after and before games, though. However, Detroit was a hotbed of protests and suffered from recurring riots. At least the Pilots didn't have to go to Philly.

June 9–11

The Pilots would have one of their most exciting games of the year on this night in the Motor City. Hard-luck Marty Pattin took the mound against World Series hero Mickey Lolich. Although Pattin was great it would appear that he would be denied his sixth win in his sixth try. Lolich struck out 16 Pilots and the game was tied 1–1 after nine. Both starters would leave after nine. The Pilots' lone run came off a homerun by Dick Simpson on the first pitch of the game. Seattle would push two runs across in the top of the 10th off reliever Pat Dobson who walked the first two Seattle batters. This was followed by a Mincher single that drove in one run and a Gil sacrifice to drive in the other. Dobson then managed to get out of the inning with the Tigers trailing 3–1. When Mincher had come to the plate he faced a right-hander while a left-hander was warming up in the bullpen. The Tigers did not make the pitching change and paid for it. When Mincher got to first base Tiger Norm Cash said to him, "Crissakes, Mayo Smith has got to be the dumbest manager in baseball."[11]

In the bottom of the 10th the Tigers showed why they were World Champions by scoring one run and loading the bases with one out against Segui, O'Donoghue, and Gelnar. But the rookie Gelnar, who had just seven innings of major-league experience, got out of the jam by striking out the dangerous Willie Horton and inducing Tommy Matchick to ground out to

Gil at second. Miraculously, the win was preserved for Pattin (6–4). Prior to the game Joe Schultz told his club, "Let's go get 'em. We're just as good as they are."[12] An outrageously bold statement, but on this day it proved true.

The following day Earl Wilson and the Bengals easily handled the Pilots, beating them 5–0 and dropping Fred Talbot to 1–1. Talbot did well through five innings, giving up just two unearned runs, but he tired and was relieved by Locker. Detroit tacked on another three runs but they didn't need to. Seattle managed only six singles and no walks.

The final game of the three-game set was another nail-biter. Mike Marshall started and pitched very well and without discomfort. Unfortunately, he drew 30-game winner Denny McLain, who matched him for five innings. Marshall's arm stiffened up on him and he was relieved by John O'Donoghue after the 5th. The game stayed tied 2–2 until it went beyond nine. John Kennedy hit a homer in the top of the tenth to put Seattle ahead 3–2; it was only his second home run of the season but it was well timed. Once again, it was up to the bullpen. O'Donoghue went out for the bottom of the 10th, he was in for his fifth inning of work and was tiring. Schultz and Maglie gambled and lost by staying with the lefty, who immediately gave up two singles. The manager was undeterred and kept O'Donoghue in. He responded by getting the first out, then giving up yet another single to Jim Northrup to tie the score at three. Amazingly, the manager still did not call on the bullpen, but O'Donoghue got Matchick to pop out. With two out now, Schultz took the walk to the mound, albeit too late. Segui came in with men on the corners and two out and the Pilots barely hanging on to a 3–3 tie. Due up was back-up catcher Bill Price, who was playing for All-Star Bill Freehan. It looked like a break for the Pilots until Price reached out and tapped a game-winning single through the hole. Almost 24,000 Tiger fans got what they paid for. After winning the opener, the Pilots lost the series to the Tigers in what can only be described as a poorly managed meeting by both teams.

One thing that baseball isn't, is fair. McLain threw nine innings of 2-run ball and came away with no decision. Dobson (2–4) pitched the 10th inning and almost blew it for Detroit by allowing Kennedy's home run, but he got the win when Detroit scored two in the bottom of the inning.

June 13–15

Members of the Pilots were excited as they got into New York for a three-game weekend series, their first games at Yankee Stadium. Many of the young players had never been to this city before. However, Milkes had his mind on other things as he dealt slumping catcher Larry Haney back to the

A's for sure-handed infielder John Donaldson. This also freed up the catching log jam a little.

It was a hot and muggy weekend in New York with frequent thunderstorms. In the first game, on Friday night, Brabender was impressive, besting All-Star Mel Stottlemyre 2–1 despite there being two rain delays. The complete game, four-hit victory brought Brabender's record up to 3–4. Gene had some incentive. Prior to the game he saw an article in the *New York Post* written by Vic Ziegel that read, "Today Mel Stottlemyre goes after his seventh victory, and Gene Brabender goes after ... whatever the Gene Brabender's of the world go after."[13] He was not happy and wanted someone to point out the writer to him. Anyway, he made the scribe eat his words.

Slick second-baseman John Donaldson was obtained on June 13 to shore up the Pilots' defense (Brace Photo).

On Saturday the Pilots eked out a 5–4 win for John Gelnar's first major-league victory. Marty Pattin started and did well until the 5th when he labored and gave up three hits and two walks. With three runs in, Pattin was relieved by O'Donoghue, who quickly got out of the inning. Winning 3–2, the Yankees tacked on another run in the 6th when O'Donoghue opened up the inning by allowing three consecutive singles. Jim Bouton came into the game with the bases loaded and no outs in his return to Yankee Stadium. He allowed just one unearned run to score and pitched a scoreless 7th inning too, he walked off the mound in both innings to standing ovations. Seattle entered the last inning down 4–2. Wayne Comer opened the frame by singling to left field. After Rich Rollins struck out, McNertney singled and Donaldson walked. With the bases loaded, Gus Gil doubled, driving in two runs to tie the game at 4–4. With first base open and only one out, Ralph Houk had Tommy Harper intentionally walked to load the bases again. Next, former Yankee Mike Hegan tapped a ball to Joe Pepitone at first base, who fired to Yanks catcher Jake Gibbs. Donaldson was forced out at home for the second out and the Yankees were close to getting out of a huge jam. Houk took a

John Gelnar gained his first Major League victory at Yankee Stadium on June 14. The photograph for his 1970 Topps card was taken at the "House That Ruth Built," as were most of the Pilots' cards (Topps).

walk to the mound and brought in recent former Pilot Jack Aker to record the final out. The Yankees were pulling out all the stops to win this game, Aker was their fourth pitcher of the inning. The Yankees' strategy quickly imploded when Aker walked Tommy Davis with the bases loaded, forcing in the fifth Pilot run. Segui pitched a 1–2–3 9th for his sixth save. Gelnar, who pitched a hitless 8th, saw his record go to 1–0; he celebrated the victory in the visitors' clubhouse with his teammates for an hour after the game. It was a tough, hard-fought game that saw a total of 33 players take part in it.

Sunday afternoon, the final game of the series, was Bat Day at Yankee Stadium. The Pilots played in front of 58,733, their largest audience of the year. Unfortunately, after a couple of rain delays Seattle lost 4–0 with former Yank Fred Talbot (1–2) getting tagged for the loss. During both delays, kids ran onto the field and slid around on the wet grass, the first time only a dozen or so, but in the sixth-inning delay about 200 kids poured onto the field. Security was not adequate and it took a long time to get the violators off the field. Additionally, they interfered with the grounds crew in their attempts to cover the infield. When the rain stopped the umpires called the game because of the deteriorated condition of the field. Schultz ran out onto the field and was furious and demanded that the Yankees forfeit the game. The score stood and an appeal to the American League was later similarly denied. Yankee started Stan Bahnsen (3–9) benefited from the abbreviated 5⅓-inning victory.

June 15

The Major League Baseball trading deadline was today. Marvin Milkes wanted to make a major deal by today but could not. Part of his problem may have been the need that he felt to make a "splash" and establish himself as a bona fide big-league GM. In order to shake things up a little he sent veteran Jim Gosger down to Vancouver and called up rookie pitcher Gary Timberlake. Gosger, who had a great spring, was hitting just .113 at the time of his demotion. He said of the move, "You know, I didn't think I was that bad a ballplayer, but they're making a believer out of me."[15]

June 16

The Pilots left New York to play their next road opponent, the Chicago White Sox, but the game wasn't in Chicago. Milwaukee businessman Bud Selig arranged for the Chisox to play a total of 20 of their home games in 1968 and 1969 at County Stadium, the vacated old home of the National League's Milwaukee Braves. Milwaukee had lost their team to Atlanta after the 1966 season and the locals hoped to prove to MLB that they were deserving of an expansion team. The Pilots' lone game at County Stadium came on Monday (6/16) during the first game of a four-game series

Veteran Jim Gosger struggled early in the season and was demoted to Vancouver (along with his .113 batting average) on June 15. However, Jim would have the last laugh over the Pilots when he was later released by the last-place team and finished out the 1969 season with the World Champion Mets. He played in the 1973 World Series with the Mets also (Topps).

(the next three games were played back in Chicago at Comiskey Park). The 13,133 fans that attended the 8–3 White Sox victory had no idea that they were watching their future Brewers. The only notable action in the game was Tommy Harper committing three errors and striking out three times. He probably wished that the team had skipped Milwaukee. Mike Marshall's woes continued as he went just 2⅓ innings and took the loss, dropping him to 3–8 on the year. Once again four relievers had to be used to get through the game. The problem with the starters' being ineffective was not just that the team was being put in holes early in games, but that it was over-taxing the relief corps, making them less effective. Although Sox starter Billy Wynne (1–0) gave up 8 hits and 6 walks he stayed in for all nine innings and gained his first Major League victory.

Kellogg's cereal 3-D baseball cards from 1970 of Harper and Mincher. The cards were inserted into cereal boxes.

June 18–19

After a travel day the Pilots and White Sox returned to Chicago to resume their series. Gene Brabender (3–5) started the first game of a doubleheader and took the loss, being bested by Gary Peters by a score of 7–3. Gene did not pitch poorly but was done in by two homers, Hopkins (solo) and Herrmann (3 run). Peters pitched a complete game and got his fifth win (5–8).

In the second game Gary Timberlake got his first Major League start. He left after 4⅓ innings, having given up six walks, but he also left with a 4–2 lead. Although he did not pitch far into the game both Schultz and Maglie were impressed with some of what they saw. However, he was relieved by an overworked Segui, who promptly allowed the Chisox to go ahead 5–4 on a home

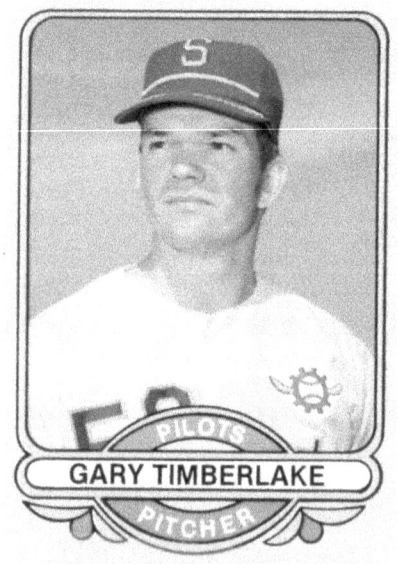

Pitcher Gary Timberlake was one of several Pilots recalled to military duty during the season (Renata Galasso Card Co.).

run by May and two doubles. Opposing the Pilots was their popular former member Gary Bell. It was a bittersweet reunion as Gary was a very well-liked teammate during his time in Seattle, but that's baseball. His pitching woes continued as he gave up four runs in just three innings of work before being relieved. In the top of the ninth with Gus Gil already on third, Tommy Davis hit a sacrifice fly to even up the score at 5–5. The White Sox failed to score in their half of the final frame and once again the Pilots went to extra innings.

In the top of the 11th Tommy Harper walked, then stole his fourth base of the game (35), putting him on second with one out. Steve Whitaker was up next and grounded to third for the second out. Tommy Davis was called on once again and he delivered with a run-scoring double over the centerfielder's head to make it 6–5. The score stood when Bob Locker (3–3) retired the White Sox in the bottom of the 11th for the win. The White Sox, who had gotten a complete game out of their starter in the first game, went through six pitchers in the nightcap. In the game John Kennedy, a usually low-key player, was ejected for arguing a called third strike. After returning to the dugout he kicked over a water cooler and threw its cover onto the field. By the end of the day Milkes looked like a genius. Bell was terrible and Locker pitched very well in both ends of the double-header.

The final game of the series was a typical back-and-forth affair that the Pilots had become accustomed to. Seattle went out ahead right away with four runs in the top of the first. Pattin, who had been pitching very well, gave it back in the bottom of the first, allowing the White Sox five runs and the lead. It was an ugly inning for the Pilots and bad fundamental baseball hurt them. Pattin allowed two walks and Oyler made an error. All three of these runners scored on two home runs, one by May and the other by Bill Melton. The Pilots quickly came back with two runs in the third to take a 6–5 lead. However, in the bottom of the same inning Pattin immediately gave up another two runs, giving the White Sox a 7–6 lead. Bouton came on and allowed another two runs before the 3rd inning was over! The score after three was an ugly 9–6. In the seventh inning the Pilots showed that they would not give up and scored four to go back on top 10–9. McNertney was having a career game keeping the Pilots in it and going 3 for 5 with 5 RBIs and a homer (6). Schultz brought in the slumping Marshall due to the bullpen's being overworked. Mike had another disappointing outing as he too gave two hits to the only two batters he faced and allowed Chicago to retake the lead. He took the loss in a frustrating 13–10 defeat. Marshall's record now stood at 3–9 and he had not won in over a month.

June 20–22

The Kansas City Royals arrived today at Sick's Stadium for a four-game weekend series that the Sorianos hoped would bring the crowds out. A nice total of 18,413 turned out to watch the Friday twi-night double-header. Fred Talbot was on the mark in the first game, beating the visitors 5–3 and evening his record to 2–2; Bob Locker came in for the final three innings and picked up his fifth save. The Pilots earned the win in come-from-behind form. Down 3–1 in the fourth, they kept pecking away with single runs until Ray Oyler hit his career-high sixth home run (one on base) in the 6th inning.

In the nightcap Gelnar (1–1) could not keep it going as the Pilots lost 6–2. Royals starter Wally Bunker handled Seattle batsmen easily again in going the distance and allowing only four hits. The Pilots' only offense was a 2-run shot by Tommy Harper in the 8th inning, his fifth homer of the season.

Fans who returned Saturday night got their money's worth. Gene Brabender pitched what may have been the best game of his career. He took a perfect game into the sixth only to have it, and the no-hitter, lost with two outs when Pat Kelly singled. Royals pitcher Roger Nelson was having himself a fine night also. The lone Pilot run came in the first when Harper singled and went to second on a wild pick-off attempt. In fact Nelson was so rattled by the fleet Harper he threw to first three times prior to the wide toss.[16] With Harper on second Nelson threw a pitch in the dirt to Gus Gil and Harper took third. On the next pitch Gus Gil singled home the only run Seattle would score today, but it would be enough. What looked like a terrible outing for Nelson turned around when the pitcher settled into a groove and did not give up another run. Inning by inning Brabender and Nelson matched each other as the fans intently watched the gem unfold. The Royals just ran out of innings as Gene got credit for the win (4–5), complete game, and 3-hit shut-out. The performance was a blessing for the Pilots' relief corps due to their being used a lot during the previous three days of five games. Royals starter Nelson also went the distance but his 5-hit complete game was good for a loss, dropping his record to 4–6. In fact, both pitchers were so stingy there were no extra-base hits in the game, which was over in 1 hour and 50 minutes.

The Pilots finished out the successful weekend on Sunday with a 5–1 win. Pattin pitched well for seven innings and picked up the win, raising his record to an impressive 7–4. The 26-year-old Pattin looked like an All-Star and possible 15-game winner, an unheard-of feat on an expansion team. No one could have imagined that he had just won his last game of the season. Bob Locker, who was becoming invaluable to the team, gained his sixth save by pitching the final 2⅔ innings.

June 23

The team lost two of its left-handed pitchers today as Steve Barber was placed on the disabled list with arm problems and Gary Timberlake was notified that he was being called up to the Army in a few days. Milkes replaced them with another left-handed pitcher, Gary Roggenburk, who was acquired off the waiver wire from Boston, and young outfielder Steve Hovley. Hovley was a talented college ballplayer who had not endeared himself to management when he told them he would not be reporting to spring training until March 22 due to college. Milkes told him he would never make the team reporting that late and Hovley replied that he did not think he was ready for the Majors anyway.[17] A high batting average at AAA made Milkes forget that conversation. Hovley had another advantage. In 1968 he was a member of the AAA Seattle Angels and was familiar with Sick's Stadium. Roggenburk had pitched some fine games during his five year up-and-down Major League career but had suffered from arm injuries. He was still only 29 and it was hoped he could stay healthy and fill the team's lefty pitching hole. Dick Simpson was also placed on the DL with leg problems.

Steve Hovley at Comiskey Park after being recalled from Vancouver on June 23 (Brace Photo).

June 24–26

After the previous day's game was rained out the Pilots were forced to play a double-header against the Chisox at Sick's Stadium. Twenty-year-old Gary Timberlake started the first game but did not make it out of the second inning. He left with the Pilots behind 4–0 and the bases loaded. It was his second, and final, appearance for Seattle as he left for a six-month mili-

As the injuries mounted, Pilots trainer Curt Rayer became a busy man (Brace Photo).

tary commitment the following day. It was a generous move by Schultz to start the young pitcher knowing that he was definitely not in the team's plans for the remainder of the season. Knuckleballer Bouton came on to relieve and recorded the final out of the inning without allowing another run to score. He retired the next nine hitters and gave the Pilots time to get back into the game. The Pilots had scored one run in the bottom of the first in typical fashion. Tommy Harper led off with a single, stole second, and went to third on a ground-out. He came home when Gerry McNertney singled. If the Pilots had offensive deficiencies, it was not with their lead-off man; he may have been the best in the Majors in 1969 in manufacturing runs. Down 4–1, the team struck in the bottom of the 5th inning to tie the score at 4–4. Donaldson singled, Rollins doubled, Gil singled, and Comer singled before the third out was made. The usually reliable Locker took over in the sixth but could not hold Chicago as they scored two free runs. Ed Herrmann led off and Locker hit him with a pitch. Bill Melton then hit a sharp grounder to Kennedy, who mishandled it; by the time he recovered the ball, Herrmann was standing on third and Melton on second. It looked like the Pilots caught a break when Ron Hanson grounded back to Locker on the mound, but when he rushed a throw to Mincher it sailed over his head, allowing both base runners to score. The score remained at 6–4 and Locker (3–4) got hung with the loss while Wilber Wood (4–2) picked up the win in 3⅓ innings of relief.

The nightcap was equally frustrating. O'Donoghue relieved Talbot with one out in the top of the 5th and held the White Sox to their 4–2 lead.

Schultz let O'Donoghue hit for himself, leading off the bottom of the 5th, and he was easily retired. Comer later followed with a 2-run home run that tied the score at 4–4. The White Sox then went ahead 6–4 but the Pilots came back again and tied it 6–6 when Mincher walked with the bases loaded in the 7th. With two outs in the top of the 9th Segui gave up a homer to Ed Herrmann that allowed the Sox to sweep the double header. Pilot hurlers also gave up a homer to May, making it a total of five Chisox round trippers in the game.

This would be the way many games would go for the team. The coaching staff would be second-guessed a lot over the course of the year and

Johnny McNamara, the Pilots' equipment manager (*Seattle Times*).

this was a perfect example of that. Should they have pinch-hit for O'Donoghue? Would Comer have gotten a 3-run home run instead? Although the real problem in this game was Bill Melton, who hit three homers and a double. Segui (6–3) took the loss while Wilber Wood (5–2) had a good day for himself, picking up another win in relief.

The Pilots were able to right themselves for the final two games of this four-game series. On June 25th John Gelnar got the start and went 6⅔ innings for the win, upping his record to 2–1. The Pilots took advantage of Sox starter Edmondson not being totally warmed up when the game started. Harper did his job again and led off with a walk, this was followed by a Comer walk. Tommy Davis then doubled in the first run. With one out Edmondson threw a wild pitch that allowed Comer to scramble home from third and Davis to go to third base. Gus Gil came up next and hit a fly ball to center that allowed Davis to easily score with the third run of the inning. Seattle would not score again today but they wouldn't have to. Locker redeemed himself, picking up his seventh save and closing out the 3–1 win.

The following day Brabender struck out ten en route to his fifth win,

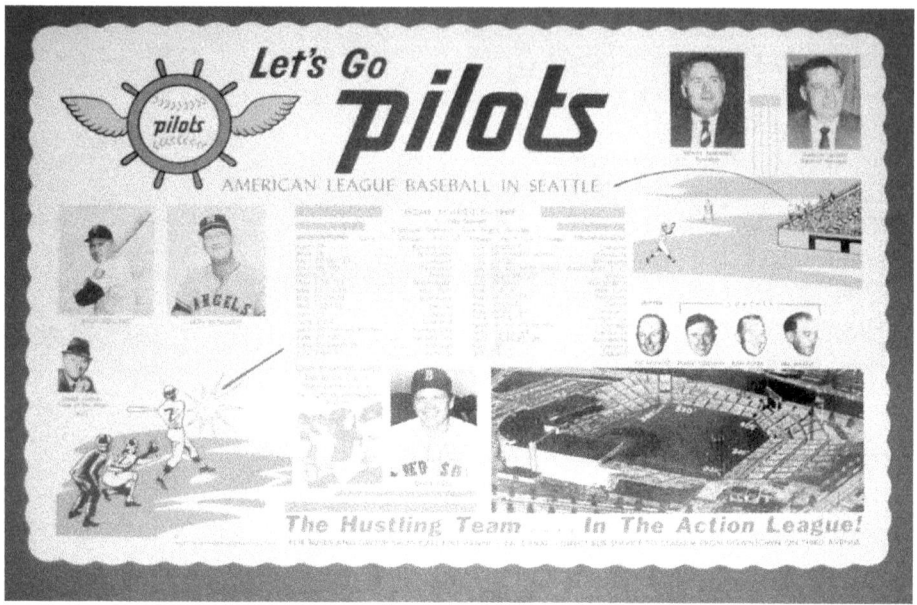

A paper diner place mat from the Seattle area circa 1969. This one is very rare, not folded, torn, or stained. It can cost $50 to $150 today.

straightening out his record to 5–5. Both teams put one run on the board in the 4th inning. The score would stay 1–1 as the game went to the 9th inning. The White Sox came to bat with Brabender still on the mound but tiring. After retiring the first batter Pete Ward walked. Gene barred down and tried to entice Pavletich into a double play; instead he lined a clean single into centerfield. Schultz now had Maglie call down to the bullpen to have a lefty and a righty start warming up. This move came a little too late; it would take a few minutes for them to be ready. Gene had to pitch to the next couple of batters. With Bill Melton up and men on first and second, Brabender pitched a little too carefully and walked him. The bases were loaded with one out now but there was still nobody loosened up enough to come in for relief. Gail Hopkins was sent in to pinch-hit and immediately lined a hit to left field. All of Chicago's runners were on the move as Mike Hegan came up with the ball cleanly and fired a beautiful throw to the plate. The first runner had already scored but McNertney blocked the plate and nailed Luis Aparicio in a collision. As McNertney walked around with trainer Kurt Raynor for a few seconds Schultz looked toward the bullpen where, amazingly, there was still nobody ready. Schultz had Brabender intentionally walk Knoop to load the bases once again. Horlen then grounded out to Oyler at second to end the threat, but the damage had already been done and Chicago led 2–1. Hovley grounded out to open the bottom of the 9th, and Seattle was down to their last two outs of what looked to be another tough loss. Wayne Comer singled to center, but then Gil hit a double-play grounder to second baseman Knoop. Knoop turned and threw to Aparico, who forced Comer and threw to first base. Some of the White Sox started to run off the field but Gil, who was running hard right out of the box, beat the throw by a split second and was called safe. Down to their last chance, Gerry McNertney, who was having the best week of his career, doubled, knocking in Gil to tie the game. The speedy Gil was given a hero's welcome back at the Pilots' dugout. While the White Sox made a pitching change and brought in starter Wilber Wood, Joe Schultz sent in John Kennedy to run for the not-so-fast McNertney. This move by the Pilots' skipper paid off when Tommy Davis greeted Wood with a single to left field on his first pitch that scored Kennedy with the winning run. Now the Pilots, Schultz included, poured onto the field, the jubilant team having turned defeat into victory. No, they were not gloating. But, for an expansion team, these team victories meant a lot. It was a process of now knowing each other and working well together.

Light-hitting shortstop John Kennedy was another one of the Pilots' many infielders. He hit .234 for the Pilots and .225 over a 12-year major league career (**Topps**).

June 27–29

The team flew back to Anaheim for a four-game weekend series vs. the Angels. They opened up on Friday with their fourth double-header in nine days. In the first game Marty Pattin (7–5) started but was not sharp and could only go three innings; he gave up five runs. Bouton and Segui combined for five scoreless innings in relief, but the Pilots' bats were quieted by Eddie Fisher (1–2), who got credit for his first win of the season. Oyler's amazing seventh home run of the season (he would have 15 in his career) was wasted in the 5–3 defeat.

The late game featured Garry Roggenburk (1–1) starting his first game since 1962. He threw six fine innings and picked up his first win since 1966 after beating the Halos 5–2. Bob Locker covered the last three innings and raised his save total to eight. After grounding out in his first Major League at-bat, Steve Hovley collected three consecutive hits including a double and a run scored.

On Saturday Fred Talbot (3–2) pitched his best game of the season, going into the ninth with a 3–0 lead. He had allowed six hits and one walk. Schultz wanted to take no chances and he went to his bullpen and brought in the reliable Segui. After a 1-2-3 9th he picked up his seventh save of the year. Rich Rollins hit his third home run in the game. As much as a surprise Oyler had been with his power, so too had Rollins, but with his lack thereof. The third baseman had been an All-Star with the powerhouse Twins in the early part of the '60s. His numbers and range had steadily declined, which prompted Minnesota to leave him exposed in the 1968 expansion draft. The Pilots took a chance on him, knowing that he would probably not be the premiere player that he had been, but his numbers and average dropped dramatically once he was in Seattle. Rollins would be out of baseball by 1970.

On Sunday the Angels, behind Andy Messersmith's (4–6) strong showing, knocked around John Gelnar (loss, 2–2), Mike Marshall, and Buzz Stephen for an 8–2 Pilot loss. The Halos' Ken Tatum picked up his third save of the year.

With the loss to the Angels on June 29 the Pilots finished the month with a 34–39 record, good enough for third place. Better yet, the Pilots were 14–15 for June and were playing .500 ball since the end of April. All things considered the season was going great for the team. The Royals had a slightly worse record (31–43) and both the Padres and Expos were having terrible seasons. The Pilots' record was a fine one for an expansion team. However, this just emboldened Milkes, who acted unsatisfied and started making more reckless statements and predictions.

July 1–3

The Pilots were back in Oakland to play a three-game series against the A's, who were chasing the Twins and fast becoming a serious powerhouse. The Pilots took the first game on Tuesday 7–1 behind a fine pitching performance by Brabender (6–5) and Mincher's 10th home run. The shutout was spoiled by Reggie Jackson's 30th homerun! In the bottom of the 1st, Bert Camaneris walked to lead off. Curiously, he tried to swipe second and was thrown out with Jackson (the league-leading home run hitter) on deck. Of course Jackson then hit a towering home run. There was already talk of Jackson breaking Maris's record; the same was being said about the Twins' Killebrew. The Pilots were impartial and trying to help both men.

When the Pilots arrived at the ballpark on Wednesday (7/2), they found themselves a mere four games under .500 and in third place. More amazing was the fact that they were just 6½ games behind the first-place Athletics. However, this day the bats of the A's awoke in a big way. The A's won 5–0 while Jackson hit three more homers (33) to pad his incredible lead. Even Oakland pitcher Blue Moon Odom (11–3) cracked a home run en route to his 11th victory. Odom only allowed Seattle's hitters five singles. Pilots starter Marty Pattin, who really only threw three bad pitches today, saw his record drop to 7–6.

Thursday's rubber game was lost by the Pilots 6–4, but there was some excitement around the team. They introduced their #1 draft pick and then let him take pre-game batting practice. The 18-year-old shortstop was named Gorman Thomas. He wound up being too big for shortstop but went on to have a fine All-Star career as an unshaven outfielder with the Brewers. While in Milwaukee he led the American League in home runs twice.

In the game Gary Roggenburk (1–2) started and gave up six runs in 4⅓ innings, the Pilots were never able to overcome the deficit. Rollie Fingers of the A's, who had now been converted to a closer, came on and shut the Pilots down for their final two innings, gaining his seventh save. Oakland, like Seattle, had lobbied the AL for years for their own team. In only their second year in Oakland the A's were probably the most exciting team in baseball. They certainly had the brightest future of all Major League teams. It was very disappointing, then, that in the first days of July the team drew an average of barely 6000 fans for this three-game series.

July 4–6

The Pilots arrived in Kansas City Thursday evening to get ready to play a weekend holiday series. Their expansion rivals had been struggling at home of late. It was a tough series; the Pilots lost a double-header on Friday, the Fourth of July, and then split the final two games to go 1–3 for the weekend. On Friday it was 95 degrees with high humidity as the teams took the field in the afternoon.[18] Talbot (3–3) started the day game and was hit hard, he allowed eight hits in 6 2/3 innings and left with the score 6–2. If Talbot was bad, Bouton was horrible: In 1⅓ innings he let in another six runs for a final shellacking of 13–2 (O'Donoghue allowed one run). Bouton gave up a grand slam to Gene Oliver.

Gelnar (2–3) pitched well in the nightcap but came out on the short end of a 3–2 loss. The Pilots were actually being shut out 3–0 when they mounted a comeback in the eighth. Hovley led the inning off and hit his first Major League home run. This was followed by singles by Comer, Hegan, and Gil, and a walk by Harper to load the bases. The rally fizzled after that, though, resulting in another frustrating loss.

On Saturday Schultz gave struggling Marshall a start after having relegated him to the bullpen for several weeks. This might have been Marshall's last chance to show management he was turning things around. At first it looked like there might not even be a game due to rain storms, but after a 1:15 delay the game got underway. It could not have gone worse for the pitcher as he gave up 10 hits in three innings and did not strike anybody out. He got hung with the 6–4 loss, dropping his record to an ugly 3–10. It was the Pilots' fifth straight loss and Marshall's final appearance in a Pilot uniform.

Although Brabender (7–5) looked good and picked up the win on Sunday, the most important news related to Hegan. He pulled his hamstring in the series opener and re-injured it in today's game. He had become a very important part of a team that was dealing with injuries to Marshall, Oyler, Kennedy, Simpson, Rollins, and Barber. The Pilots were hitting .234 and were looking at the loss of a .300 hitter.

It all happened very quickly for the Pilots. In the bottom of the 1st inning Harper popped out and then Hegan reached on an error. Wayne Comer walked, pushing Hegan to second. Next, Tommy Davis stepped to the plate and doubled to right. On his way around third, Hegan did something to his leg but scored the first run of the game, and Comer scored right behind him. When the Pilots took the field in the bottom of the inning it was with a 2–0 lead. Royals first baseman Fiore drove a ball to the centerfield fence for a double. On the play Tommy Harper ran into the wall and cut his face above his right eye. Hovley replaced Harper, who had to be removed from the game and taken to a hospital, where he received five stitches. During the break in play Hegan's leg tightened up on him and he also left the game and was replaced by Mincher, who was being given a day off (a short one). As these things often go, Mincher went 3 for 4 with two home runs, a double, and four RBIs while Hovley also went 3 for 4 with a double and an RBI. When the dust finally settled the Pilots had themselves a 9–3 win. Segui relieved Brabender and finished out the game for his eighth save, but fortunately the rest of the bullpen was rested. A crowd of 26,480 went home disappointed.

July 7–9

On Monday evening the Pilots were home for a quick four-game home stand hosting the Angels, who were in last place in the AL West. After this series Seattle would be playing 11 games against the A's and Twins, so it was hoped that they could pick up at least three wins here.

Marty Pattin, who had shown signs of breaking out of his funk, was given the assignment of starting the first game. The Pilots scored one in the first inning but were shut down the rest of the way and wound up losing 5–1. Pattin's record now evened at 7–7; it was his third straight loss. This was another game that he did not deserve to lose: Pattin went seven innings and struck out seven while giving up six hits and three runs. Unfortunately, the Pilots once again could not figure out Andy Messersmith (6–6), who pitched a complete game 4-hitter. Steve Hovley accounted for two of the Pilots' four hits.

The next day it was the Angels who would jump out to a 1–0 lead in the first, compliments of a Jay Johnstone (5) home run. Local fans were familiar with the free-spirited Johnstone from his days with the PCL's Seattle Angels. Their lead was short-lived, though, as Don Mincher (14) hit a three-run homer in the bottom of the opening frame, putting Seattle up 3–1. And that was it; no more runs were scored that day. Garry Roggenburk (2–2) pitched a gem, going all the way for a complete game 5-hitter; he would finish his Major League career in 1969 with just six victories, but this one was his best. Once again it came just in time for the overworked bullpen.

On Wednesday the teams were set to play a double-header with pitcher Fred Talbot getting the start in the first game. Now it was Talbot's turn to shine in what was easily the finest game of his Major League career. He tossed a 3-hit shutout and smacked a sixth-inning grand slam in the 8–0 win. Talbot also had a single for good measure to go with his four RBIs and two runs scored. Interestingly, the Pilots ran a contest all season called Home Run for the Money. The name of a fan is drawn from entries and he is assigned a particular hitter for that game. If the hitter hits a home run the fan wins money; if it is a grand slam the prize money is significantly more. Additionally, the home run must come in a specific inning determined just prior to the game. When today's fan was assigned the pitcher's spot in the batting order he probably didn't even bother to pay attention. The chance that Fred Talbot would even come up with the bases loaded in the sixth inning was miniscule. The chance of him then hitting a grand slam was astronomical. But with knuckleball pitcher Eddie Fisher's help, Talbot accomplished the unbelievable. A Pilot fan from Oregon won $27,000.[19] How do you think Marvin Milkes and the Sorianos felt watching that ball sail over the Sick's Stadium fence? The Pilots won big with Tommy Harper stealing his 44th base but pulling a leg muscle in the process. Donaldson went 3 for 4 with an RBI and run. Milkes went into motion after the game and brought up infielder Ron Clark. He made room for him by sending down badly struggling Mike Marshall (3–10) and recalled rookie Dick Baney to fill an empty roster spot. By all

accounts Marshall was actually glad to be gone, even for the minors.[20] He was never on board with Pilot management's philosophy.

That evening, the Pilots were shut out by the Angels and veteran pitcher George Brunet (5–6). Brunet had been around since the mid–1950s and held several minor-league career pitching records. He looked tough in allowing Seattle seven hits and no runs over nine innings, was Milkes watching? Gelnar (2–4) was done in in the top of the 1st inning when he allowed three runs to score on three singles, a walk, and an error. He pitched well after that but still received a loss.

July 11–13

The Pilots flew into Minneapolis for their second trip to Metropolitan Stadium, where they were swept at the end of April. Hoping to quickly end their problems in the Twin Cities, Schultz gave Brabender the start in the Friday night opener. Gene was a hard-

Top: In one of the Pilots' best moves, Bob Locker was obtained from the Chisox on July 8. He would finish the year with a 3.14 ERA. *Bottom:* Later that night, Gene Brabender would lose 10–0 in his homecoming versus Baltimore (both photographs: Photo File).

Top: On July 8, Gordy Lund is thrown out at third when tagged by the Angels' Aurelio Rodriquez. *Bottom:* On July 9, pitcher Fred Talbot is congratulated at home by Lund, Donaldson, and McNertney after hitting a grand slam (both photographs: *Seattle Times*).

When Harper went down on July 9 with leg problems, Milkes recalled infielder Ron Clark. Clark, an interesting character who knocked around the Majors for 10 years, was actually a cowboy (Renata Galasso Card Co.).

throwing fast-baller who could throw it by free-swinging big hitters most of the time. He would need to, as most of the Twins lineup was capable of hitting the long ball. Brabender had just won four in a row, bolstering the Pilots' hopes in him. However, on this night Gene would give up seven runs in 4⅔ innings, including two home runs and a hit batsman. O'Donoghue relieved Brabender and finished the 7th, having pitched well, but down 7–3 with just two innings to go against the Twins, the game looked out of reach. This was a good opportunity to get Dick Baney some Major League experience. All Major Leaguers remember their first game but Harmon Killebrew made sure Baney wouldn't forget it. On his second Major League pitch the future Hall of Famer creamed the ball 407 feet. Rattled, Baney next gave up a triple to Rich Reese and then a single to Johnny Roseboro that drove home Reese. Baney was lucky to get out of the inning with having given up just two runs. The score held there at 9–3. Killebrew hit two home runs in the game, upping his amazing RBI total to 90. Killer also had a double and four RBIs and three runs scored. Killebrew, Jackson, Melton, and every other home run hitter in the American League were very thankful for the 1969 expansion. Brabender picked up the loss, dropping to 7–6.

On Saturday the Pilots' fortunes did not improve. Marty Pattin started and pitched poorly, picking up his fourth straight loss (7–8). He put 10 men on base and allowed six to score in four innings of work. O'Donoghue and Bouton relieved and did equally as poorly. The final was an embarrassing 11–1 loss with the Twins out-hitting the Pilots 14 to 5.

On Sunday the 13th the teams met to play what was the Pilots' ninth double-header of the season already. Garry Roggenburk was given the start in the first game and he did not have a good outing. He couldn't stop the team's slide when he gave up nine hits including homers by Frank Quilici (1) and Cesar Tovar (2), two of the Twins that were actually not power-hitters. All-Star Jim Kaat (9–6) started for Minnesota and went the distance, pick-

A very rare Pilots coaster and stirrer set that was sold at Sick's Stadium and through the yearbook. If you want one today with all eight pieces and the original box, it will cost you $80 to $110.

ing up win in the 5–2 victory. He helped his own cause with a double and a single. The only damage done by Seattle was a home run by McNertney (7) in the 9th inning with two outs.

The nightcap was a game that could only be described as a total disaster and disheartening. Fred Talbot was strong once again, pitching a three-hit shutout going into the bottom of the eighth with a 4–0 lead. He got Cesar Tovar to ground out to open the inning, and it looked like the Pilots' losing streak would end today. Tony Oliva was the next batter and he singled, chasing a tired Talbot, who was relieved by Locker. Locker's first pitch was driven into left-field for a single by Killebrew. Chuck Manuel then doubled in two runs but Locker managed to get out of the inning with the 4–2 lead preserved. In the bottom of the ninth Schultz stayed with Locker to finish off the Twins. The Twins, however, had different ideas and quickly pounded the reliever. Leo Cardenas led off with a double, then the Twins' pitcher, Ron Perranoski, was called back into the dugout for a pinch hitter. Rod Carew did not start the game due to a military call-up; he was not even in the stadium until the late innings. He came in now as the pinch hitter and clubbed a single to drive in a run and make it a 4–3 ballgame. O'Donoghue relieved

Locker but only pitched to one batter and got Ted Uhlaender out on a sacrifice that moved Carew to second. Segui now replaced O'Donoghue and faced Cesar Tovar with one out. Tovar hit what looked like an easy grounder to shortstop but it was misplayed by Gordy Lund for an error. Actually, Lund came up with the ball but instead of getting the sure out at first he went to third and hit Carew in the back with the ball. With men on the corners, Tony Oliva singled, driving in Carew to tie the game at 4–4. Up next was Killebrew, who by now should have been known as the Pilot Killer. It was an easy decision to intentionally walk him to load the bases with still only one out. The Pilots got what looked like a huge break when Reese hit a sharp liner right at the shortstop Lund for the second out. The runners were unable to move up. Segui needed only to get one out to send the game into extra innings. Every member of the Pilots not on the field was standing on the top step of their dugout. They got to watch Chuck Manual crack a game-winning single to right field and Cesar Tovar just walk home with the Twins' fifth run. The Twins had a 5–4 victory while Segui (6–4) took the very tough loss. It was one of those games that tests a team; less than 20 minutes earlier the Pilots had a four-run lead and were shutting out the Twins. The Pilots were now walking off the field 0–6 at Metropolitan Stadium and 0–7 against Minnesota. The players could not wait to get back to Seattle for a seven-game home stand that preceded the All-Star break.

July 15–17

The Pilots, who now appeared to be fading in the July heat, came home to Sick's after a road trip that saw their record drop to 4–11 on the month. Unfortunately, they were coming home to the Oakland A's. Gelnar, Brabender, and Pattin, now the team's three most reliable starters, had lost three consecutive games. The only bright spot was Mincher, who hit a homer in each of them. Don had now hit 8 home runs in the month, raising his total to 17 and removing any doubt as to his being recovered from the '68 beaning.

In the first game on Tuesday night the young Gelnar pitched well until the sixth when he left with the score tied at 2–2. Segui came on in relief and promptly gave up a three-run home run to A's pitcher John Blue Moon Odom, two of those runs being charged to Gelnar. The A's got one more run off Bouton for a final score of 6–2. Odom threw a complete game and saw his pitching record improve to 13–3; he was 2 for 4 at-bat with four RBIs. Odom had hit three home runs and eleven RBIs off the Pilots this year. The rookie Gelnar's record dropped to an undeserved 2–5. Mincher was 2 for 3 including his 15th home run and a walk plus two RBIs.

On Wednesday Brabender (7–7) labored through his start, losing handily to Lew Krausse (4–4) 6–1. Brabender wasn't terrible but he put 10 men on base in six innings, and four of them scored. He was a victim of no run support, the lone Pilot run coming in the 2nd inning on Mincher's 16th round-tripper.

The following day Marty Pattin (7–9) continued his, and his team's, slide, dropping the series finale 8–2. Pattin was sluggish and was relieved in the 5th inning by Dick Baney. Baney's second Major League outing was almost as bad as his first! Dick pitched 1⅔ innings and gave up 3 hits, 3 walks and allowed 4 earned runs. He was lifted in the 7th in favor of Bouton. None of this seemed to be bothering Minch, who was 2 for 4 with two RBIs and his 17th home run. Sal Bando went 5 for 5 with four RBIs for Oakland and Catfish Hunter (8–7) got the complete game win.

Besides getting swept in the series, the Pilots had now lost eight in a row and were 19½ games out of first but somehow still in third place.

July 18–20

In what must have seemed like a bad joke to the Pilots, the A's left town only to be replaced by the Twins, who were 7–0 vs. Seattle. On Friday's (7/18) double-header the Pilot players showed their grit and professionalism by not letting the Twins intimidate them. Seattle pitchers were tired, the team was in desperate need of a well-pitched game, or at least one in which their starter went deep into it. Because of injuries and a juggled staff, Diego Segui was given the start in the first game, his first since April 22nd. He responded with one of the best-pitched Seattle games in a while. Diego went all nine innings, striking out seven while walking two and allowing only one run. It was his first complete game in three years. His timing could not have been better. Over on the Twins side starter Bob Miller was putting on his own show; this would not be an easy victory for the Pilots. Going into the bottom of the 9th the score was tied at 1–1. The Twins brought in Ron Perranoski to start the bottom of the inning and hold the Pilots to one run. Wayne Comer led off with a single. Gerry McNertney sacrificed Comer to second for the first out. Ron Clark was walked intentionally to set up a double play. Gordy Lund flied out to right for the second out of the inning. At this point Perranoski must have lost the plate somehow. Tommy Harper came up and walked to load the bases with two outs. Steve Hovley came up, looked out at the mound, and waited for the first pitch. After five pitches the count was full; Perranoski had to throw a strike. Hovley fouled off four consecutive pitches. For the fans and players time was now standing still. Perranoski threw his tenth pitch of the duel and the rookie Hovley had the confidence to take it... BALL FOUR! Steve threw his bat down and jogged to first while Wayne Comer crossed the plate with the winning run. Segui (7–4) ran out to find Hovley and congratulate him.

There would be little time for celebration; just a light meal, shower, and suit up again. In the night game Fred Talbot would face Dave Boswell. Although Fred gave up ten hits he ate up seven innings too. He allowed only two runs and the bullpen continued to rest. Locker had to pitch 1⅔ innings of hitless ball and O'Donoghue retired the final batter for his fourth save. Seattle won 3–2 thanks to Hovley's second homer of his career. Talbot got the win and went to 5–3. Beating the Twins twice in the same day, and both times by one run, must have been sweet satisfaction for the players and Joe Schultz.

On Saturday night the teams played a little-noticed game one day before the All-Star break; the minds of all Americans were somewhere else this evening. Indeed, the game itself was halted for 20 minutes in the 6th inning so everyone, fans and players alike, could listen to the Apollo astronauts' moon landing. [21]

Jim Bouton was given a rare start and did not fare well. He did not have a good feel for his knuckleball and was hammered for five runs (2 HRs) in 3 2/3 innings. Going to the bottom of the 9th with Seattle down 6–3, Hovley and Gil led off with singles. Next, Davis hit into a fielder's choice and Mincher grounded out, 2 outs. Jim Pagliaroni then pinch-hit a single that drove in two runs to make it a 6–5 game. McNertney stepped to the plate hit a hopper to Carew at second, who booted it for a rare error. Little-used Ron Clark came up next and singled to right field, driving home Pagliaroni with the tying run. Oyler grounded out to send the game into extra innings. The 12,069 fans present thought they had just witnessed something special but they hadn't seen anything yet.

The game slowly progressed five more innings without any player crossing the plate. It was well after midnight and the outside of Sick's Stadium was eerily quiet; downtown Seattle was dark. Gene Brabender had come for the start of the 9th inning and was still out there when the 15th began, so far having pitched six scoreless innings of relief. Brabender retired Carew to lead off the inning but then walked Manuel. Reese singled to left field, sending Manuel to third base. John Roseboro grounded to second base and Gus Gil scooped the ball and threw to Oyler covering second for the sure out. This may have not been the right time to play fundamental baseball. Reese was forced out at second for the second out but Manuel scored the go-ahead run. Did any fans get up and leave now? As discouraging as this may have been, the Pilots came up in the bottom of the 15th losing 7–6 but hoping for just one run (but probably two). Don Mincher grounded out for the first out.

Jim Pagliaroni, who helped send the game into extra innings, hit a solo home run to tie the game again. The next two batters were easily retired and the game went to the 16th inning. The 16th was a scoreless affair but the umpires suspended play for the league's 1:00 AM curfew at the conclusion of the inning. It would be completed prior to tomorrow's game. The exhausted players, who had been at the stadium since 4:00 PM, quietly showered and headed out.

Early Sunday afternoon saw John Gelnar and Jim Perry taking the mound to continue the struggle prior to the regularly scheduled game. It would only last 2 innings. Gelnar (2–6) got tagged for the loss in allowing four Twins to cross

The Pilots' All-Star first-baseman Don Mincher at Sick's. He was also the team's player representative (Photo File).

the plate in the 18th for a final score of 11–7. It would have been a crushing defeat for either team but it was the Pilots that had to live with it. Jim Perry raised his record to 10–4; the pitcher actually started the rally in the 18th with a double. The Pilots had out-hit the Twins 20–16 and a then-record of 44 runners had been stranded. A total of 41 players participated in the game.

After only pitching less than 2 innings Schultz decided to stay with Gelnar for the second game. The Twins' manager did likewise. The fates were not kind to young Gelnar who, although pitching a great game, came up short against the man of the day, Jim Perry. Gelnar (2–7) had picked up two losses today while Perry (11–7) came away with two wins. The Twins won 4–0 on homers by Mitterwald (4) and Tovar (3), both off Gelnar. Gelnar threw seven innings and struck out four with no walks; he only allowed five hits but two of those were the homers. Perry had pitched a total of eleven innings today.

As Sunday afternoon gave way to nightfall, members of the Pilots packed up their belongings and left Sick's Stadium. The three-day All-Star break could not have come sooner for the free-falling team. After playing respectable

.500 ball for two months, the team's record now stood at 40–55, good enough for fourth place in the AL West and 18½ games out of first.

The only Pilot who would not have off would be first baseman Don Mincher. His 17 home runs, 50 RBIs and .253 batting average would be going to Washington, D.C., as a member of the 1969 American League All-Star team. Don will go down in history as the only man to be able to say he was a Pilot All-Star. Actually, Mike Hegan was originally slated to go but Milkes would not let him due to his hamstring injury.[22] Once in Washington the weather turned ugly during Monday's off-day. Tuesday's scheduled game had to be postponed until Wednesday's off-day. This drove down the attendance for the game, including President Nixon, who had to attend a reception for the astronauts instead. Mincher finally got to play, though, pinch-hitting for Tigers pitcher Denny McLain in the fourth inning. He struck out against Cardinals Hall of Famer Bob Gibson; Mincher had singled off Gipson pinch-hitting in the '67 All-Star game.

Chapter 8

The Season Continues

As the Pilots' season resumed on Thursday, July 24th, there was no longer very much optimism. The injuries were still there, the fans were still not there, and now the mounting problems in the team's hierarchy began to unravel.

July 24–27

The Pilots opened up the second half of the season with a 10-game home stand against the Red Sox, Senators, and Yankees. At least they would not have to see either the Twins or A's until September. Thursday the Pilots began a four-game set versus the Bosox and scored seven early runs. The hitting star was McNertney, who clubbed two doubles and drove in three. The Pilots tacked on one more, allowing Brabender to cruise to his eighth victory (8–7). After tiring in the sixth inning and walking the first two batters, Gene was replaced by Locker, who allowed Boston to get back into the game. Bob walked the first batter he faced, and the Red Sox now had the bases loaded without the benefit of a hit. That would change as soon as Carl Yastrzemski stepped to the plate. Carl singled to right field but the ball was misplayed by Hovley; all three base runners scored, making it an 8–6 game. Locker was lifted for O'Donoghue, who put the fire out while getting his fifth save.

On Friday the GM was about to place Mike Hegan on the disabled list due to his hamstring injury, but this became unnecessary when he was called up for military service. He was replaced by Greg Goossen, who had 18 home runs at Vancouver, prior to the game. Goossen was what is known as a AAAA player. He was a minor-league phenom who had several call-ups with the Mets but couldn't get it done at the Major League level. When he was a 20-year-old rookie his manager Casey Stengel said of his future, "In ten years he has a chance to be 30."[1] He was also a bit of a character and fit nicely onto the

Top and bottom: As the second half of the season progressed, rookies Greg Goossen and Steve Hovley emerged as quality players. Both would see more playing time (both photographs: Topps).

Pilots stage. That night Diego Segui started again and was uncharacteristically bad. He was removed in the third inning, having given up seven hits including a home run by Tony Conigliaro, and replaced by Gelnar. John did great over five innings and had the Pilots up 5–4 in the eighth when he began to tire. The script was all too familiar to the team as Gary Roggenburk gave up a three-run homer to Russ Gibson, making it 7–5 in favor of Boston. Making it even worse was the Pilots' staging a comeback in the bottom of the ninth but being able to only score one run. It would not be a stretch to say that it was unfair that Gelnar (2–8) got hung for the loss in this 7–6 game. Goossen went 3 for 4 with a long home run in his first game as a Pilot. One oddity in the game: Tony Conigliaro pulled his back badly while swinging and hitting a home run. He had to walk around the bases slowly to cross home plate before being replaced by Joe Lahoud.

The next day Talbot started but was removed after 4⅔ innings with the score 5–0 Boston. Jim Bouton relieved him and recorded four straight outs before being lifted for a pinch-hitter during an eighth-inning rally. Gerry McNertney's three-run home run was the big blow as the Pilots turned the tables and came all the way back, winning 8–5. Bouton (2–0) was the beneficiary, getting credit for the win while Locker (9) picked up the save. In the game infielder Ron Clark was run over by big George Scott at second base, requiring thirteen stitches in his lip and jaw. Clark stood little chance against Scott, who weighed 70 lbs. more than he did.

On July 24, Don Mincher scores ahead of the throw to Red Sox catcher Tom Satriano on Gerry McNertney's three-run double (*Seattle Times*).

In what was a very telling sign, only 9000 fans showed up for a beautiful Sunday afternoon game in the middle of the summer vs. the Red Sox. And that small number was an above-average crowd for a Pilots game in 1969. About the only time the team could bring in a good attendance now was on give-away days. But the fans that came today got their money's worth: 20 innings of baseball. Had any of them been at last weekend's 18-inning game?

Marty Pattin pitched another great game on July 27 only to be beaten by the Red Sox in 20 innings (Brace Photo).

Marty Pattin started and pitched a great game, giving up only one run through eight innings on a Reggie Smith (21) home run. The score was tied 1–1 and would remain so until the 19th inning. Eighteen innings of great pitching looked wasted when the Bosox pushed a run across in the top of the 19th on a Yastrzemski double, but not so fast Red Sox fans! In the bottom of the 19th, Steve Hovley walked to lead off. Next, Greg Goossen sacrificed Hovley to second, and that was followed by a Pagliaroni single that drove him in. The inning ended that way with the score now tied at 2–2. This was strangely similar to the 16th inning of the eighteen-inning game on July 19th.

Almost immediately the Pilots gave the game back to Boston. Jim Lonborg, a pitcher, led off the 20th with a single and was then sacrificed to second. Joe LaHoud stepped to the plate and stunned the crowd with a 2-run homer to right field off Bob Locker for a 4–2 Boston lead. Adding insult to injury, the Red Sox were able to tack on a 5th run.

In the bottom of the 20th, Boston got 2 quick outs to start the inning. The Pilots had so few players left on the bench that Gene Brabender was used as a pinch-hitter; he struck out. Down to their last out, Tommy Harper hit a solo home run (6). John Donaldson then walked, bringing Hovley to the plate, who represented the tying run. He tapped the ball back to second base, ending what was probably the Pilots' toughest loss of the season. Locker got credit for the loss (3–5) and Jim Lonborg got the win. This game seemed to follow a pattern: when the Pilots' pitchers threw great games, they suffered from a lack of run support. Conversely, when the pitching staff gave up a lot of runs, the team would have a big day at the plate. As the season wore on it became increasingly frustrating to lose games either by scores of 2–1 or 10–9.

The Pilots closed out the month with a 3-game series at home against the Senators in which they were only able to win one game. Their record for a disastrous July was 9–20. Marvin Milkes was now making repeated statements to the press, insisting the team had better take third place, this posturing was making Joe Schultz uncomfortable and adding to his stress.[2]

The first half of August went as about expected. The team was 5–7 until August 15th managing to somehow hang onto third place in the AL West.

July 29–31

The Pilots continued their home stand with three games against the Senators, who they were 5–1 against so far this season. Seattle jumped out to a two-run lead but Brabender could not hold it. He gave up four runs over eight innings and got no run support. Losing 4–2 in the bottom of the ninth, John Donaldson singled with two outs. Mike Hegan hit a long fly ball to right that

Despite losing a 20-inning game on July 27, Bob Locker had a fine season for the Pilots, compiling a 2.18 ERA after coming over from the White Sox (Topps).

looked as if it was going out only to be caught at the fence by Ed Stroud. It was another frustrating game for Seattle players and fans. Senators starter Joe Coleman pitched a complete game and allowed Seattle just five hits.

The following day Segui started and got the win, raising his team best record to 8–4 while Gelnar got his second save. Greg Goossen was quickly making Milkes look good by hitting two more home runs in the 4–3 victory. Pagliaroni also hit a home run, his third.

One unusual move caught all of the players by surprise prior to the game. That morning Gary Roggenburk got up, packed his bags, walked into Milkes' office and quit. After just five years in the majors, the 29 year old was done with the game; he wanted to go home to his family.[3] Marvin Milkes tried to talk him out of it because the team was very thin on left-handed pitching, but to no avail.[4] The GM wasted no time and immediately purchased lefty George Brunet from the Angels for $20,000. Brunet was a 34 year old who first came up to the majors in 1956. He had a lot of innings in his arm and even held some minor-league career pitching records for years. He was reportedly still pitching in Mexico in the 1980s.

The Pilots just could not get anything going as they lost the third, and final, game of the series 7–6. It was another tough loss for Seattle. In the bottom of the ninth, down 7–4, the Pilots loaded the bases. With two outs and John Donaldson due up, Joe Schultz curiously pinch-hit for him with Gerry McNertney. Although Donaldson was not known as a dangerous hitter he was 2 for 3 today and was hitting .364 over the past nine games. McNertney was also the last available hitter on the bench. The move momentarily paid off when Gerry singled home two runs, bringing the Pilots to within one (7–6). This would have actually tied the game were it not for Frank Howard hitting his 35th home run in the top of the 9th with no one on. Now, however, with no available pinch-hitters, the very weak-hitting Steve Barber was due up. He was actually pinch-hit for with the slightly better hitting pitcher John Gelnar. Washington pitcher Darold Knowles struck Gelnar out on three pitches.

The Pilots, beset with injuries, had just finished their worst month of the season, going 9–20. One could have assumed that this would be their toughest month of the season but the worst was yet to come. Amazingly, at 43–59 they still found themselves in third place. GM Marvin Milkes was still insisting that the team win 70 games and finish their inaugural season in third place.[5] At this point the Sorianos should have overruled their GM and insisted the Pilots look at their younger players and unload some of their veterans. Besides trying to overcome the injuries, a poor stadium, and money problems, the reality was that the Pilots just were not going to catch the Twins or A's, who had power and pitching. Milkes' insistence that the Pilots come in third no longer made any sense. Originally he believed that the Seattle fans would not support a young, developing team but these mystery fans failed to appear after the opening home series. Clinging to the original goal now was just hurting the team's long range chances.

August 1–3

The Pilots began the month with a weekend series against the Yankees at Sick's. Before Friday night's game Joe Schultz gathered the players and told them, "Let's keep our minds on the game. And let's remember we're the same as everybody else. Let's go out there, kick the s**t out of them and come back in and enjoy the beer."[6] In his memoir Jim Bouton added, "We went out there, got two hits and lost 4–2. The beer was great."[7]

In that game Marty Pattin's problems continued as he could not get out of the second inning. He gave up a three-run homer to long-time Yankee outfielder Roy White (6), walked three, and picked up his fifth straight loss, dropping his record to 7–10. He was relieved by Bouton, who gave up just one run, a Joe Pepitone (21) home run. Still, the Pilot hurlers only gave up four runs in the game. They lacked run support yet again. Yankee starter Bill Burbach was wild and after four walks and a wild pitch was lifted at the beginning of the third inning. The Pilots' hitters could not capitalize on this and scored only two runs in the game.

In Saturday's game George Brunet (6–8) got his first start as a Pilot. Things were going well until the fifth inning, when the Yanks broke open a scoreless game with Pepitone's (22) 3-run shot. Yankee back-up catcher Frank Fernandez also touched Brunet for a home run (9). The Pilots mounted a comeback when Pagliaroni (5) and Mincher (18) both hit homers, but it fell short with a final score of 5–4.

The Pilots hoped to salvage the last game of the series on Sunday. It was a beautiful day and also the team's second Bat Day; 23,657 showed up. This was the type of crowd that Pacific Northwest Sports thought would show up every weekend but came to realize that was very optimistic.[8] It took promotions, and a visit by either the Yankees, Orioles, or Tigers, to get that number. Steve Barber took the mound and lasted one-third of an inning while giving up five runs. He walked three and said while his arm felt fine his rhythm was off. Down 5–0, Barber (2–2) was relieved by Gelnar, Talbot, and Segui, who combined to throw eight scoreless innings. Once again great pitching was wasted, as the Pilots could only muster three runs for a 5–3 loss and a series sweep by New York. Tommy Harper's seventh homer was the only fireworks in the game for Seattle. On the homestand Seattle was 5–12. At least they had a travel day to look forward to.

August 5–7

In Boston, Brabender pitched a complete game and received lots of run support in winning 9–2 and upping his record to 9–8. He defeated 15-game winner Ray Culp and helped himself with his second career home run. After a slow start Big Gene had become the workhorse of the staff. In the game rookie Steve Hovley had three hits including a homer (3) and Tommy Davis' three hits extended his hitting streak to ten games. It was a good way to open the nine-game road trip.

The following night the Pilots did the unusual and came from behind to win in extra innings. Segui started but could not make it out of the third inning. Reggie Smith (another Pilot killer) cracked a 3-run homer five batters into the game. Diego was relieved by Pattin, who was equally ineffective; he left in the fifth with the bases loaded and the Pilots losing 4–2. Jim Bouton came on and threw one pitch, inducing a double play to end the inning. Bouton was lifted for a pinch-hitter and was replaced on the mound by

Barber. In Seattle's half of the eighth, Comer led off with a walk, followed by Davis double. Hegan then singled them home, tying the game at 4–4. But that would be all for the Pilots in the eighth as Bosox pitcher Jim Lonborg was relieved by Sparky Lyle, who shut them down to get out of the inning. In a surprising move, Schultz sent Barber up to lead off the top of the ninth. His risky move was rewarded when Steve lined what looked like a single to center. The Pilots caught a break when Reggie Smith, running in hard, dove for the ball and came up short. By the time Tony Conigliaro retrieved it, Barber was on third. Tommy Harper hit a sacrifice fly to bring him in, putting the Pilots up 5–4.

In the bottom of the ninth Barber went back out to the mound to complete a badly needed win for his team. A two-game winning streak isn't much but the Pilots desperately needed something to click. As with all things with the Pilots, it did not come easily. The Red Sox's Dick Schofield led the inning off with a walk. Control had been Barber's biggest problem this season but Schultz still did not pull him. Mike Andrews moved the runner to second, then weak-hitting Dalton Jones singled him home for a 5–5 tie. Barber then proceeded to load the bases before manager Schultz finally removed him. Bob

On August 1, Yankee Horace Clark steals third as Harper tries to handle the throw (*Seattle Times*).

Locker was summoned and managed to get out of the inning without allowing another Boston run to cross the plate. On to the tenth they went; Red Sox hurler Vincente Romo replaced Lyle. Comer, who started the rally in the eighth, now led off with a double. This was immediately followed by a McNertney double that drove him in, giving the Pilots a 6–5 victory with Locker (4–5) picking up the win. It made a loser out of Romo (3–8).

The Pilots looked to turn things around with a sweep of Boston and sent out Fred Talbot for the finale. He turned in another fine game and even hit a homerun in the top of the ninth to give Seattle a 4–2 lead. As Talbot took the mound in the last frame the Pilots players could almost feel the pressure being lifted from them. Then disaster struck. Big George Scott led off with a double and Schultz wasted no time tonight in bringing in yesterday's hero Bob Locker. Sox catcher Gerry Moses hit a sacrifice fly, pushing Scott to third. Up next was Dick Schofield, who was pinch-hitting for pitcher Lee Stange; he lined a single to center, making the score 4–3. Mike Andrews then singled and Locker was relieved by O'Donoghue. John O'Donoghue struck out Don Lock for the second out and then had to face Carl Yastrzemski with runners on the corners. The future Hall of Famer was all that stood between the Pilots and their second sweep of the season. By now you know the rest of the story. O'Donoghue got Yaz to do what he wanted: He hit a grounder right to Oyler at shortstop, who had been inserted for defensive purposes. Oyler misplayed the ball, and just like that, the score was tied with runners still on the corners. Reggie Smith followed with a game-winning bloop single and the Pilots walked off the field to a very quiet clubhouse. It seemed that every time things were beginning to click for the Pilots the team imploded. The usually successful Locker's record dropped to 4–6, and the Pilots caught a plane for Washington.

August 8–10

On Friday night George Brunet got his second start as a Pilot in the capital city. He pitched well until the sixth inning when he gave up four runs and was pulled with his team down 4–3. It looked like it was developing into another close, heartbreaking loss, but another pitching change took care of that. Schultz elected to bring in Pattin, who had been demoted to the bullpen. Pattin made quick work of it, giving up six earned runs in two-thirds of an inning. Barber and O'Donoghue also came in and got hit. Only Bouton, who pitched the ninth, was not scored on. Brunet picked up the loss (6–9) in the 10–3 debacle. There seemed to be a pattern emerging with Brunet: He appeared to be a good five-inning pitcher. After that you ran a big risk of

On August 10, Tommy Harper can't handle the throw as the Senators' Lee Maye slides in safely for a bases-clearing triple at RFK Stadium. Both teams would be gone in two years (©Bettman/CORBIS).

him losing something off his ball. Don Mincher hit his 19th home run in the losing cause.

Saturday's game start was given to John Gelnar. The rookie had been demoted to the bullpen, along with his 2–8 record, but had pitched very well recently. Joe Schultz and Sal Maglie both thought he had earned another start, but he lasted one inning and gave up five runs. Although he put his team in a hole early, the Pilots chipped away until they tied the game at 6–6 in the 7th inning. In the eighth Comer singled with two out and then Davis worked out a walk. Goossen, who was having his best season in the majors, came up and drove a long double to left, scoring both runners, sealing an 8–6 victory. Locker (5–6), who was being used a lot, picked up the win. Today's game was typical, with a parade of pitchers taking the mound. This was a huge problem for the Pilots. Too many of the starters were either old, injured, or inexperienced. The bullpen corps was very overused and tired, thus they had largely become ineffective also. Putting injured and ineffective starters in the bullpen did not solve those individual pitchers' problems either; it only made the bullpen worse. It was a cycle that the Pilots never pulled out of all season. Both Goossen and Donaldson had three hits today.

On Sunday afternoon the Pilots played their final game against the Senators this season. The back and forth game of little importance ended in a 7–5 Senator victory. Brabender started and could only go four innings but it was the apparently cursed John Gelnar (2–9) who picked up the loss even though he pitched just ⅔ of an inning. Tommy Harper had three hits and stole his 52nd and 53rd bases. The Pilots became the first major league team of the twentieth century to relocate and change names after only a year in existence. As both the Pilots and Senators walked off the field at R.F.K. Stadium on this summer afternoon, could any of their respective fans have imagined that both of these teams would cease to exist in just two years?

August 11–13

Mike Hegan returned to the team after having been called up for military duty for a couple of weeks, bad hamstring and all. In order to clear a spot for him, Milkes traded infielder Gordy Lund to the Angels. Lund had proved to be a versatile utility infielder with a dependable bat (.263), so the decision to rid themselves of the 28-year-old Lund, instead of some of the other infielders, was a curious one.

The Pilots opened up a three-game series vs. the Tribe on Monday night with Bud Daley, Dewey Soriano, and Marvin Milkes in attendance.[9] Diego Segui started against Luis Tiant and had a great game. The jack-of-all-trades pitcher went all nine innings and gave up just six hits. His only mistake came in the 4th inning when he allowed a solo home run to light-hitting Frank Baker. With the score tied 2–2 in the sixth inning Don Mincher hit a grand slam to put Seattle ahead for good. With that homer Don had reached the 20 HR plateau for the fourth time in his career. Segui even hit a two-run single in the ninth for insurance and picked up his ninth win (9–4); he had three RBIs on the night. The great Tiant dropped to 8–14 on a woeful Cleveland team. The Indians were actually drawing fewer fans than the Pilots (4658 tonight).

On Tuesday night Fred Talbot was ineffective and removed in the fourth with his team behind 6–1. He had given up three walks and eight hits, including a homer to Hawk Harrelson, and was now out of gas. A group of relievers held the Indians scoreless as the Pilots mounted a comeback over several innings. Down by one run in the 9th inning, Seattle hitters put men on the corners with two outs. As Ron Clark walked to the plate, Indians manager Alvin Dark walked to the mound. Veteran Stan Williams was brought in to try to get the last out, and he did his job, inducing Clark to pop to second base. In another heartbreaking game, the Pilots came up short, losing 6–5. It was one more tease, another tough loss.

George Brunet (7–9) threw a complete game victory on Wednesday, which was a big break for the bullpen, especially considering it preceded a travel day, giving all of the pitchers two days off. He allowed nine hits and no homers in outlasting hard-luck Tribe pitcher Steve Hargan (4–10). Actually, any pitcher on the 1969 Indians was a hard-luck one. Brunet had not done well since being acquired, but this is what Milkes had expected from him: not an All-Star performer but somebody who was a tough pitcher who could eat up innings. The Pilots won 5–3 on eight singles. A total of 18,342 paid to see all three games between these two teams who were both twenty games under .500. The team left the stadium and headed home after a 5–4 road trip. Relatively, this would have to be considered a success, but it easily could have been 7–2 and energized the young players for a late-season push. It would have helped, as the

Top: Mike Hegan had one of the few fine seasons for the Pilots despite its being interrupted several times for military commitments and leg injuries (Photo File). *Bottom:* When he returned to the team on August 11, valuable reserve infielder Gordy Lund was sent packing to the Angels (National Baseball Hall of Fame Library, Cooperstown, N.Y.).

Pilots' first seven games of the ten-game home stand were against the Orioles and Tigers.

August 15

The Pilots recalled 36-year-old outfielder Billy Williams. Although he would never figure in the team's future it was still a feel-good story for the Pilots and their fans as it was the very first major league game for the 17-year minor-league vet. He would play in 4 games and not record a hit, reaching base just once on a walk. Williams would never play in the majors after 1969.

August 15–18

Game 1 of the 4-game set against the Orioles in Seattle featured Brabender and 15-game winner Mike Cuellar. Brabender, by now the Pilots' ace, pitched another great game; unfortunately so did Cuellar. Down 2–1 in the seventh, Gerry McNertney singled to open the inning. He was lifted for pinch-runner Billy Williams, who was playing his first Major League game. The next two batters proceeded to strike out before Jim Pagliaroni singled, sending Williams to third. With the tying run on third, the fleet Tommy Harper laid down a bunt. Mike Cuellar, caught by surprise, ran in for the ball and shoveled it in his mitt back to the catcher Elrod Hendricks. Williams appeared to slide under Hendricks' tag but was called out by the umpire. An incensed Joe Schultz raced out of the dugout and argued to no avail. The Pilots would not threaten again and an excellent performance by Brabender (9–9) would be recorded as a 2–1 Pilot loss.

Saturday's game would not be such a heartbreaker. The light-hitting Chico Salmon, who had been a

Career minor-leaguer Billy Williams got his one major league shot with the Pilots. The 36-year-old outfielder was recalled on August 15 after 17 years in the minors (National Baseball Hall of Fame Library, Cooperstown, N.Y.).

Pilot in spring training, had four hits, two home runs and drove in six runs. Segui was hit hard in the start and finally had to admit he had a sore back. The staff could ill afford the loss of Segui but he was put on the two-week disabled list. Four Seattle relievers could fare no better as the Oriole assault continued, Blair (25) and Powell (33) each homered and Etchebarren collected four hits. Seattle lost 15–3 with Segui (9–5) getting the decision and Oriole flamethrower Dave McNally upping his impressive record to 17–2.

The Pilots lost again on Sunday despite a decent game pitched by Talbot (5–6), if you could call it that. He gave up eight hits but three of them were hit out of the park in the 4–1 loss. The only Pilot run came on Mincher's 21st home run in the 9th, spoiling the shutout for Tom Phoebus, who still got the win (12–4). The frustration level must have been enormous by now as almost every well-pitched game was wasted. Others have said that the team actually loosened up as the losses mounted and they fell farther out of contention.[10] It was no secret among the American League in 1969 that the Pilots were a team filled with characters who tended to enjoy themselves. Not every player on the team, of course, but it was certainly a team that tended to have fun and good times.[11] This loose atmosphere permeated the clubhouse, with Joe Schultz not being known as a party pooper.

By now it was routine. On Monday George Brunet (7–10) gave up eight runs in the second inning as the Pilots lost 12–3 to Baltimore and Jim Palmer (12–2). Palmer had thrown a no-hitter in his previous start and a crowd of 19,000 Seattleites showed up to witness the possibility of back-to-back no-no's. The only thing they saw was their team get slammed again. Comer (11) and Davis (4) actually managed to each hit a homer against Palmer but they couldn't make a dent in the continued punishment Baltimore was giving the Pilots.

The fact that it was the Orioles did not make getting swept any easier. By now, with their emerging young pitching staff, Baltimore was probably the best team in the majors. They outscored the Pilots 33–8 in the series. Six different Orioles had home runs. At the time Fred Talbot said, "We got no business scheduling these guys."[12] After the first game the Pilots used up all of their relievers once again, and now would also be without Segui.

August 19–21

The Orioles left town but the buzz saw would continue with the arrival of the Tigers for a three-game series. For the first game Joe Schultz started Steve Barber. His faith in the former All-Star seemed to be limitless. There may have also been pressure from upstairs to keep running him out there, since Milkes had built this staff with Barber as its ace. He gave up three runs in the first inning and two more in the fourth when he was removed. A string of Pilot relievers did well, giving up just one hit, and Harper (8) and Pagliaroni (6) both homered, but it wasn't enough; Seattle lost 5–3 with Barber dropping to 2–3. The Tigers of the late '60s had some terrific pitchers but the Pilots were satisfied losing to Mike Kilkenny (3–3).

For the second game the Pilots' best, Gene Brabender, hooked up with World Series MVP Mickey Lolich, who was already 15–6 on the season. Brabender (9–10) once again pitched a great game but was just out-dueled by Lolich, who struck out fourteen Pilots. Seattle was down 4–2 in the ninth and managed to push across another run but went down in frustrating fashion again. With Comer standing on first, Goossen popped out to end it, and the score stood at 4–3.

With the score tied at six in the eighth inning of the third game, George Brunet was relieved by Jim Bouton. Mickey Stanley was the first batter Bouton faced and he tried to throw a fastball by him. The result was a solo home run and a 7–6 Tiger lead. All season long Bouton (2–1) had tried to convince the Pilot management that his knuckleball was for real, and he did very well with it. By his own admission it was a mistake to try to use his fastball with his injured arm, he paid for that tonight and so did his team.[13] Jim picked up his first loss of the season and the Pilots' losing streak extended to seven.

August 22–24

With the team mired in a seven-game losing streak and attendance plummeting, Dewey Soriano came up with an idea for a gate attraction. Tommy Harper's 61 stolen bases were good enough to lead the majors; in fact, he was the only Pilot leading the league in anything. This Friday night would be Tommy Harper Night at Sick's Stadium as the Pilots took on the Indians. With Olympic hero Jesse Owens in attendance, the team gave Harper an award and a trip to Hawaii for him and his wife during an on-field pre-game ceremony. The attendance of just 6,720 fans probably took the last bit of air out of Soriano's balloon. Here he was, a local boy who gave the people of Seattle what they had asked for for years, and they just would not embrace it. Before the game Schultz held a team meeting in which he told the players to ignore anything they read in the papers or heard. He said he did not want the players putting too much pressure on themselves with the talk about them having to finish third. He also acknowledged for the first time that his job might be in jeopardy and he did not know who would be leading the club next year. This, he also told his players, was not their worry either.[14] Schultz had been around the game for a long time and was a realist.

If it seemed like it could not get worse, it did when the game started.

On August 23, pitcher Marty Pattin fouls one back while trying a bunt. He later strikes out—and so do the Pilots, losing to Indians' fire-baller Sam McDowell. Tribe catcher is Duke Sims (*Seattle Times*).

Fred Talbot started and after two pitches the Tribe had a 2–0 lead. Although the Pilots came right back and tied it, Cleveland went ahead 8–4 in a seesaw game and that's how it stood going into the ninth. Bouton came on in relief and gave up a home run to Tony Horton (his second of the night) before striking out the next two batters, then inducing a pop-out to the third. At the time it didn't really seem to matter, but the Pilots came to bat in the bottom of the ninth down 9–4 and unbelievably managed to score four runs. The team had runners on second and third with just one out before Gil and Pagliaroni struck out to end the game. The Pacific Northwest Sports officials could not have been feeling very good about things as they drove home tonight.

The Pilots lost to the Indians again on Saturday (7–3) when Marty Pattin (7–11) gave up a bases-clearing double to Cleveland starter Sudden Sam McDowell and Tony Horton's 25th home run. After the game Pattin was placed on the disabled list by the team. He had struggled for a long time and now he would have a chance to rest and rehab. McDowell (15–10) went all the way, limiting Seattle to five hits.

The following afternoon the Pilots made it three series sweeps in a row by dropping another one-run game. They actually had a 3–0 lead and fell behind 4–3 and then came back to tie it 4–4 on a Goossen HR. But the pitching staff was completely decimated and Schultz had to use starters Talbot and Brunet to finish the game after Barber could only go three innings. The Indians struck for two runs in the top of the 9th off Talbot to go ahead 6–4. In the bottom of the final frame Wayne Comer led off with a solo home run. After the next two batters were retired, Donaldson and Pagliaroni both singled. Dick Simpson batted for Oyler and popped out to the infield to end the game. The final was 6–5 and Talbot (5–8) had lost twice in three days now. There could not have been a more frustrating way to lose a game. The Pilots just seemed to have a knack at this and it must have taken its toll on the players to some degree. Worse, in the three losses to Cleveland, Schultz had used 14 pitchers! And he had nothing to show for it.

After the game (8/24), that extended the losing streak to 10, knuckleballer Jim Bouton was shipped to the Astros for pitcher Dooley Womack. Bouton had done an okay job out of the bullpen but some of the coaching staff just didn't believe in his knuckleball. Bouton's own brashness did not help him ingratiate himself with some of the members of the team either.

August 26–28

The Pilots arrived in Baltimore to play a three-game mid-week series, hoping to somehow stop the bleeding. Former Oriole Gene Brabender would once again make the O's pay for trading him. With little run support Big Gene pitched a complete game 2–1 win, the Pilots' first since August 13th. Tommy Davis (5) hit a solo home run and an RBI single to lift his team to a very needed victory.

For the second game of the series starter George Brunet drew 17-game winner Mike Cuellar. It would have been a tough assignment even if Brunet had pitched well, but he did not. The Pilots dropped the game 7–2 and Brunet dropped to 7–11 (1–4 as a Pilot). He went four innings and gave up six runs. The Orioles continued to hit home runs off Seattle's pitchers at a shocking rate; Frank Robinson (29) and Elrod Hendricks (10) connected today. After 10 losses in a row the Pilots' winning streak lasted 1 game.

The final game of the set was more of a classic Seattle heartbreaker. Talbot started and was relieved by Locker in the sixth with the score 3–3. Bob was his reliable self and finished out the 9th frame without giving up a run; the score remained even at three. Dooley Womack came in to start the 10th in what was his first appearance for Seattle and threw a 1-2-3 inning. In the bottom of the 11th Curt Motton lead off pinch-hitting for the Orioles' pitcher

Left-handed pitcher Bob Meyer was another in-season acquisition by Milkes. He would play just six games for the Pilots and 38 in his major league career (National Baseball Hall of Fame Library, Cooperstown, N.Y.).

Eddie Watt; he singled. Don Buford sacrificed him to second, then Mark Belanger grounded out to Donaldson at second, moving Motton to third. With two outs and a runner on third, Frank Robinson was intentionally walked, bringing up ex–Pilot Chico Salmon. He surprised everyone by bunting down the third base line. Motton quickly crossed the plate while the fleet-footed Salmon ran easily to first. The only choice third baseman Tommy Harper and Womack had was to hover over the ball and hope for it to go foul. The ball rolled down the field on top of the white line and actually came to rest directly on it. A frustrated Womack picked up the ball and walked off the field with the rest of his team. Womack's record quickly was 0–1 while long-time O's reliever Eddie Watts went to 4–1.

After dropping the final two games of the series, Milkes sent Fred Talbot to the A's for minor leaguers Bob Meyer, who would join the team, and Pete Koegel, who was sent to the minors. Talbot had only pitched so-so during the year but could be counted on for innings and had remained uninjured, which was a plus on this team.

August 29–31

The team finished out the month with a three-game series in Detroit. The floodgates appeared to be open now as the Pilots got swept. If July had been rough, August was a complete disaster. The team compiled a 6–22 record for the month; add that to July and they were 15–42 for the summer. A loss to the Yankees on September 1st dropped the Pilots to sixth (last) place, where they would finish the season.

In game one of the Tiger series the Pilots drew Bengal hurler Mickey Lolich. The Pilots threw Steve Barber (2–4) at Detroit with the usual results: He was ineffective (4 IP, 5 H, 3 R) and walked away with his fourth loss of the season in the 6–1 defeat. Lolich, for his part, continued to feast not only on donuts but the Pilots as well. He struck out 12 Pilots (his three-game total vs. Seattle was 42 strikeouts) and reached 100 career victories.

In the second game Denny McLain got his 21st win as the Tigers squeezed out a 4–3 win in which the Pilots had led. Gelnar started and did well but left after the 5th inning leading 3–2. Four relievers finished out the game for Seattle but could not beat McLain, who was masterful (9 IP, 5H, 3 R). O'Donoghue (1–2) got tagged for two runs and the loss. After the game popular Tommy Davis was traded to the Astros, where he would join Bouton. The Pilots in return got little-used outfielder Sandy Valdespino and minor-league prospect Danny Walton, another outfielder, who was the key to the deal. The trade upset Davis a lot; he actually wanted to stay in Seattle![15] After being traded around the past few years he thought he had found himself a home with a starting job and popularity with the fans. Walton was tearing up the AAA American Association and would wind up being the 1969 Minor League Player of the Year. His career now had much promise, but he would turn out to be another AAAA player: too good for the minors but not good enough for the Majors. This may actually be a bit unfair. Walton's career would be beset with injuries that would limit his at-bats and yo-yo him up and down from the minors. Since the rosters would be expanding on September 1st, both players joined the team. Milkes also promoted promising pitcher Miguel Fuentes; he was 8–2 with a 1.46 ERA in the minors.

For the closeout game of the series, Gene Brabender just did not have his good fastball. He got beat by Earl Wilson (12–8) 7–2 and saw his record drop below .500 (10–11). Gene may have been wearing out at this point in the season; he went five innings and gave up three homers, two to Willie Horton and one to Don Wert. The staff was not getting any run support either: The Pilots had scored 12 runs in their last six games. The Pilots were now 49–81 and in sole possession of sixth (last) place, and they were 1–15 since August 15. Infielder Fred Stanley was recalled after the game, which was his first Major League look.

The local press was now asking Milkes how safe Joe Schultz's job was. Milkes refused to give his manager any support nor guarantee his return. Needless to say the entire coaching staff had to feel at least uneasy about their future.[16]

Other problems were quickly mounting for the year-old organization. Their future stadium project should have been well under way by this time. Not only had clearing and construction not begun, the site had not yet been chosen! There was no way the stadium would be completed by the original agreed-upon date now. The most likely site was Seattle Center near downtown, but residents formed a Committee to Save Seattle Center and filed court papers to prevent the construction. As the summer was winding down and the Pilots' hopes for a third-place finish were dashed, visions of a new stadium were growing dim too.

However, the Pilots had much more immediate woes. Forget about their future stadium, they were in jeopardy of losing their present one. The constant behind-the-scenes battle between the City of Seattle officials and Pacific Northwest Sport Inc. came to a head and erupted into the press during the first week of September when Mayor Floyd Miller threatened to evict the team from Sick's Stadium.[17] As if the team's playing woes weren't enough it now appeared that Seattle's own mayor and its citizens were openly working *against* their new Major League team. The team owed the city money but felt the city had not lived up to its part of the bargain by failing to bring the stadium up to standards. A double-header vs. the White Sox on September 8th was put in doubt with the possibility of the city locking the Pilots out. Distracting matters were the circling sharks in the form of Arlington, Texas and Milwaukee, Wisconsin. Both cities immediately offered the team their own baseball fields, Turnpike Stadium and County Stadium respectively, in which to finish out the season and possibly help them procure a major-league team. Both offers were rebuffed by the league. However, the immediate problem persisted with the City of Seattle insisting that Soriano and Daley put up a $600,000 letter of credit from a bank to cover four years' rent.[18] No bank would cooperate because Pacific Northwest Sports had either run out of money or was about to do so. The banks, and the city, knew that it was now mathematically impossible for the Pilots to break even in 1969.

Mayor Miller met with representatives from the American League and agreed to stay the eviction. AL President Cronin went to Seattle and met with both Daley and city officials. After this meeting Daley and Soriano had a press conference in which Daley angrily stated, "Seattle has one more year to prove itself."[19] His frustration with the season's attendance was understandable but this comment appeared repeatedly in the local press and just served to further alienate the fans.

September 1–2

The Pilots limped into New York for their final series against the Yankees after getting swept by the Tigers and bested by the O's. Normally, after being humiliated by powerful teams like Detroit and Baltimore, the Pilots would have been happy to play weaker teams such as the Yanks. However, it now meant little. Finishing in third had been given up on weeks ago, the manager was on thin ice, and so was the organization itself. With management finally realizing its mistake, rookies were now being played regularly at most positions, not just in the bullpen. Indeed, if some of the veterans seemed to have lost interest, who could blame them?

The Pilots showed up at Yankee Stadium for a twi-night double header with George Brunet set to face New York ace Mel Stottlemyre. Brunet got things turned around, pitching well but leaving after six innings, losing 3–1. John O'Donoghue came on and was hit hard for his third straight outing, but Brunet got tagged for the loss, dropping to 7–12. After this 6–1 loss the Pilots were 1–15 over their last 16 games.

It couldn't go on forever. Just when it seemed the Pilots would lose every game the rest of the season they won in exciting form. Recently acquired Bob Meyer started in what was his first appearance for Seattle. Although he would finish his brief Major League career with a 2–12 record, tonight he was masterful, giving up just one run in nine innings. He actually may have lost the game were it not for ex–Yank Mike Hegan singling in the top of the 9th with Harper on second to tie the game 1–1. In the top of the 13th light-hitting Ron Clark singled with one out. Donaldson came to the plate next and struck out for the second out, and it looked like the Yankees would have another free shot to win. However, Harper walked and up stepped young Steve Hovley. The rookie was having a fine season and he was not intimidated by the house that Ruth built. Steve singled on the first pitch, Clark scored, and the Pilots led 2–1. That would have been enough tonight but Hegan came up for the second time and hit a three-run home run to give Seattle a 5–1 lead, where it would remain. Hegan had exacted his revenge on the Yankees for leaving him exposed in the expansion draft. It must have been even sweeter because just two years after the draft, the Bombers could have used a player of Hegan's ability; in fact, they wound up getting him back in a trade a couple of years later. Dooley Womack (3–2), another former Yankee, got credited with the win, his first as a Pilot.

The Pilots' last game ever at Yankee Stadium was another long one. A string of pitchers got the team to the 13th inning with the score tied 3–3. Danny Walton showed his potential by hitting a go-ahead solo homer in that frame. The overused Brabender was brought into the game by Schultz, who wanted to win this one very badly and make it two victories in a row. It was another panic move that resulted in disaster. Horace "Hoss" Clarke led off with a single and stole second. He went to third on a groundout and then got caught up in a controversial play. Roy White grounded to Donaldson at second, who fired home to beat Clarke, except that Clarke had turned tail and headed back to third. McNertney ran him back and fired to Harper. Brabender and Oyler joined in the rundown when Clarke finally scrambled toward home. When he did, Horace ran into Brabender and was called safe at home on interference. The Yanks tied the score and won it in the following inning 5–4. If nothing else the Pilots had to lead baseball in frustrating losses. It could also be said that the Pilots did not give up on themselves and just throw in the towel.

September 4–7

The Pilots came home to Sick's Stadium after a discouraging 2–7 road trip. For most teams this would have been a relief but the Pilots had a 14-game losing streak at home to deal with. The streak would go to 15 as the team lost the first of four games to their expansion rivals the Royals. It was an unremarkable game that saw John Gelnar's record drop to 2–10. Seattle

On September 6, Greg Goossen crosses the plate after homering. He is congratulated by Jim Pagliaroni (*Seattle Times*).

batsmen could only scratch out five hits off winner Dick Drago (8–11). In the bottom of the 9th the Pilots were losing 5–1 when Steve Hovley led off with a single. Don Mincher stepped into the batter's box and hit his 23rd home run of the season. The next three batters grounded out. How many times could a team have late rallies only to fall short? There appeared to be no good news for Pacific Northwest Sports as the attendance for the evening was 3958. The owners knew that they were not going to break even now but it was a Thursday night at the end of the summer; it appeared that any fans that the Pilots had earlier in the season had lost interest.

The following night was Friday and the teams had perfect weather for baseball. Like so many times before, Gene Brabender was called on to turn things around and he did so once more. The youngsters Goossen (6) and Walton (2) were the stars tonight as they hit back-to-back home runs in the third. Down 4–3 in the seventh, Walton came up with the bases loaded and hit a sac fly to tie it. He was followed again by Goossen, who singled in the winning run. The score stayed 5–4 and the Pilots finally came away with a home win. Brabender upped his record to 11–12, his 11 wins represented 22% of his team's victories.

The Pilots lost on Saturday evening as Bob Meyer (0–1) started and got his first loss. He was wild and gave up six hits and three walks against no strikeouts in 3⅔ innings. It mattered little now but the bullpen was used extensively in this 6–2 loss; but at least there were a few new rookie arms out there. The Saturday night game drew 4744 customers.

On Sunday's day game Brunet started and was very ineffective again. He avoided another loss thanks to Royals starter Moe Drabowsky's being equally bad. After 9 innings the score was tied 5–5. The Royals managed to get a run across in the top of the 10th on three singles. It looked like another demoralizing defeat until Harper tripled with two out in the bottom of the frame with Donaldson on first to tie the game. Hovley was up next and walked and was followed by Wayne Comer. He lined a single to right field as Harper crossed the plate for a 7–6 Pilot win. Segui, who was off the disabled list and threw three innings, picked up the win and his record now stood at 10–5, not bad for a pitcher whose team was 33 games under .500. Only 4653 fans witnessed a great Sunday afternoon of baseball.

September 8

The 5th-place White Sox came to town for a one-day series doubleheader. Remarkably, unbelievably, over 10,000 fans showed up. In the first game Steve Barber was given another start. In the bottom of the first Steve Whitaker (4) hit a solo home run to stake the Pilots to an early, albeit slim, lead. It proved not to be enough as Barber gave it right back in the top of the second on a Buddy Braford homer. One could not blame Seattle fans for being frustrated and anticipating another come-from-behind loss. However, today Steve Barber flashed his old 20-game-winner form and went the rest of the way without giving up another run. He had no room for error either, since the Pilots would only score once more on four walks in the third inning. The score stood at 2–1 and Barber (3–4) won for the first time since June 3rd. It was also the first time in over a month that Seattle had won consecutive games.

On September 8, rookie Miguel Fuentes pitches his way to a seven-hit victory in his major league debut. He was the Pilots' most prized prospect, but his story would be the club's most tragic (*Seattle Times*).

In the nightcap the Pilots started recently recalled rookie Miguel Fuentes. Next to Gorman Thomas he was perhaps the most highly touted minor-leaguer in the Pilots' system. The youngster did not disappoint while giving the team's fans something to cheer for and hope for the future. Through the first six innings he was throwing a three-hit shutout. When he came to bat in the bottom of the 6th he was given a standing ovation and responded with a single. Meanwhile the Pilots had scored five times to support the pitcher's effort. Rookie Steve Hovley went 4 for 5 with two doubles. Other rookies kicked in, too; Comer and Walton had two hits and an RBI each and Goossen added another hit and RBI. This is exactly what the Pilots' management should be doing at this point in the season. They could not change how the season had gone thus far but they could figure out their plans for the future with auditions. It was also a valuable confidence booster and experience for the young players. In the 8th inning Miguel finally gave up a run on a couple of hits but he did not become unnerved and finished the game. When the final out was recorded his teammates ran out to the mound and surrounded him and walked him back to the clubhouse. Additionally, the Pilots had now won three in a row and were just ½ game from climbing out of last place.

September 10–11

The Pilots took a short flight to Oakland for a quick two-game series. Although the team was not exactly storming back in the American League, the demeanor in the clubhouse had changed with the last three wins and the presence of a group of wide-eyed rookies. Also, the A's, who earlier in the season looked invincible, had just lost 12 of their last 15 and were letting the Twins pull ahead.

In the first game Brabender (11–12) faced Chuck Dobson (14–11), both were workhorse type pitchers with roughly .500 records. Although Brabender did not have his best stuff today he outlasted Dobson with fine relief help from Segui, who picked up his 9th save of the year. Wayne Comer hit his 13th homer of the season to put the Pilots on top in the eventual 9–4 victory. This was Seattle's fourth straight victory, their longest winning streak since early May. They were also 6–4 for September so far, the six victories matching their entire total for August. If nothing else, the pressure was off the players now; they proved that they could still win and there were no longer any expectations on them at this point. The same security was not afforded to Schultz.

The following day the Pilots were back at Oakland-Alameda Stadium with the young Bob Meyer taking the mound and trying to extend the team's winning streak. He lasted five innings, giving up eight hits, including two doubles and a pair of home runs to Sal Bando and Bob Johnson. The Athletics easily got by Seattle 6–3 and Meyer's record dropped to 0–2. Fred Talbot came on to pitch 2⅔ innings of scoreless relief against his old team to earn the only save of his career.

September 12–14

The Pilots returned home and would play back-to-back double-headers and a single game against the Angels. In the first game of the first doubleheader George Brunet (2–5) had his best showing as a Pilot in throwing a complete game, 5-hitter, the only run coming off a fifth-inning solo HR by Aurelio Rodriguez. Brunet picked up the win and even stroked his only home run of the year against his old team in the 4–1 victory. Tommy Harper stole 3 bases to raise his league-leading total to 70 and rookies Greg Goossen (three hits) and Wayne Comer (14th HR) had good games. Hovley continued to impress by going 2 for 4.

The nightcap also showcased rookies as the Pilots' only hope now was to look toward the future. Skip Lockwood started (third rookie this week to start) and pitched a shutout through seven. Segui and Locker relieved him

Tommy Harper slides into second ahead of the Angels' Jim Fregosi for his seventieth steal of the season (*Seattle Times*).

and pitched a scoreless game the rest of the way. With the score tied 1–1 in the tenth, rain stopped the contest, which would be replayed prior to the next day's regularly scheduled game; however, all individual records from the game counted. Recently called up Fred Stanley, who would go on to play 15 years in the majors, went 3 for 3 with a walk.

The next afternoon the teams took the field to play the unexpected extra game. Marty Pattin started and was average, giving his team five innings of five-hit ball and surrendering three runs (all earned). Angels starter Tom Murphy was worse, giving up nine hits and six runs, dropping his record to 9–14. Segui pitched four innings of relief and got credit for the win, upping his amazing record to 11–5 (and 9 saves). Hovley/Mincher/Walton went 6 for 11 in the middle of the order, helping their team to a 6–4 win.

An hour after the first game Miguel Fuentes walked out to the mound in front of 11,000 enthusiastic Seattle fans. Coming off his great debut, Miguel pitched another good game, going 5⅓ innings and giving up three runs, all earned. This, however, wasn't enough. Eddie Fisher was a reliever who had been in the Majors since 1959 with several teams. By 1969 he had pitched in 600 games but had not started one since 1964. He pitched in 52 games in 1969 but today would be his only start of the season. The Pilots would have expected that he would not be able to go long into the game, they were in for a surprise. Fisher gave up three hits and no walks in eight full innings. In the bottom of the 9th inning he went back out, just three outs away from a shutout and a 4–0 lead against Seattle. Fred Stanley led off with a triple to centerfield. Steve Whitaker batted for John Gelnar and singled to drive home

Stanley. At this point Halos manager Lefty Phillips came out to the mound to get Fisher. As he walked back to California's dugout the Seattle fans rose and applauded him.

After recording two outs, Ken Tatum allowed Hovley an RBI single, but then got Walton on called strikes to end the game. Fisher got the well-deserved win (2–2) and Tatum the save (19). Miguel got hung for somewhat of a tough-luck loss as the Angels beat the Pilots 4–2, splitting the double-header. The Pilots were held to 6 hits, but 2 of them belonged to Hovley, who was 10 for 23 over the last six games.

On Sunday the Pilots played a day game to close out the long series before going on their last road trip of the season. Steve Barber, who had quietly gotten back into the rotation, started and was able to go 6⅓ innings. His season-long problem of giving up too many hits continued as the Angels recorded 10 safeties including an Aurelio Rodriguez (7) homer. California was able to bang out a total of 14 hits but was somehow held to just 4 runs. That break went for naught as Andy Messersmith (15–9) struck out eleven Pilots and held them to 3 hits, winning by a 4–2 margin with Barber dropping to 3–5.

September 15–16

The Pilots arrived in Kansas City to play their final two games against the AL's other expansion team. At this point in the season the Pilots' record stood at 57–88 and in sixth (last) place while the Royals were 61–84 and in fourth place. Both teams would finish the year exactly as they stood right now. In the first game of a two-game set Gene Brabender started against recently recalled Royals rookie Jerry Cram. Gene was in his old form, going seven innings and giving up just three hits and two runs before tiring. However, the Royals freshman had matched Brabender, also going seven and giving up two runs on four hits. In the top of the eighth Schultz elected to stay with Brabender, who was to lead off; Big Gene responded with a single. Tommy Harper sacrificed him to second with a bunt, followed by Donaldson flying out to right with Brabender tagging to third. With two out Comer was solid again, singling to center to knock in Brabender and give the Pilots the lead. Brabender, who had been running back and forth on the basepath for 15 minutes, tried to continue in the bottom of the eighth but walked the first batter and was removed for Diego Segui, who closed the door and picked up his 10th save. The Pilots were now 9–8 in September and Brabender's record stood at 13–12. To have a winning record on this team was impressive enough but even more so when your first win did not come until May 21st. With his 13th victory, Gene also set the record for most wins for a pitcher on an expansion team, a record (12 wins) previously held by Bennie Daniels of the 1961 Washington Senators.

The following night was an overcast, chilly evening in Kansas City. It had rained overnight and during the day but stopped in time for the game to be played. What remained was a heavy infield and an outfield full of puddles; the time when owners had much concern for their players' safety had not arrived yet. Bob Meyer took the mound hoping that his hard luck would stop tonight and not his team's winning streak. He pitched well enough to win, but not on the Pilots. After seven and a half innings the score stood tied at one with the Royals coming to bat in the bottom of the frame. Bob Oliver led off with a single and was followed by KC starter Wally Bunker. It was at this point that the condition of the field affected the outcome of the game. Bunker reached out and slapped a single to left field with Danny Walton giving chase. As he got to the ball he hit one of the puddles, fell and slid 10 feet as the ball rolled past him to the outfield wall. By the time it was retrieved and thrown in, Oliver had crossed the plate and Bunker was on second. The score stood at 2–1 in favor of Kansas City. Meyer, to his credit, did not let it affect him and retired every batter he faced after that. The score held and Meyer had to settle for a complete game 5-hit loss. Bunker (11–10) also threw a complete game 4-hitter but came away with the win. It was another one of those games that the Pilots had gotten so used to. Making it a little worse was the fact that the first Royal run scored on a Lou Piniella sacrifice. After the game the Pilots boarded a bus to Chicago for a single double-header.

Lou Piniella, about to be tagged out by Gerry McNertney, would come back to haunt the Pilots (Milwaukee Brewers).

September 17

In the first game of the day Marty Pattin was sluggish, giving up four hits and three walks in five innings. After allowing three runs he was removed for Miguel Fuentes' first relief outing. This was another questionable move by Schultz and Maglie as Fuentes had always been a starter and other pitchers were available. Miguel quickly got into trouble in his new role and was pulled after giving up three runs in one inning. A string of Pilot relievers followed him. Despite a 3-run Seattle ninth, the team fell short, losing 6–4. Pattin fell to 7–12, his once-promising season now a disaster.

In the second game rookie Skip Lockwood was another victim of no run support. He pitched six fine innings, striking out four, walking none, and giving up just two runs. The White Sox were able to manufacture a run in each of the first two innings but were shut down the rest of the way. Diego Segui pitched the final two innings without allowing a run either. In the third inning John Donaldson hit a solo HR but there would be no scoring after that. Billy Wynne (6–6) started for Chicago and went all the way, giving up just four hits and getting credit for the 2–1 victory. It was the best game of Wynne's career; his final Major League record would be 8–11. In 1969 mediocre pitchers seemed to have a habit of having the best games of their careers while facing the Pilots. The Pilots had already played 20 games in September and they were tired, it had been a long season for the players. If they needed any more discouragement, they had 13 games left, 7 of which were against the Twins and 3 against the A's. The team's record stood at 58–91, the main goal had suddenly become to avoid 100 losses. All they would need to do was go 5–8 the rest of the way. This was not exactly what Milkes and Soriano had envisioned in March.

Skip Lockwood was a late-season call-up who pitched in six games for the team. He was one of only six Pilots who would play in the majors into the 1980s (National Baseball Hall of Fame Library, Cooperstown, N.Y.).

September 19–21

The Pilots left Chicago and took a short flight to Minneapolis, where they had a day off to lick their wounds before a weekend series. After starting out the month so well they had just lost three in a row and were set to play the Twins, against whom they were 2–9, 0–6 at Metropolitan Stadium. Steve

Twins slugger Bob Allison bats against the Pilots on September 21 at Metropolitan Stadium. Seattle did not play well at all in Minnesota. The Pilots' catcher is Gerry McNertney (©Bettman/CORBIS).

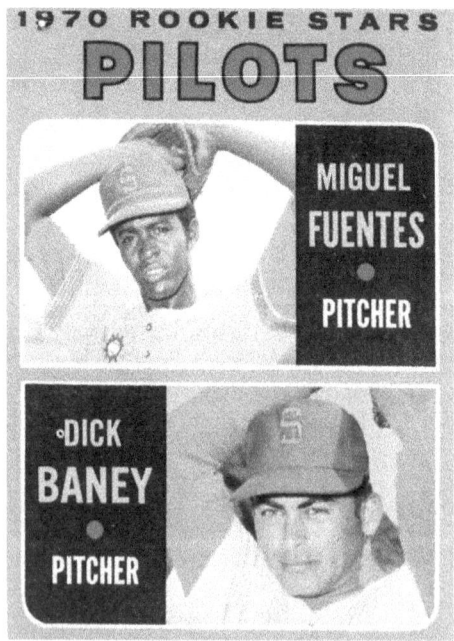

Barber, who was finally doing better—not great, but better—started and had another decent game. He was starting to get the feeling of his pitches again. Steve was able to go five innings and gave up two runs, one earned. He walked none but his old Achilles heel did him in, he allowed seven hits. Steve had an almost insurmountable task anyway as Twins All-Star Dave Boswell (18–11) struck out 14 Pilots and walked only 1 while going the distance and winning 2–1.

On Saturday afternoon the

The Pilots finally started to use younger pitchers in September. Fuentes and Baney started on consecutive days against the mighty Twins during the season's final games (Topps).

8. The Season Continues

Pilots faced another All-Star in 19-game winner Jim Perry. However, Seattle sent out their ace in Gene Brabender. Gene did not have his best stuff but after 6½ innings the Pilots led 2–0. Jim Perry led off the bottom of the 7th by grounding out. Could Seattle eke out a win? The next batter, Ted Uhlaender, tripled. Rod Carew followed and singled home Uhlaender to make it a 2–1 ballgame. Tony Oliva singled to center, chasing Brabender from the game. Schultz brought in the reliable Segui, who promptly struck out Killebrew for the second out. However, the next batter, Rich Reese, singled, bringing home Carew to tie the game at 2–2. Cesar Tovar came to bat looking to knock in the go-ahead run. He hit a sharp grounder to third base and John Kennedy opted to go home with the ball. McNertney just tagged Oliva out in time to hold the game at a tie. The way Perry was pitching the Pilots would have to get lucky; either team could win the game on one bad pitch. In the bottom of the 9th, Segui retired Uhlaender for the first out. In the course of the next minute Carew would single and Oliva would double him home. Some of the Pilots were stunned, others just dejected; they had seen this before. Seattle was now 0–8 at Metropolitan Stadium with one game remaining. The next day Dan Meyer (0–3) would face former All-Star and 20-game winner Dean Chance.

The Pilots showed up on Sunday (they had no choice) hoping to avoid the ignominy of going 0 for Minneapolis. In the top of the first, Tommy Harper singled and then stole second. Danny Walton then singled to third but Harper had to stay put. On the very next pitch the Pilots pulled off a double steal and now had second and third with no outs. (This was Harper's 73rd and final stolen base.) All of the Pilots were now standing on the dugout steps. But just as quickly as their hopes were raised they were also dashed. Whitaker struck out and Hovley lined into a double play. In the bottom of the first, Harmon Killebrew hit a monstrous home run off Meyer. A few minutes earlier the Pilots thought they were going to jump out to a several-run lead and now they were actually losing 1–0. One could have understood the Pilots' throwing in the towel right now but that is something they never did all season. The Pilots scored two in the top of the fourth to go ahead 2–1, briefly. In the bottom of the inning Meyer showed that he did not learn much today when Killebrew hit his second tape-measure HR. Both teams pushed one more run across (3–3) and that is how it stood going into the 9th inning. Jim Kaat, a starter who came on in relief, got two quick outs in the top of the frame. Down to their last out, light-hitting John Kennedy shocked Kaat and the Twins with his 4th homer of the year and second in two days. He came back to his jubilant teammates, who had spilled out onto the field to greet him. In the bottom of the ninth all of the Pilots must have either held their breath, bit their lip, or smoked a cigarette as John O'Donoghue retired the Twins 1–2–3. It may have been a case of a great amount of satisfaction in a small event but the Pilots took it. This one game, if nothing else, showed that this team of cast-offs and hopefuls were professional players who would not give up even at the end of a hopelessly lost season. It was a testament to their love of the game.

September 22–24

The Pilots arrived in Anaheim to play three games that were their final away series of the season. Since the acquisition of George Brunet, the veteran pitcher was unsteady, pitching some very good games but more often poor ones. His last decision was a victory on September 12th, also against his former team, and it was his best game of the year. Right from the start of today's game it was obvious that he would not repeat that feat. George labored through four innings, giving up four hits and three walks, leaving with the score tied 2–2. The Pilots were still in the game thanks to a Danny Walton home run, his third of the year. Womack (2–1) relieved Brunet and picked up the win when the Pilots rallied in the 5th. Segui got credit for his 11th save.

On Tuesday night Miguel Fuentes (1–2) started and was hit hard, the Angels put 10 men on base in 5⅔ innings. Whether or not his ill-advised relief appearance threw him off will never be known. The Pilots managed to keep it close but lost 5–4. In the eighth inning there was an unusual string of events that hurt the Pilots even further. With one out Don Mincher, who earlier had hit his 24th HR, singled to right but pulled a leg muscle running to first. Don was removed from the game and replaced by a pinch-runner, Mike Hegan. The irony in this was that Hegan was having one of the few good years offensively on the team but missed significant time due to leg muscle strains himself. The Pilots now had a man on first with one out and rookie sensation Danny Walton coming up. Walton swung at the first pitch and grounded to third for an inning-ending double play. However, as the Angels ran from the field their catcher Randy Brown stood over Walton, who was crumpled on the ground at home plate. The rookie had twisted his knee badly and it would require a cast. For a team that was loaded with injury-plagued vets, having one of their youngsters go down with a possible serious injury was the worst possible scenario, especially as they looked toward the future.

On Wednesday evening the Pilots played their final road game and could only manage four hits against Rudy May (10–13). Brabender (13–13) pitched well enough to win but picked up the loss, which dropped his record to .500 again. The team flew back to Seattle, where they had just seven games remaining. With their record at 60–95 they would have to go 3–4 the rest of the way to avoid 100 losses.

September 25–28

As the 1969 season mercifully drew to a close for the Pilots, they had to face the first-place Twins once again for a four-game series at Sick's Stadium. So far this season the Pilots were 3–11 against Minnesota. After the Twins left, the A's would come to town to finish out Seattle's season. Three wins almost didn't seem possible, but having already clinched the division, the Twins were resting some of their regulars for the AL Playoff. By some miracle the Pilots turned the tables on the Twins and beat them in three of four, thus ensuring they would not lose triple digits. It was the one goal that the team was able to deliver, albeit an adjusted goal.

Steve Barber (4–6) pitched the first game and had his best performance of the year. He struck out 10 over eight innings en route to an easy 5–1 victory. O'Donoghue came on for the ninth and was his usual effective self, gaining his sixth save. Greg Goossen also put on a one-man show, hitting a double and two home runs (7 & 8) and driving in three.

On Friday (9/26) night's game Lockwood once again pitched great and was supported by Goossen's 9th HR. However, it was only good for a tie and the game continued on to the bottom of the 14th. With two out, Wayne Comer stepped to the plate. It was just after midnight and not many of the 6,586 who attended were left to see some excitement at the end of a disappointing season. Comer swung at Tom Hall's first pitch, sending it into the left-field bleachers and guaranteeing Gelnar (3–10) his first victory in over three months. Harmon Killebrew's league-leading 48th home run was wasted.

The Pilots continued to get a look at their up-and-coming players as they started rookies in the final two games of the series, which were played on Sunday due to a rainout the day before. Miguel Fuentes (1–3) lost and Dick Baney (1–0) got his first major-league win.

In the first game Fuentes failed to get out of the second inning and was removed for John O'Donoghue with his team down 3–1. O'Donoghue was great again, pitching a scoreless 5+ innings, but the Pilots could never get back in the game and lost 5–2.

In the evening game Dick Baney (1–0) pitched perhaps the best game of his career. He went eight innings, striking out five and walking just one and giving up just a single run. Segui came on for the ninth and got his 12th and final save, good enough to lead the team in that category. Their one final goal had been achieved. With tonight's win the Pilots were 63–96 with three games left to play; 100 losses had been avoided. In the third inning Mincher hit his 25th, and final, home run, which also paced the club. His three RBIs gave him 78, good enough for second among Pilots. Don had a very good season, better than most observers had expected after his serious injury in '68. The Pilots could have only wished that the other infirm vets had bounced back like Mincher. With their eye on the future, Schultz gave Don, and his still sore leg, a breather the rest of the way and started Goossen at first base for all three remaining games.

September 30–October 2

The Oakland A's came to town for what no one knew would be the Pilots' last series ever. The A's quickly jumped out in front and won the first game 8–4, dropping Brabender to 13–14. Over the course of the long season Gene had been the staff's workhorse and had to be a bit worn out by now. It showed today as he could not get an out in the fourth inning; still, he did not deserve to be below .500. It's hard not to imagine what Brabender's record would have been had he still been a member of the AL Champion Orioles and enjoyed all of their run support; Gene probably wondered this too. Goossen, who was on fire, hit his 10th home run along with another three RBIs.

A total of 2937 fans showed up for the game. Despite the fact that it was a Tuesday night, the Pilots were guaranteed to finish last, and the summer weather was gone, this was still a shocking number for a Major League ballgame, especially for a team's inaugural year. It was the second worst home attendance for the Pilots, the worst (1,954) coming on Tuesday, April 29, vs. Cal. For the record, the Pilots went 14–16 in Septem-

Steve Whitaker went out with a bang, hitting home runs in the Pilots' last two games. His homer on October 2 was the Pilots' final hit and run scored (National Baseball Hall of Fame Library, Cooperstown, N.Y.).

ber with the help of several young players. This was considerably better than July and August.

The following night just 3,612 fans would witness the Pilots' last victory for the season. This figure represented the team's 4th worst-attended home game of the year. George Brunet started and although he was not sharp he bulled his way through eight innings and passed off a one-run lead to Segui. Diego Segui upped his fine record to 12–6 (with 12 saves), although he did that by giving up a run in his one inning of work that allowed the A's to tie the game. When former Pilot Fred Talbot gave up the winning run in the bottom of the ninth, Segui came away with a victory, although Brunet probably wasn't too happy with the turn of events. Little-used Steve Whitaker, who had earlier hit his 5th HR, scored that winning run, giving the Pilots a 4–3 win.

Thursday night, October 2nd, was a cold and damp typical Seattle fall evening. Through the turnstiles that night passed 5,473 paying customers, a symbol of the team's season. An anemic total of 12,022 customers came to see the Pilots' last series of the year. In 1969 there were 13 Major League teams that averaged more than that per game. One can be sure that Marvin Milkes and the Sorianos knew all of these figures too. But it was not a baseball night and summer seemed like a faraway distant memory.

The A's led 3–0 for most of the game and the Pilots looked to be shut out to close out their inaugural season. Steve Barber started and his recent success escaped him. He lasted just two innings and, in typical Pilots fashion, was followed by a parade of four relievers. With one out in the bottom of the ninth, Steve Whitaker managed to crack a solo homer; the Pilots' last home run, hit, and run. Did anyone even applaud or did they just stay wrapped under their blankets? Two quick outs later it was over. Steve Barber (4–7), who was supposed to anchor the team's pitching staff, took the loss in the club's final decision.

The fans slowly stood up, collected their belongings, and walked down the aisles heading toward the exits. And the Pilots players... They too collected their gear, walked off the Sick's Stadium field, headed back into the clubhouse and into baseball history. The ballpark was now silent and for twenty minutes the powerful lights lit up the night sky heavy with mist. Then the lights were turned off and the stadium went dark.

Chapter 9

The Failure

> I want to assure the baseball world and Pacific Northwest fans that this will be a stable organization and we can expect to see Major League Baseball here for many years to come.
> —GM Marvin Milkes, November 24, 1969[1]

With the season over the players went home, the Pilots faded from the fans' thoughts, and management went to work on the many issues that surrounded the team. There were many questions facing the Pilots, would there be as many answers?

The season, while frustrating, had not been a total loss. Last place is to be expected for an expansion team, and the Pilots kept up their end of the bargain. However, things must be taken in context; if the inaugural Pilots season was bad, then the Padres' and Expos' seasons were horrendous. Both teams posted a record of 52–110 compared to Seattle's 64–98. All three finished in 6th place (last) in their respective divisions, but while the Pilots wound up 33 games back, the Padres were 41 games back and the Expos ended up 48 back! Only the Royals fared better among the four expansion teams, 69–93, 4th AL West, and 28 games back from the first-place Twins. Also, one saving grace was the Indians, who at 62–99, 6th in the AL East, 46.5 games back, prevented the Pilots from having the worst record in the American League.

There were also bright spots on the Pilots roster. Starting with their All-Star, Don Mincher had ended any doubt about his injuries from the '68 beaning. He hit .246 while reaching 25 home runs and 78 RBI, and the unspeedy Mincher also managed to steal 10 bases. Tommy Harper proved to be a capable leadoff man and wound up leading baseball with 73 stolen bases. Mike Hegan, although hampered by injury, brought experience to the club and hit .292. Behind the plate Gerry McNertney's .241 average and 55 RBIs were more than the team had expected from him and he handled the pitching staff very well.

The Pilots had to be very pleased with the youngsters Wayne Comer and Steve Hovley in the outfield, who both had fine seasons. Rookies who were called up during the season that the club was excited about included Goossen (10 HR, .309), Fred Stanley (.279), and Danny Walton (3 HR, .217, 1969 Minor League Player of the Year). Where the team was very thin was the bench, with most of the roll players hitting poorly. Players such as Rollins, Oyler, Gil, Clark, Kennedy, and Simpson appeared to be on their way out or were already finished and helped pull the team's batting average down to an unacceptable .234.

On the pitching side there seemed to be one general theme: get younger, and for that matter, better. The team's ERA of 4.35 would not get it done in 1960s/'70s baseball. They needed a more durable starting staff so the manager would not have to deplete the bullpen so often. Gene Brabender was the only dependable starter on the staff. Marshall and Pattin had started out well and it was hoped that they would rebound. Gelnar, Meyer, Fuentes, Lockwood, and Baney all looked very promising. About the only strong point on the Pilots' staff had been their relief corps, when not abused, with Locker (2.18, 6 saves), O'Donoghue (2.96, 6 saves), and team pitching MVP Diego Segui (3.35, 12–6, 12 saves). By the end of the season 53 players had worn a Seattle Pilots uniform. Through the 1995 season only one team had ever had that many players on it during a single season, the 1915 Philadelphia A's with 56. Since 1996 nine teams have bested the Pilots' 53, but this has been due to expanded rosters, multiple

Danny Walton, the 1969 Minor League Player of the Year. After a decent 1970 season with Milwaukee his career fizzled because of high strikeouts and many injuries (Photo File).

relief specialists on every team, and players' no longer fearing going on the disabled list. By 1969 standards 53 was a startling number of players for one team. Some of the Pilots said that this did not help the team's cohesiveness. The roster was in a constant state of flux. In some cases management did not realize what they had in some of the players that were traded away. Others were never able to settle in; they were given too quick of a hook after just a brief look.

Milkes wasted no time in assigning blame and making moves. By the first week of November he released the entire coaching staff: Crosetti, Plaza, Maglie, and O'Brien. Since Schultz was not informed prior to his coaches' being fired, he assumed it was just a matter of time for him too, and he was right. On November 20th Milkes made it official and fired the Pilots' first manager. Interestingly, neither the Expos' nor Padres' managers were fired despite much worse seasons. Preston Gomez would go on to manage the Padres into the 1972 season and Gene Mauch would continue to lead the Expos through the 1975 season. However, back in the AL, the Royals manager Joe Gordon would retire after leading his team to the best record among the four expansion teams.

Top: Big Gene wound up leading the staff with 13 wins. He also led the team with 14 losses (Topps). *Bottom:* Fred Stanley, a September rookie call-up, would become a utility player on great Yankee teams of the '70s and '80s (National Baseball Hall of Fame Library, Cooperstown, N.Y.).

Naming a new Pilots manager for the 1970 season was something that needed to be done quickly and Milkes had already drawn up a list of candidates. The list, which had actually included Schultz initially, was narrowed down to Dave Bristol (former manager of the Cincinnati Reds and the PCL's San Diego Padres), Billy Martin (recently fired Twins manager), Bob Lemon (the Pilots' AAA manager at Vancouver), and Warren Spahn (manager of Tulsa AAA). On November 24th, Milkes settled on Bristol, a no-nonsense, serious type who could be said to be the exact opposite of Schultz. At the time, however, it was thought to be a dubious move since Bristol, like Schultz, was a career National Leaguer and that was what some believed to be part of the problem with Joe. But in the game of baseball a disciplinarian is usually replaced by a player's manager and vice versa. Bristol fit the bill. The fact that he was switching leagues did not seem to bother Bristol, who said at his press conference, "It's all baseball and it's predicated on one thing—winning."[2]

On November 20, Joe Schultz's lifelong dream of managing in the majors came to an abrupt end when he became the final casualty for the team's poor season. Opinions vary as to whether he did a good job at the helm of the Pilots or whether he deserved this fate. Joe would go on to coach for a few more seasons and even briefly served as interim manager of the Tigers in 1973 (28 games, 14–14). But he was never a serious managerial candidate again (Brace Photo).

Upon being named manager Bristol got on board with the getting-younger movement. "Sure, we intend to do some trading. You know Marvin. But mostly, we have to build from within. A lot of patience will be required. I think we have a chance to climb in the standings." Bristol continued, "Pennant? Well, the Mets proved an expansion team finally can arrive. Only I hope it does not take until our ninth year. I think I can promise that the Pilots will be competitive in 1970."[3]

Wes Stock was quickly named the pitching coach along with Cal Ermer (another former Twins manager), who was named third base coach. Next,

Hired to replace Joe Schultz, Dave Bristol was never a regular season manager of the Pilots. This 1970 Topps card photo was taken during spring training of that year just before the move to Milwaukee (Topps).

long-time NL infielder Roy McMillan was named first base coach and Jackie Moore bullpen coach. With that, the leadership was set and a big step for Seattle's 1970 season was in place. But hold on: Would there be a 1970 season in Seattle?

As baseball fans intently watched the 1969 miracle Mets capture the World Series, the Pilots teetered on bankruptcy. They had been quickly running out of money toward the end of the season and were trying to cover it up. Most baseball owners wanted both Daley and, especially, Soriano to divest themselves of their interests in the team by selling to new local Seattle ownership.[4] They were tired of the problems and the excuses. The club did not field a good team nor did it ever get together with the city to fix the problems at Sick's Stadium.

These problems led to a lack of attendance that led to low revenues, which in turn led to the club's not being able to pay its bills and rent. The league also felt that management was inept in never getting a local television contract. Initially, Soriano had demanded $15,000 per game, which was turned down by Seattle area stations.[5] He had overplayed his hand. As the season progressed, Soriano kept lowering his price all the way to $5,000 per game, but by then it was too late. The Pilots got off to a bad start and attendance was down almost from the beginning. The T.V. stations took the view that this was not a product that would draw in viewers. The lack of a T.V. affiliate just served to further alienate local area fans that could not connect with their team unless they actually attended games. When they did attend games, fans found the highest concession prices in the American League along with the highest ticket prices; and for seats that for the most part had bad views, were uncovered, or in the case of the newly constructed bleachers, were so far away the batter looked like a dot. The bottom line was the league wanted to start fresh in 1970, but still in Seattle.

During the winter meetings in 1969 AL owners discussed all of the problems surrounding the Pilots. After finances it was felt that the biggest issue was the lack of progress on a new stadium. This was something else in which Soriano had completely failed. Actual construction was supposed to begin by the last day of 1970 but that was a pipe dream now, a new site had not even been chosen yet as 1969 came to a close. Once a site was picked it would have to be condemned, demolished, and cleared prior to construction. Architectural firms would have to be contacted, interviewed, submit bids, and present plans. The plans would have to be approved by both the City of Seattle and Pacific Northwest Sports, after which many permits would have to be procured. The reality of the circumstances was that it may not have been Soriano's fault. Of the dozen sites that were initially on the drawing board the team and the city settled on one, the downtown Seattle Center. What should have been a step forward in the process became a quagmire as area residents formed the Committee to Save the Seattle Center. Their goal was to prevent construction of the stadium here and they would throw up lawsuits to stop it. This may have led some exasperated AL owners to wonder if Seattleites wanted a major-league team or not.

Just as things looked grim a savior appeared out of nowhere. Fred Danz, a Seattle businessman who owned a chain of theaters, stepped forward with an offer to buy the team for $10 million.[6] After several meetings with him, owners and AL President Cronin liked what they heard, the Pilots would be saved and stay in Seattle and everyone involved would have closure to this mess. The AL had a standing offer from Milwaukee interests, headed by car salesman Bud Selig, to purchase the team for $13.7 million.[7] It was a very tempting offer to turn down. In addition to the added money, Milwaukee had a ready-made major-league park in County Stadium. But the league did not want to deal with the embarrassment or lawsuits that would erupt from moving a franchise after just one lone season.

Once Danz took over, all systems would be a GO, but sadly Dewey Soriano would be bought out and step aside. Sportswriters, Seattleites, and officials could say all the negative things they wanted about Dewey's running of the club, but the bottom line was there would have been no Major League Baseball in Seattle in 1969 (or even 1977) if it was not for him. A local boy and baseball lifer, he poured his heart and energy into the team, but he would be out. William Daley, by the way, would retain part ownership under the Danz group. Daley's interest in the team would drop from 60% to 25% and he would become a minority stockholder. Daley agreed to this at Danz's behest; as a new owner he would need Daley's experience.

Just prior to acquiring the team Danz and his numerous partners and investors began to wonder if they had made a mistake. One of the first problems that they had to deal with was Seattle's new mayor, Wes Uhlman. The construction of the new stadium was a huge issue but more pressing was all of the money that the team owed the city for the use of Sick's Stadium in 1969 and 1970. Danz agreed to post $750,000.00 in letters of credit and bonds to the City of Seattle. Uhlman in turn agreed to send in a team of his employees to evaluate the ballpark and make repairs and add more bleachers.[8]

The Pilots were much more in debt than Danz was led to believe and worse yet, the Bank of California called in a $3.5 million loan that was originally taken out to purchase the team.[9] Meetings and more meetings were held that dragged on into spring training; all the while Selig and his partners waited on the sidelines observing the developments. Danz's suggestion to the bank that he be allowed to pay the debt in installments was rejected. Now Danz and his group were out of money. It was obvious to everyone that Pacific Northwest Sports Inc. had no money either and that the walls were closing in around the Pilots. Danz and his partners could not cover the additional $3.5 million so his offer to purchase the team fell through. And if you weren't aware of the team's condition at this point it should have become obvious when the AL loaned them $650,000 to pay for spring training (1970) and for back salaries.[10]

The Pilots' 1970 season was already underway and had been since mid–February in Tempe, Arizona. In what had become a regular theme for the franchise, this would not be without problems either. The owner of the facility threatened to lock the Pilots out unless certain promised projects got underway. E.B. Smith also demanded a $500,000.00 promissory note for back rent and future rent.[11] Soriano found local contractors to pave a new parking lot and access roads to the spring training stadium, but the team was there now on a day-to-day basis only.

For his part Milkes somehow stayed above the fray and continued to do his job. During the off-season, catcher Jim Pagliaroni and pitcher Steve Barber were released. While Pags would never play again, Barber rebounded and had five good seasons in a new role as a reliever. Next, injured Mike Marshall was sent packing to the Astros. Milkes had so little regard for the future Cy Young Award winner that he simply sold him to Houston for nothing in return.

The number one priority for the team was to obtain a healthy shortstop who was at least an average hitter; Oyler's .165 clip in the eight slot in front of the pitcher led to a huge hole in the Pilots line-up. It was almost sure outs in the 8–9 spots every time they came around. Milkes pulled the trigger on a big deal sending Oyler and Diego Segui to the A's for SS Ted Kubiak and pitcher George Lauzerique. The GM had ridded himself of Oyler and picked up an excellent fielder and decent hitter in Kubiak. The downside was losing Segui, who might have been the Pilots' best pitcher; the A's owner Charlie Finley regretted losing him in '68 and now he had him back. Segui would go on to play eight more years, becoming a footnote in Seattle baseball trivia. In 1977 he was obtained by the expansion Mariners from the Angels and became the only man to play for both of Seattle's Major League Baseball teams. Lauzerique, like Segui, was both a starter and reliever.

Milkes' second big trade occurred when he sent his All-Star, Don Mincher, and infielder Ron Clark to the A's for pitchers Lew Krause and Ken Sanders, catcher Phil Roof and outfielder Mike Hershberger. Beginning with trades during the season, the two teams had created an Oakland-to-Seattle shuttle. The Pilots were high on former prospect Greg Goossen and felt that he had finally blossomed. He had led the Pilots with a .309 average and hit .363 over the winter in the Arizona Instructional League. There was now a logjam at first base with Mincher, Goossen, and the experienced Hegan, who also had a solid year and proved himself to be a bona fide major leaguer. Mincher was the oldest, and of the three, the player for whom they could get the most in return. He was the natural choice to go, but die-hard fans didn't see it that way.

Krause was another serviceable starter/reliever who was young and already proven; he would be an upgrade in the bullpen. In Hershberger, Milkes got an excellent outfielder with one of the best arms in the game and a good bat. The outfield was now covered with Hershberger in left or center, Walton in right, Comer in center, and Hovley in right. One of the last three would become the fourth outfielder. Sanders was more or less a throw-in, as was Clark.

Although the team looked better on paper Milkes had now traded away the team's three most accomplished and popular players in Mincher, Segui, and Davis. These improvements, while necessary, may have turned more fans away.

The most shocking development of the Pilots' off-season happened on January 29, 1970, thousands of miles away from Seattle. Tragically, the young and promising pitcher Miguel Fuentes was shot three times in the chest and killed during a bar fight in his native Puerto Rico.

Miguel Fuentes (National Baseball Hall of Fame Library, Cooperstown, N.Y.).

Chapter 10

The End

On March 17, 1970, the AL owners met in Tampa, Florida, to make a final determination regarding the Pilots. The decision was to approve the transfer of the team to Milwaukee. However, they were served with a court order obtained by the State of Washington and the City of Seattle preventing the relocation of the team. The order was issued at the request of Alfred Schweppe, a Seattle attorney. His position was that he would be suffering damages if the Pilots left Seattle. Schweppe had purchased two season tickets and a parking spot for the 1970 season totaling $775.00.[1] He further stated that he was also representing the people of Seattle. This legal missile completely blindsided the AL owners. The court forbade the league from changing the schedule of its games and Pacific Northwest Sports from moving any equipment from the team's Tempe, Arizona, spring training facility or changing/canceling their radio broadcasts.

The owners' hands were now tied as the Seattle Pilots lived on. The AL, though, put their lawyers immediately to work and they hauled everyone into federal bankruptcy court. During the hearings the Pilots' treasurer Max Soriano told the court that the team had lost $1 million in 1969 and that they expected to lose $1.5 million in 1970.[2] Max said that if the team was forced to play in Seattle in 1970 it would be catastrophic. The Pilots' debts totaled $8.3 million and they had less than $100,000 ($87,000) in the bank. In two days $216,000 in loan payments were due. The average monthly overhead to operate the team was $300,000.[3] Milkes himself admitted that there was no money to pay the players their bonuses. Once they were 10 days late the players would automatically become free agents. He further stated there was no money to pay the civilian employees and the coaching staff their salaries.[4] The Pilots' own GM had made the court's decision easy. At 5:00 PM on March 30, 1970 (the last day of spring training), Judge Sidney Volinn signed an order allowing the transfer of the team to Milwaukee.[5] He stayed the order for one day in the last-ditch hope that somebody from the Seattle area would step forward with a concrete offer to purchase the team. On the morning of April 1st the Pilots ceased to exist. A moving truck, which had left Tempe, Arizona, loaded with team equipment, was parked in Utah waiting for instructions; they were contacted and told to turn east, head for Milwaukee.

Examining how the courts and the league went about the transfer, one thing is clear: Seattle was given every opportunity to retain their team. Other ideas were looked at to save the Pilots. Washington State Attorney William Dwyer wanted the team to file for bankruptcy and appoint a trustee to run the club. In this case the American League would take over the Pilots and keep them in Seattle. They could run the club, since the league itself was not bankrupt, until a suitable area buyer was found. However, after giving it some consideration the AL decided that it did not want the responsibility or delicate entanglements that would come with running a team. (The Pilots' eventual owner Bud Selig would have no such reservations when he purchased the Expos for Major League Baseball 32 years later. That move turned out to be a complete and utter failure.) Edward Carlson, chairman of Western Hotels, put forth a plan to buy the team and run it as a non-profit entity. His investors would supply the team with a $2.5 million line of credit and Pacific Northwest Sports would continue to run the team. Their employees would be paid but the entity PNWS would not profit. Any money made, after paying expenses and costs, would go to local community service and educational groups.[6] A team designed to not make a profit surprisingly did not go over too well with the other owners, who turned down the idea. One judge sitting on one of the Pilots' many bankruptcy hearings stated that "nobody seems to want it [the team]."

Pilot fans, although few in number, were stunned and saddened by the loss of their team. Their shock was understandable, despite the numbers problems with the club: No modern-day Major League Baseball team had lasted just one year. The Houston Colt .45s were only around three years (1962–1964), but that doesn't count because they were the same organization in 1965, just with a different name (Astros) and a new stadium (Astrodome). Houston did not lose its ball team.

The most short-lived teams since 1902 were the 13-year runs of both the Milwaukee Braves (1953–1965) and the Kansas City A's (1955–1967). However, if one went all the way back to the earliest days of the Dead Ball Era, there was one other one-year team in the AL when many still considered it a bush league. The American League's inaugural season was 1901, when it started play with eight charter teams. In what can only be considered strangely ironic, the fledgling Milwaukee Brewers collapsed and moved to St. Louis, where they became the Browns in 1902.

The quickly-thrown-together 1970 Brewers yearbook. The players' photographs were in their Pilots uniforms but the words PILOTS and SEATTLE had been air-brushed out.

On April 7th, 1970, the Milwaukee Brewers played their first game under an overcast sky with a threat of snow. Were it not for the 37,237 fans in attendance it could have been Seattle. Now Bud Selig was the hero of the day; he had become the Emil Sick of Milwaukee. And if the Brewers looked liked the Pilots it was because they were wearing their uniforms. The equipment staff got out their razors and hastily cut off the words "Pilots" and "Seattle" and replaced them with "Brewers" and "Milwaukee." The distinctive Pilots logos were tossed in the trash. To this day the Brewers' color scheme dates to the Pilots. Selig had been savvy enough to have tickets printed up and to line up staff to be hired well prior to April. He even had the stadium cleaned up and the playing field ready. The only satisfaction Seattle baseball fans had this day was the Brewers' 12–0 loss to the Angels. The Brewers' new ace and opening-day starter, Lew Krause, could only go three innings and was removed after giving up four runs. He was followed by the relief parade of four pitchers, who gave up another eight runs. Yes, it definitely had the feel of a Pilots game. The Pilots, excuse me, Brewers would have been 1-hit by Andy Messersmith were it not for Steve Hovley picking up where he left off and going 3 for 3.

The following day, on April 8th, a crowd gathered at Sick's Stadium for one final Pilots event. In Pacific Northwest Sports' last act a fire sale was held at the entrance to the ballpark. Caps, helmets, baseball cards, tee-shirts, yearbooks, and pennants were sold at cut-rate prices.

A rare 1970 Media Guide that somehow survived. Sold for over $200, a 1969 version sells for less than half.

Toward the end of spring training the following short article appeared in *The Sporting News*.

> Baseball is not a sport—it's big business claim the realists. Yet what has been happening in Seattle would make any businessman, big or small, wince. Since

Tommy Harper models the Brewers' new (Pilots' old) uniform at Milwaukee County Stadium in April 1970 (©Bettman/CORBIS).

the American League awarded a franchise to Seattle for the 1969 season, the Pilots situation has inspired a lot of descriptive terms, including Mickey Mouse. But never has the Seattle operation been called businesslike. Maybe that's the root of the entire tragi-comedy unfolding in the Northwest.

The Seattle fiasco should provide lessons aplenty for the American League, Seattle's political and business leaders and the Pilots management. It appears that all must shoulder some of the blame for the most glaring flop since baseball pushed the expansion button in 1960. As this is written Seattle is still in the Major League picture, but just barely. If the city wins a reprieve, it will have to improve on its 1969 performance to attain permanent Major League status. If it loses the Pilots in the current showdown, Seattle can't cry foul with much conviction. Seattle's most affluent and influential citizens confined their participation largely to expressions of delight at the arrival of a Major League Baseball team. They failed to fund the team or even attend games. William Daley was the largest single investor in the Pilots original ownership group (60%). It was commonly known that Daley preferred a lesser position and share in the club and repeatedly asked Seattle money men to invest in the Pilots—to no avail. Meanwhile, brothers Dewey and Max Soriano borrowed heavily to acquire their 35% interest in the club.

In the future the Majors had better take a hard look at the whole picture before granting new franchises or okaying the sale or transfer of existing ones. The league would be wise to insist on ironclad, written contracts spelling out the obligations of both city and club. And stronger financial credentials for prospective franchise investors seem imperative too.[7]

While the Pilots' story is unique and interesting it certainly isn't hard to figure out what happened. Seattle probably should not have been awarded a Major League Baseball franchise in 1969; they weren't ready. But undue pressure was brought to bear on MLB by powerful Washington senators Jackson and Magnunson.[8] Complicating matters was the date change of expansion from 1971 to 1969. This gave Pacific Northwest Sports, Inc., who owned the Pilots, little time to shore up support for their enterprise. They began the season very under-capitalized, partially due to not having a television affiliate. Once the season started the team got off to a bad start and attendance plum-

10. The End

meted; that loss in revenue was something the Pilots never recovered from.

Before the season began, Dewey Soriano predicted a first-year attendance of over 1 million.[9] What he based this on is anybody's guess but he should not have counted on that money. The team finished the year with a final attendance figure of 677,944. It would be difficult, if not impossible, for any business to survive on two-thirds of its anticipated income. Usually the top 10–20% is the profit margin, so you can do the math and see what the Pilots were up against.

However, this alone cannot be blamed for the Pilots' failure. There was a dramatic downward trend in baseball attendance in the second half of the 1960s and Seattle was not last in that tally in 1969. The woeful Padres showed a figure of 512,970, followed by the Phillies with 519,414. In the AL the White Sox had 589,546 turn the gates, followed by the Indians with 619,790. The star-studded, AL Champion Orioles hit the one million mark on the last game of the season. What these teams (except the Padres) had going for them that Seattle did not was that they were already established organizations. Being so, they could withstand problems better. They had management staffs that had been around the Major Leagues longer and knew what to expect. They did not overestimate and budgeted money better. Also, they did not have the start-up costs that the Pilots had. These additional costs to Pacific Northwest Sports really put them in a hole, one they could not climb out of.

The Padres, although an expansion team as well, were better funded. They did not have to pay the banks as much money on the 1st of every month. They were also playing in a new stadium that needed no upgrades or repairs. In fact, they would play in their original ballpark for 34 years. Like the Pilots, the Royals were in an old stadium, but it was an old Major League stadium. It held

An unused full ticket for a June 1970 game that was never played by the Pilots. The Brewers played the Orioles at County Stadium instead. Pilots tickets command $25 to $75 depending on condition and if they are full. The 1969 home opener tickets are worth $150 to $200.

Above: Pilots patches, including three cap patches that were intended for, but never used on, cheap souvenir hats. *Right:* A child's T-shirt sold at souvenir stands at Sick's Stadium. The shirt is still in its original plastic wrapper that also has a Pilots logo.

Left: A bobbing head doll. These are rare in any condition and variation although some are more valuable than others. *Above:* The holy grail of Pilots memorabilia? Perhaps. Children's plastic batting helmets began to be sold at Major League ballparks in 1969. A Pilots variation is extremely hard to find, especially in an unscratched condition with all of the stickers intact. Today they are usually priced between $125 and $225.

more fans and was better suited for the Show. Additionally, construction on their new stadium had already begun, giving their fans something to look forward to. This optimism led to an attendance figure of 902,414 for the '69 Royals. And the Expos? Well, somehow Canada's first Major League team managed to have a final attendance count of 1,212,608 in 1969! Almost twice what Seattle had. They were playing in a 60-year-old facility that was not even built for baseball. Jarry Park had no upper deck and was totally uncovered too. Perhaps it was the excitement of big-league baseball or maybe it was just better marketing. If Milkes and company had been able to attract over one million fans in 1969 we'd still be watching Pilots games.

The Pilots never did expand Sick's Stadium to the agreed-upon figure of 28,500, instead ending up at 25,420.[10] While this upset the league it really had no impact on the Pilots' failure, as the largest crowd they had for the year was 21,900.

No, the Pilots' weak link in the chain was upper management, a.k.a. Pacific Northwest Sports, Inc. Their unorganized administration has to be held accountable for making baseball history. A well-financed organization can withstand low attendance; a thinly capitalized club cannot. As one Pilot fan lamented during the souvenir clearance sale, "Maybe next time there will be a little better planning before a big-league team is brought here."[11]

The story of Major League Baseball in Seattle could have ended there but it didn't. As soon as the Pilots fled, the finger pointing began. The politicians blamed the league, the city blamed the Sorianos, the league blamed the city and the mayor, and so on.

As Jimi Hendrix and Janis Joplin played at Sick's Stadium in July of 1970, the City of Seattle and King County filed a $32 million anti-trust lawsuit against the American League. The suit dragged on until 1976, when it was settled out of court; the AL agreed to grant Seattle a team in the upcoming 1977 round of expansion.[12] Since 1970, Seattle had wisely gone ahead with the domed stadium project and completed the Kingdome, home of the NFL's Seahawks. Without that stadium there would have been no Mariners, who began play in April 1977 along with the Toronto Blue Jays.

In 1970, the Brewers managed just 1 more win than the '69 Pilots. More importantly, though, they increased attendance 38% (933,690) over the previous year largely due to their fine major-league-level ballpark, County Stadium. That ballpark had been home to the Milwaukee Braves until 1965 and had hosted two World Series. Through the 2004 season the Brewers (including the 1969 Pilots season) had compiled a record of 2680–3019. Good enough for a .470 winning percentage. It is better than the Pilots' .395, but not that much better. The Brewers may have survived longer than the Pilots but the organization continues to be an exercise in futility. The team's lone World

Series appearance came in 1982 when they lost a 7-game thriller to the Cardinals. A good guess would be that Joe Schultz rooted for St. Louis.

Milwaukee's 34-year run without a World Series Championship is longer than that of every American League team except the Indians (1948). But, as far as keeping their fans interested, the Indians have had two World Series appearances and three other playoff appearances since the Brewers were in the World Series. The Brewers have never been in the post-season except for '82 and they never seem to be in the playoff race either. The Brewers are the oldest American League team to have never won a World Series. While some things change, others remain the same. The Brewers' finances have almost always been shaky but have gotten much worse in the past half-dozen years. The organization claims that it has lost money every year for almost a dozen seasons. This squeeze has prevented the team from going after big-name free agents or upgrading the roster in any meaningful way. The result has been 12 consecutive losing seasons. Sound familiar? This franchise seems to have gotten by for 35 seasons without really being able to establish themselves as a serious, sound franchise. In 2004 Allen "Bud Selig" and his family sold the Milwaukee Brewers for a reported $223 million (a cool $210 million profit!).[13] At the time Selig was the longest continuous owner in baseball.

The Pilots may have faded into history but they will never be completely forgotten, thanks in part to their dissolving after just one season, a feat thought unimaginable up until that point in time. And a feat that will never happen again, thanks to the safeguards put in place by Major League Baseball to guard against just that. Fool me once, shame on you; fool me twice.... Also, could there ever be another uniform like the Pilots? Doubtful. Nothing has ever come close. There is a third reason too for the team's lasting interest and intrigue.

On August 24th relief pitcher Jim Bouton was sent packing to Houston, where he finished his career during the 1970 season (released August 12). Bouton was a controversial character who, while he did have some friends on the team, had rubbed others the wrong way. Throughout the '69 campaign, members of the Pilots saw him engaging in an activity that many found curious but most didn't think too much about. Bouton was taking notes.[14] He would take notes after the game while sitting near his locker, he would take notes on the team bus and on flights, he would even whip out a small pad and jot things down in the bullpen and while standing around the batting cage. As the season wore on, players became more inquisitive as to his purpose, especially because he would not let anybody see what he was writing. It became somewhat of a joke that "Bouton's writin' a book." The joke ended abruptly when Bouton's *Ball Four* was published during the 1970 season, less than one year after the Pilots' final game.

Top: A vacant Sick's Stadium in 1979, just before demolition... *Bottom:* ...and after (both photographs Rainier Valley Historical Society, Seattle).

One of only two known photographs of the Seattle Pilots. Both were taken at Sick's Stadium. This one in front of the centerfield scoreboard before a game against the Red Sox (*Baseball Bulletin*).

Bouton had basically chronicled the day-to-day life of a Major Leaguer, using the 1969 Pilots (and briefly the '69 Astros) as his subjects. In it he named names and activities that, while not criminal, were embarrassing to baseball and to families of some of his fellow players. He told the story of young ballplayers and what they would do during their many, long off-hours. He also went back to his New York days and wrote about Yankee legends in not-so-complementary terms.

The book literally sold out in days; it flew off the shelves. The baseball world was rocked. Never before had the public gotten an inside look into the sport. Bouton was immediately called into Commissioner Bowie Kuhn's office. An irate Kuhn told Bouton to refute what he had written and to tell the public that he had lied in the book. Bouton refused.[15]

What some saw as gutsy, others viewed as foolhardy, irresponsible, and selfish. Bouton became an instant pariah in the baseball world. To this day many of his former teammates will not talk to him. In 1971, while working as a journalist covering spring training, Bouton happened across Joe Schultz, now a coach for the Tigers. His old manager refused to even acknowledge his hello and refused to talk to him.[16] In the book Bouton had documented many times over the colorful language and love for Budweiser of his salty manager. He also crucified the entire coaching staff.

10. The End

Baseball returned to Sick's Stadium in 1972 in the form of a class A team in the Cincinnati Reds organization. The newly named Rainiers played for five seasons with little fan support until 1976, when they were displaced by the Mariners. After standing vacant, ignored, and overgrown with weeds for another three years, Sick's Stadium was torn down in early 1979. The last evidence of the Pilots in Seattle was gone.

Back in Milwaukee, the former Pilots slowly faded from the baseball scene. Some retired, some were released, and most others were quickly traded away. None of the coaching staff had been retained. GM Marvin Milkes was fired after the 1970 season. The trainer, equipment manager and traveling secretary were gone after one or two seasons also. Pitcher Skip Lockwood had only appeared in six games as a Pilot but by the end of the 1973 season he was the lone survivor. After the season he was traded to the Angels. However, Mike Hegan came back to the Brewers via a trade from the Yankees for the 1974 campaign. He was now the lone Brewer that had once worn a gold "S" and scrambled eggs on his hat. On July 15, 1977, the first baseman/DH was released, any connection that the team had with the Pilots had ceased.

For the record, Fred Stanley was the last Pilot standing. After playing eight years for the New York Yankees as a quiet, hardly noticeable utility player during their Bronx Zoo Championship days, he was traded to the A's. On October 1, 1982, he played his final game while with Oakland. The Pilots had totally passed into history.

Appendix A
Pilots Interviews

The following appendix features 16 interviews with members of the Seattle Pilots, both players and staff. Some of the players were members of the team for almost a year and a half, others for mere months. However, since details about the Pilots and their season are difficult to come by, first-hand accounts, however brief, are of value to the baseball historian and have been included here.

JIM GOSGER

Q. *What was your reaction when you first found out that you were drafted by the Pilots?*

A. I figured that by going to a team like that I had a shot of playing everyday but it didn't work out that way. Most of us were platooned except the established players. Right from spring training I could see it was like A ball. One day I was playing in the outfield and got hit with a low liner. While I'm rolling around on the ground in pain Schultz walks out and asks, "What happened?" I told him that I got hit with the ball and he says, "Just drag him off the field." This is my manager, I couldn't believe it. It was real bush league.

Q. *What did you think of Sick's Stadium?*

A. Not much. We had little cubicles for lockers and we were all crammed in there. There wasn't a whole lot of money put into it. It was like a nice high school field or average college stadium. I played in AAA places that were much nicer.

Q. *Any thoughts on the Pilots uniforms?*

A. (Laughs) We weren't as sharp as the uniforms. The colors were nice. I thought they were sharp looking. I had come from the K.C. and Oakland A's with Charlie Finley as the owner. We had three different uniforms in green and yellow. With the Pilots we just had home and away.

Q. *The Pilots were an expansion team so essentially the members had never played with each other before. Do you feel they lived up to expectations or should have played better than their 64–98 record?*

A. Any time you have an expansion team you have to start with pitching, but we had no young guys. We just did not have any pitcher that you could rely on every 4th day. They were using the bullpen way too much. I felt we never did come together as a team.

Q. *How well organized was the Pilots organization?*

A. It was different than any other Major League team that I played for. When you walk in on opening day and you see that big crane there and they are still putting the stadium seats together, you kinda wonder what's going to go on here. I've never been associated with a team like that, it was chaos.

Q. *Was there a failure on some level by the Pilots organization to support the players?*

A. There is no question that Milkes was the weak link. We went out to get a sandwich in Cleveland one night after a game and when we came back to the hotel and Milkes was standing there in a bellhop uniform to check on us. I got up to my room and Aker says to me, do you believe that?

Jim Gosger (Photo File).

Q. *How were the Seattle fans?*

A. Very nice people and very enthusiastic. Win or lose they were cheering for us. I liked the area other than it rained all the time.

On Joe Schultz:

Joe just couldn't communicate with anybody. It seemed like he just wanted the games to be over quickly. One day we were playing the Twins and some kid was pitching and getting into trouble. So Joe comes out and has a meeting on the mound and says to this kid, "Keep it down and off the plate." I wanted to say, Geez, no kidding. If he could do that every pitch he'd be in the Hall of Fame.

On the team's move to Milwaukee:

No, I was not really surprised. Milwaukee was a place that had success before. They needed an established area. There was no way that they were going to survive in that park [Sick's].

Q. *Looking back on the whole experience are you glad that you were a Pilot?*
A. Yeah, sure I was. They were only there for 1 year and you were there for it. It's like history and you were a part of it.

STEVE BARBER

Q. *How did you become a Pilot and what was your reaction when you first heard it?*
A. I fully expected it. I wasn't pitching the last month of the season in '68. Houk [Yankees manager] told me I was going [being exposed in the expansion draft]. They were trying to hide me. I didn't look at it as an opportunity to pitch more, if I had been pitching well I would have been pitching more. Maglie helped me with my delivery, a minor tip that really helped me. It was the one good thing I got from Seattle. I could throw strikes again.

On Sick's Stadium and the facilities:
It was sick [laughs]. It wasn't a bad playing field though. The weather wasn't a pleasant experience; it was overcast for 6 months.

On the Pilots uniforms:
I thought it was unique but not all that bad. It was different. Especially those hats.

Q. *Do you feel that the Pilots lived up to expectations or should have done better than their 64–98 record?*
A. We weren't all that bad of a club until a few injuries hit. However, we had no depth. The club was supposed to be built around me and Gary Bell. It just so happened that Bell was at the end of his career and I couldn't pitch most of the year. I thought we could have done better if things had gone as planned or without injuries. There were a few bright spots in the season, a few

Steve Barber (Photo File).

young guys that were called up and did a good job. There should have been more of that but they were trying to get it done with veterans.

On the Seattle fans:
I noticed a lack of fans but they liked baseball.

Q. *How well organized was the Pilots organization?*
A. They were in pretty decent shape. They seemed to have a fair idea but there was some favoritism to native sons like [coach] O'Brien.

Q. *When the season ended was there any sense that the team would not be back?*
A. No, none of the rumors had started yet.

Q. *What was the feeling in camp during that second spring training in 1970?*
A. We were just doing our jobs and playing the game. We didn't think about it, there was no doom and gloom. All we heard all spring training was Seattle or Milwaukee, that was all that was talked about. So I wasn't surprised they moved.

Q. *Was it a good thing that the team moved from Seattle?*
A. At that particular time, yes. At least when the Mariners went in it was a Major League setup. Plus at that time (1969) Seattle was a pretty depressed area. Boeing had just gotten hit with a lot of layoffs.

Q. *Looking back on the whole experience are you glad that you were a Pilot?*
A. I had a lot of fun up there and it was a good bunch of guys. My second daughter was born in Seattle too. I'm glad I was a Pilot but I would not have been disappointed if I hadn't been either.

Q. *What happened to you after the Pilots moved to Milwaukee?*
A. Well, the Pilots released me toward the end of spring training (1970). But I came back and had a second career as a reliever. I actually made Fireman of the Year for the Angels organization in 1972. One of the perks after playing 10 years in the majors is that you get a lifetime pass, but the last time I went to a game was right after they opened Camden Yards [1993]. I loved playing. Honestly, I was never a fan. I enjoyed playing and the competition, the total integrity of the situation. It is just you and the hitter.

JOHN DONALDSON

Q. *How did you become a Seattle Pilot?*
A. I was traded in June for Larry Haney. We had a good club and were in second or third for a long time.

Reaction on becoming a Pilot:
I didn't know what was going on, it was kind of last minute. I met the team [Pilots] in New York. I'd been with the A's organization since 1964. I was

John Donaldson (National Baseball Hall of Fame Library, Cooperstown, N.Y.).

weak from a stomach operation so the A's traded me. I played most of the year with the Pilots and they gave me a raise for 1970, then they traded me back to the A's.

On Sick's Stadium and the facilities:
I'd played AAA ball there, I was in the coast league [PCL] for a few years. It definitely was not a major-league ballpark. It was not good from where I came from [Oakland]. They built a set of bleachers in the outfield and we drew good at first but it tailed off as we started losing.

On the Pilots uniforms:
Personally, I liked them. Especially the hat, in fact I still have one. I lot of people didn't like them but I did. I wish I had a shirt.

Q. *The Pilots were an expansion team and not expected to finish high. Do you feel they lived up to expectations or do you feel they should have done better than their 64–98 record?*
A. I think we should have done better with the players we had. They were all veteran players. I think toward the end it got to be a joke, guys were missing curfew. Mincher tried to keep us in line, he was sort of the person that kept it all together. It would have been worse if he wasn't there.

Q. *How well organized was the Pilots organization?*
A. I would say not very good. A couple of times they were short on the meal money. Back then guys really used that, they'd have it spent right away.

On the Seattle fans:
They were great at first then they gave us hell. The bullpen and fans got into some fights.

Q. *When the season ended was there any sense that the team would not be back?*
A. I think everybody wanted to get out of there. Nobody was sure what was going to happen. At spring training [1970] we thought we thought we were going back to Seattle though.

Q. *What did you think of Joe Schultz being fired as manager?*
A. I knew that would probably happen, things got out of hand with him. I liked him as a manager though. In July we had a team meeting and went over the A's hitters. Schultz told the pitchers not to throw Jackson any strikes and he hit 3 home runs that night. He hit a ball over my head at second for a home run, it was a liner that I thought I could catch at first. It just took off.

On the team moving to Milwaukee:
Everyone was surprised. Bristol sent me down on the last day to Vancouver but then I was traded back to the A's. I was angry because they had told me the job was mine.

Q. *Do you think it was a good thing or did you miss Seattle?*
A. Yes I did think it was good. I guess because of the stadium, they hadn't done anything to it.

On his time as Pilot:
To be honest with you, it was an experience. I'd do it again but I would have done things different. I was having a lot of trouble with left-handers and I should have worked harder.

Mike Marshall

Q. *How did you become a member of the Pilots and what was your reaction when you heard it?*
A. I was selected in the expansion draft from Detroit. Because I did not have any say in the matter, I did not care one way or the other.

Q. *How was that first spring training?*
A. It was hot in Tempe, Arizona.

On Sick's Stadium and the facilities:
It was minor league.

Q. *And what about the Pilots uniforms?*
A. Goofy.

Q. *As an expansion team do you feel the Pilots lived up to expectations or do you think they should have done better than their 64–98 record?*
A. I was not present for the full season, but when I was there, we did as poorly as I expected.

Q. *After playing .500 ball for May and June and early July the Pilots were beset with injuries. How much would you say this affected the team?*
A. I was one of those injuries. Until my injury, I had a 3.08 earned run average.

Q. *How well organized was the Pilots organization?*
A. Not.

Q. *How were the Seattle fans?*
A. Uninterested.

Q. *What did you think of Joe Schultz being fired?*
A. He got what he deserved.

Q. *Looking back on it, are you glad that you were a Pilot?*
A. I had no choice. It made no difference.

One final observation:
"The Pilots were a joke."[1]

Gary Bell

Q. *How did you become a Pilot?*
A. I was with the Red Sox and when the two new teams came into the league, I wasn't protected. They got screwed on me [laughs]. I didn't have the same stuff as the year before, I think I just lost my fastball over the winter.

Bell's reaction upon hearing he had been drafted by the Pilots:
I enjoyed my stay with Boston and didn't want to leave. We had just been in the World Series [1967] and I liked Boston. Back then you had no say in the matter so I just went.

On the Pilots' first spring training:
The thing I remember about spring training in '69 was Piniella. The manager didn't like him and said he would never hit Major League pitching so they got rid of him. Two-thousand hits later he proved him wrong [laughs].

On Sick's Stadium and its facilities:
I had played there about 13 years earlier in the PCL when I was coming up. It was a hard park to pitch in, it was close all around. The park had been there forever and was just an old stadium.

On the Pilots uniforms and hats:
I thought they were going to give us a boat with that cap. I didn't particularly like all of that stuff on the bill. They were unusual.

Q. *As an expansion team do you think the Pilots lived up to expectations or should have done better than their 64–98 record?*

Gary Bell (Photo File).

A. We had some good players that could still play, like Mincher. But the pitching was spotty. Diego Segui was great. But we were just average as a team. Let's face it, the other teams aren't going to give us their best guys.

Q. *How well organized was the Pilots organization?*
A. We thought it was O.K. We didn't know at the time but they were strapped big time. They had run out of money during the season. That's why they moved to Milwaukee.

Q. *Was there a failure on some level by the organization to support the players?*
A. No. We had a good manager and the coaches were good. We never had any interference from upstairs.

On Seattle's fans:
They were great. They were happy to have a big league team. The people were friendly and Seattle was a nice city.

On Joe Schultz getting fired?
I loved Joe Schultz. He was a character and a good baseball guy. He kept the team loose. He had been in the game for like forty years.

Q. *Were you surprised when the team moved to Milwaukee?*
A. Yeah, good Lord, you get a major league team and the league can't even keep them beyond one year? It was a surprise.

Q. *Do you have any thoughts about your time with the Pilots?*
A. Well, I tricked them [laughs]. After that first game they thought I was going to be great. I think I won one game after that.

DON MINCHER

Mincher was the lone representative of the Pilots at the All-Star game. Inserted as a pinch-hitter, he struck out against the Cardinals' Bob Gibson. In Don's other All-Star game (1967) he also pinch-hit against Gibson, hitting a single. "I felt great because I got a hit against one of the best pitchers in the league," Mincher says. "But I struck out the second time, and that wasn't so good."

On becoming a Pilot:
I was the first player drafted and was very excited about it. I went on a tour of Seattle and met all of the people. The weather wasn't what I was used to, everywhere I played it was hot.

On Sick's Stadium and the facilities:
Well, when we got there they were still building it! I'll say this, though, until the day they put me in the grave, I don't care what anybody says, Sick's Sta-

dium had the best infield I ever played on. Not being a fan I can't say about the concessions and other things. The construction was distracting though.

On the Pilots uniforms:
I thought it was good. I would have changed the caps. The uniform itself was fine but I'd have taken all the stuff off the hats.

Q. *As an expansion team do you feel the Pilots lived up to expectations or do you think they should have done better than their 64–98 record?*
A. I feel like we did as expected. People wanted us to win 75–80 games before the season, but that was not realistic. We won as many as we could. Some guys were a little over-the-hill or less talented.

Q. *How well organized was the Pilots organization?*

Don Mincher (Topps).

A. It was in a little disarray, which was natural because they didn't know what to expect. There was early enthusiasm and lots of fans, then we started losing and they stayed away, I guess because of the stadium a little too. The front office people were nice but overwhelmed.

On the Seattle fans:
They were fine but the combination of the ballpark and the luster of having an expansion team wore off during the season. As a ballplayer you don't pay as much attention to that stuff as you do until after you get out of the game. But by the end of the season the empty seats were noticeable. I was the player representative and just tried to get the players to concentrate on the game.

Q. *When the season ended was there any sense that the team would not be back?*
A. Well, it really was a sense that it was being talked about but it was not conceivable. It did not come to the forefront until the next spring.

On manager Joe Schultz:
I thought the world of Joe Schultz. I remember being disappointed when it [his firing] happened.

Q. *Were you surprised when the team moved to Milwaukee?*
A. Somewhat, but by the time they left I was not too surprised. It had been talked about so much that by the time they moved all the players did expect it.

Don's thoughts on the franchise moving to Milwaukee:
It was a good thing for ownership and baseball itself. I think it gave Seattle time to recover and do things necessary to be ready for a big-league club, like building the Kingdome. It let them catch their breath. More people showed up that first year in Milwaukee than would have for that second year in Seattle.

Q. *Looking back on the whole experience are you glad that you were a Pilot?*
A. Absolutely. I loved the area and enjoyed my time there. I made some great friends, the guys were great. I got to know guys very well who I had played against. I'm glad I was there but you move on and I did that. I just went on to the next club.

Mincher on the terrible August losing streak:
You can't blame the front office for being unhappy with all of those defeats. But how do you think the players felt? We don't want to lose. Joe Schultz didn't want to lose. But what could he do? He kept us fighting, kept us up through the worst of the losing streak.

Gerry McNertney

On how he became a Seattle Pilot and his reaction to it:
I was drafted 4th round from the Chicago White Sox. I was very surprised! I never thought any other clubs were interested. I was very apprehensive, I'd been in the Chicago organization for 11 years. I didn't know if I would make friends easily but I had a wonderful experience.

On Sick's Stadium and its facilities:
It was a minor-league facility that they tried to update with more seating, but I enjoyed every minute of it.

On the Pilots uniforms:
I liked the hats and wings more every time I wore them.

Q. *As an expansion team do you feel that the Pilots lived up to expectations or do you feel they should have done better than their 64–98 record?*
A. Thought we played well early, but after they traded Tommy Davis I thought our club lost enthusiasm. Davis was our leader.

Q *Was there failure on some level by the organization to support the players?*
A. Don't think so, I believe they tried to get an older club so as to be competitive.

On the Seattle fans:
Great fans! They supported us, wonderful people!

Q. *When the season ended was there any sense that the team would not be back?*
A. No, in fact I left all of my apartment things stored. I'm glad they made a decision but I didn't have the problems that the married guys had moving their families.

Q. *What did you think of Joe Schultz being fired?*
A. Surprised. I thought Joe kept the players relaxed and focused. But it didn't work with him in there, at least management didn't think so.

Q. *Did you think the move was a good thing or did you miss Seattle?*
A. Missed Seattle. But the Milwaukee fans and players wound up being great too.

Gerry McNertney (Photo File).

Q. *Looking back on the whole experience are you glad that you were a Pilot?*
A. Very much so. I get most of my fan mail wanting Pilots memorabilia.

Q. *There is some speculation that GM Marvin Milkes was too quick to trade, demote, or release players during the season. Do you think this affected the team's stability?*
A. I believe he wanted to win more games and just be competitive. That's tough for an expansion club.

Q. *Anything else?*
A. We really had some fun personalities on that club! Brabender, Comer, Mincher, Donaldson, Marshall, Bouton, Gosger, Hovley, Kennedy, Oyler, Pattin, Segvi, Rollins. I wouldn't have missed that experience. [Laughs] The guys on the team knew I was an outdoorsman. A lot of times when management was looking for a player and they didn't know where he was, when they'd finally find him he'd say, "Oh, I was with McNertney hunting or I was with McNertney fishing" [laughs]."

DICK BANEY

On how he became a Pilot and his reaction to it:
Sal Maglie used to come down to Pittsfield, Massachusetts and watch me pitch, he liked me a lot. It was 1968 and it was a Red Sox AA team. He told me about the upcoming expansion. I was excited [when I got picked in the draft by Seattle]. I was practicing baseball and my mom came out to the field and told me. She had seen it on TV. I thought it was a good opportunity. The best pitching we had, though, was Miguel Fuentes, it was a shame what happened to him.

Q. *Do you remember the particulars of that incident?*
A. Sure, it was during the off season and he was in a bar in his native Puerto Rico. There was something wrong with the bathroom or it was full so he went outside into an alley to urinate. He was near some guy's jeep and the guy came out and was yelling that he was going on or near his tire and he just pulled out a gun and shot him three times in the chest.

Q. *How was that first spring training?*
A. I liked it a lot. Joe Schultz liked me and I figured I was going to go with the team but my knee locked up on me. An old football injury. That was the deciding factor that sent me to AAA.

On Sick's Stadium and the facilities:
Well, it wasn't what I expected. You had rusty, metal, fold-up chairs. The outfield grass was too rich, too healthy, always mushy from the rain. We got Achilles injuries on it from sprinting on it.

Q. *What did you think of the Pilots uniforms?*
A. At that time they were 100% wool and playing in the heat was tough. We wore the same type uniform at home and on the road. I never thought too much of the uniforms, I don't think any of us felt very professional out there. Even to be called a Pilot was way off base. None of us could relate to those uniforms. I was the only guy to have my uniform tailored. My first time out on the mound for them I felt like a clown, my uniform was so baggy. The organization just didn't have it together. When I walked in there they just handed me a uniform. Nobody even asked me my size! [laughs] So I snuck it out of the park and took it to a tailor and paid for it myself. Psychologically I felt better. Bouton stopped me and asked me, "What's different about you?" I said, "Look at my uniform." But nothing belonged to you back then, it was all the property of the team. All you got when you were called up was one free pair of baseball shoes and one mitt.

Q. *As an expansion team do you feel the Pilots lived up to expectations or should have done better than their 64–98 record?*

A. It's not negative, it's a fact. Alcohol was such a big factor on our team I was surprised we ever won. Schultz would always say, "Let's go pound those Budweisers after all the games." Win or lose! I think that it was too loosely handled. The intellectuals were outcasts, if you were a college guy or didn't drink you were looked down on. It seems unbelievable now, but back then in baseball you did not want to be different. Being different was definitely looked down on. You didn't even want to wear your socks too high. It had just started where you could tailor your uniform a little thanks to Mays. Willie Mays wore his tight and pulled his baseball socks way up. But as for our team, you were either a prospect or a suspect. Guys were either on the way up or on the way out.

Dick Baney (Renata Galasso Card Co.).

Q. *How well organized was the Pilots organization?*
A. I can only tell you from AAA and the Major League level. Things are not going to be organized if you don't have money. If you don't have the cash you don't have the flash and it doesn't take long for people to recognize that. We had to ask the team for our meal money a few times, they would say things like the paperwork is being processed, it will be here in a couple of days. That wasn't a good sign. The atmosphere was not real serious. On other teams if you wanted game tickets there were always plenty available, they were always around. On the Pilots you had to ask for tickets and you were lucky to get two, they were that tight. I was lucky to get them for my mom and dad.

Q. *When the season ended was there any sense that the team would not be back?*
A. There were a lot of rumors. Nobody wanted to trade with us, that was a signal. The players talked about it all the time: "Is this the big leagues?"

On manager Joe Schultz:
He didn't create a winning atmosphere. I don't think he had full control on the field, he was definitely better as a third base coach. For someone

at the end of their career it was a free ride [being on the Pilots], it was very loose.

Q. *What did you think about GM Marvin Milkes and the job that he did?*
A. I liked him but his hands were tied. The Seattle Pilots were a AAA/Major League team. We had no theme but our theme was "Let's go pound those Budweisers."

On coach Frank Crosetti:
Frank was a very knowledgeable baseball guy who had been with all of those great Yankee teams. But we all thought that his main job was to prevent you from giving balls to the fans. He was real old-school baseball. If he saw you throw a foul ball into the stands to a fan he came running down screaming threatening to fine you.

On Don Mincher:
Mincher came from the Twins, which were a championship organization. Mincher knew what it took to win. He couldn't understand the looseness of the team, he really wanted to win.

WAYNE COMER

On become a Pilot and his reaction to it:
1969 was the year of the expansion draft and there were four teams involved. I was picked by the Pilots, but I went low in the draft. Well, when I heard it I was excited. I thought I'd finally get a shot to play regularly. I was the 25th man on the Tigers. I wanted to see what I could do on the Major League level.

Q. *How was that first spring training?*
A. It was different. It was in Tempe, Arizona, and the Tigers had trained in Florida. They [the Pilots] had drafted a bunch of older players, they wanted to try and win right away. The Royals went after younger guys. At the time I was just a young kid fulfilling my dream of being a Major League ballplayer. '68 was my first full year and I got a World Championship ring, I was excited. I had an at-bat in the World Series and got a single, I hit one-thousand! [laughs]. But I knew I was the sixth outfielder on the Tigers. I had a very good spring [1969] and won the starting outfield job right out of spring training.

On Sick's Stadium and the facilities:
[Laughs] It was different. It wasn't even a AAA ballpark, it was a minor-league ballpark. After seeing Tiger Stadium, Yankee Stadium, and Fenway Park it was different. It was still being constructed with the cranes in the

bleacher area and a tarp on the outfield wall. We had to play with all of this going on. But it was still the Major Leagues and I didn't care. I had no problems with the playing field. The outfield was short, though, and not suitable for the majors.

On the Pilots uniforms:
I thought they were different. They had the wings on the left chest and everything. The uniform doesn't mean a whole lot to me, I just wanted to play. In Detroit we had the more traditional ones, though.

Q. *What was your salary that year?*
A. Just the minimum or a little more, I think. The minimum back then was $7500. It's gotten out of hand today.

Q. *Do you believe the Pilots lived up to expectations or do you think they should have done better than their 64–98 record?*
A. I thought we should have done a little better. We had some proven players: Rollins, Mincher, Tommy Davis, Tommy Harper. We were doing OK until the middle of the season. We were better than the Expos and Padres. The Royals were better but just by a little, the injuries got us.

Q. *How well organized was the Pilots organization?*
A. It was terrible. I didn't get involved with what was going on. That second spring training [1970] we did not know what was going on; they didn't tell us until the last day where we were going, Milwaukee or Seattle. My family was already in Seattle, we had rented an apartment, so I wanted to stay there. I never got involved with Milkes or the Sorianos, I didn't see them around too much.

On the Seattle area fans:
I thought they were great and supportive, what few we had. We were an expansion team and they fell in love with us. I think they got a raw deal when Soriano moved the team. That's a great area up there.

Q. *Did you think the team would be back the following season?*
A. I thought that we would be back and that they would have improved the facilities a bit, make the stadium nicer.

Q. *What did you think of Joe Schultz being fired?*
A. Well, I thought he got a raw deal. He didn't have a whole lot to work with. Dave Bristol was a bigger name than Schultz and I guess that's why the move was made. I ended my career back with the Tigers in '72. He [Schultz] was Billy Martin's third base coach then, he was bitter over what happened in Seattle.

On the team moving to Milwaukee:
We kept hearing from people during the spring training that the team was

going to move but I didn't believe it. The team told us nothing. It was a real surprise to me.

Q. *Did you think it was a good thing or did you miss Seattle?*
A. It was a better facility than there was in Seattle, old Milwaukee County Stadium, the old home of the Braves. I just didn't think one year was enough time to prove ourselves.

Q. *Looking back on the whole experience are you glad that you were a Seattle Pilot?*
A. Well, yeah. [laughs] It was the only year that the team existed, once a Pilot always a Pilot. I got 1970 Pilots tickets and other memorabilia. We had a great bunch of guys and had a lot of fun playing together and being around each other.

Q. *You had a very good rookie year in '69 and were expected to carry that over into 1970. What happened to the rest of your career after the Pilots?*
A. I went from starter to sitting on the bench in 1970. I didn't get along with Bristol and was in his doghouse. I got traded on Mother's Day in 1970 to Washington and played for Ted Williams. He could hit but that was it. He liked to talk about fishing and hunting more than baseball. Bill Short, the Senators' owner, brought him in to get people coming back to games, but it didn't work out that way. I got out of baseball after the '73 season, I had two young boys going to school and wanted to be around them. The Tigers offered me minor-league coaching positions but my family and I decided that it was time to make a career move. I still get fan mail daily and try to answer it. I don't charge for my autograph. I do some good causes when they come up, like Mothers Against Drunk Driving. Otherwise, I no longer go to Players Association things except for Tigers reunions we have every five years in Detroit.

BOB LOCKER

On how he became a Pilot:
I became a Pilot because I wasn't doing so well with the White Sox and got traded for Gary Bell. I was throwing well but the White Sox didn't know that [laughs]. I had the worst streak of my career but I found it. But by going to the Pilots I was reunited with Gerry McNertney, who I go all the way back to college with. He was my catcher and would also take me fishing.

Q. *What was your reaction when you first heard about the trade?*
A. I'm sure I was devastated to be traded, I was hurt a little but there was no option. Ed Short [White Sox G.M.] was short sighted. I enjoyed my year with the Pilots very much, it was a fun bunch of guys. There was a very laid back, semi-pro approach on that team. Very loose, it was like, go get 'em,

then let's throw back some beers. There was some very good talent on that team, though: Marshall; Brabender got to show his stuff; Diego Segui. Don Mincher's a very good guy, a good citizen. I have a high regard for him.

On Sick's Stadium and the facilities:
Well, as I recall it was obviously more of a minor-league stadium. The short porches scared a lot of pitchers, I was a sinkerball pitcher and it did not effect me that much. I was always a reliever too. I went to college and threw in the service also, so by the time I got to the Majors I was a little older and wasn't a starter.

On the Pilots uniforms:
I thought they were kind of neat but I don't have one. I know I have a couple of little uniforms from father-son games that my boys wore. But I was an old-school guy and never tried to sneak anything out. Back then at the end of the season they told you to put all your uniforms back in here and we just did it.

Q. *Do you feel the Pilots lived up to expectations or do you feel they should have done better than their 64–98 record?*
A. No, I thought they played up to their abilities for the first four months. There was a realization that, "Oh my God, we're in third place!" and it just faded from there.

Q. *How well organized was the Pilots organization?*
A. It *was* in the Major Leagues and we *did* play the other guys. Despite how few fans were there we were in the same circuit and did play the other teams. I saw no evidence of it being organized, though [laughs].

On Seattle and the fans:
I liked the area, I liked the fans. I loved the people of Seattle, no negatives about that. I really liked beating the Yankees.

Q. *When the season ended was there any sense that the team would not be back?*
A. When you're a young player you don't worry about it or even know it was brewing [laughs after realizing his unintentional joke]. After it happened it was upsetting to move my family. Only shortly into the 1970 season I was traded to Oakland and had to move a very understanding wife and kids again. But I had a great opportunity with Oakland. Seattle deserved a team and it was a new area, I would have loved to have stayed there. We could have built something. It was groundwork for future things.

On Joe Schultz:
I liked Joe Schultz very much. Not that he was a brilliant man but he was just a nice old baseball guy. He didn't deserve to get fired for taking a rag-tag bunch of players and doing well for a few months.

Q. *Looking back on the whole experience are you glad that you were a Pilot?*
A. I am, absolutely. I loved my short time there; loved the players, Seattle, and the Northwest. No negatives at all. The Seattle fans proved their mettle and got a very successful franchise.

One final thought:
I love the game but I have not stayed close to baseball. We should all be happy that we played Major League Baseball.

DOOLEY WOMACK

Q *How did you become a Pilot?*
A I was traded for Jim Bouton in August [24th]. I was in St. Louis playing the Cardinals and we were one-half game out of first place. They wanted to trade me because a reporter around the batting cage asked me, "What do you think about being so close to first place, Dooley?" I said that I'd like to lose a few games once in a while so I could get into a game. I was kidding, of course, but the Astros thought that I was a problem after that. I went 30 days without getting on the mound at one point. But that was Harry Walker [Houston manager], I did not care for him. Once you get into a manager's doghouse you're done.

Q. *Were you disappointed with being traded?*
A. Yes and no. Your Major League career continues but I was in the pennant race. But I got into a few games with those guys [Pilots]. I think I was 2–1 with an ERA of three-something.

Q. *When you got there from the National League what did you think about Sick's Stadium?*
A. It was a minor-league ballpark but you paid Major League prices [laughs]. We had metal folding chairs, I remember talking about that with the other players. There wasn't much there.

Q. *Do you think the Pilots played to their abilities or were a better team than their record?*
A. I think they were a better team than 64–98. There were some castoffs but they had some damn good pitchers. Segiu, O'Donoghue, and Locker was very good. Maybe I was a castoff! [laughs].

Q. *After having played for the Yankees, did you find the Pilots organization disorganized?*
A. I wasn't there long enough to see any of that. But I know that if you lose it can become terminal. Hard work is the only thing that is going to change things. Joe [Schultz] was a player's manager [laughs]. Maybe he wasn't strict

enough, being they were a first-year team. With 25 personalities you have to know who to pat on the back and who to kick in the rear.

On the Pilots uniforms:
They were different, especially the braiding on the caps. I've got one of the hats still. We didn't get to keep anything back then. The only one I was going to keep was the old A's uniform with all those different colors. At the end of the season I had a set all folded and in my duffel bag and I was going to walk out with it. Then the clubhouse guy says that anybody that didn't return all of their uniforms would not get their last paycheck sent to them. I went back to my locker and just threw my bag in there and left. I guess I needed that check more. I probably should have taken them anyway, they'd be worth more than that check today.

Dooley Womack (Topps).

I get letters from attorneys about any Seattle Pilots memorabilia or uniforms that I have. And all of my stuff from my other teams too. They represent collectors. People call me all the time and ask about my old memorabilia and things. You hate to give something to somebody for their children only to hear it was sold on eBay. I've gotten mad and put the fan mail on the side for a few weeks but then say to myself, that's not right. I'm saving my things for my own children. I'm not a computer person but a friend of mine told me recently that I've got thirteen items on eBay, photos and baseball cards and things.

Q. *Were you surprised when the Pilots moved to Milwaukee?*
A. Yes, I sure was. It was the stadium, I figured. If they moved to Milwaukee they'd be in a Major League stadium. An older, used one but it would still be better [than Sick's].

Q. *Looking back on it were you glad that you were a member of the Pilots?*
A. Well, I was just happy to be in the majors. I spent eight years in the minors. Scouts would say to my parents, "Why don't you take Dooley home? He doesn't have what it takes for the majors." I was in the Marine Corps and

that helped me gain confidence in baseball. I went in in '61 and got out in April of '62. If you train as a Marine you can do anything in life.

I was a nobody, it was an honor and a thrill to play for the greatest team in the majors [the Yankees, not the Pilots]. Playing for New York was the greatest thrill of my life. Winning the game when Mantle hit his 500th home run was great. I came in and pitched 3½ innings. Back then relievers pitched as long as they could go, as long as you were needed. After that game Mickey came up to me in the clubhouse and said, "Dooley, I just want to thank you for allowing me the opportunity of celebrating my 500th home run. If we had lost I wouldn't have been able to enjoy it." He was my idol, he was so down to earth.

I was glad I was able to do this for my parents. When they came to see me in Houston my father said to me, "Thank you for allowing us to see the Eighth Wonder of the World." One thing about the Astrodome that I remember was when it rained the people in the stands would actually break out umbrellas! The roof leaked like a sieve. I just did what I had to do, what I was taught to do. The loyalty isn't there today, it is a business.

SANDY VALDESPINO

Q. How did you become a member of the Pilots?
A. I was only there for the last four or five weeks of the season. Houston needed a power, right-handed hitter and they got Tommy Davis. Tommy Davis went to the Astros for me and Danny Walton. He [Walton] had spent the year at AAA. Danny Walton had some great year [at Oklahoma City as Minor League Player of the Year]. They wanted him and he played a lot but they used me just to pinch-hit. I hardly played.

Q. What was your reaction when you first heard about it?
A. Well, I felt terrible, we were half a game out of first place. I went from first place to last place [laughs]. The ballpark was very old and it was raining every day. I didn't like it too much. But you were still in the majors.

Q. When you got there what did you think of Sick's Stadium?
A. It was a AAA ballpark, very, very bad. It had no kind of facilities at all. No kind of place where you could practice and a small clubhouse. It was no good.

Q. What did you think of those uniforms, especially the hats?
A. Well, I think they wanted to go into the Major Leagues with a different style than anybody else, like Charlie Finley with the Kansas City A's, to draw people to the stadium. It was something different [laughs].

Q. Did that work? The Pilots did not seem to draw very well. How were the Seattle fans?

A. I think there were some. With five or six thousand people in the stands we had a full house. But I never thought the league would approve the move to Milwaukee unless the new stadium wasn't coming.

Q. *You were surprised when the franchise moved to Milwaukee?*
A. Yeah, I was surprised. We all went to spring training in Tempe with the Pilots. Less than one week before we break for Seattle they told us the club was sold. Everybody was kind of upset because they had their wives and apartments already, especially the guys that were there last year.

Q. *When you came over to the Pilots did you feel that the franchise was disorganized in any way?*
A. I went over at the end of the season. I did not see anything that unusual but I don't know what went on before I got there. All I saw was a lot of losing, we didn't have a lot of talent.

Q. *What did you think about your new manager Joe Schultz?*
A. [Laughs] We did not have anybody. No pitching, no fielding, no hitting. What can he do? He can not pitch, he can not field, he can not bat for us. [laughs]

Q. *When you came over from Houston did you have an occasion to meet Marvin Milkes?*
A. He was not around very much. I had him as a GM in Charleston in 1960. Then I saw him again with the expansion team. He treated us very good as far as the hotels and flying, and he talked to us. I think he was a nice guy.

Q. *You stayed with the team over the winter and started 1970 with the Brewers?*
A. Yes, it was not a very good stadium [Sick's]. It was rainy and cold in Seattle so they decided to sell the team to the Milwaukee Brewers. I was only there for one month too [laughs], they sent me down to the Portland club. I didn't like Milwaukee either, it was rainy and cold also [laughs]. I was a hot weather ballplayer from Cuba.

Q. *What happened to your career after the Pilots?*

Sandy Valdespino (Topps).

A. Well, as I said, I had been in the pennant race before the trade. But I was still in the majors anyway. I finished up with Kansas City in '71. After I stopped playing I went to work for George [laughs]. I was a minor-league hitting instructor for the Yankees from 1974–1979. We worked very hard with the good quality players that we had. We traded most of them away to other teams, though. We had Mattingly, Willie Magee, Otto Velez, Fred McGriff, Damaso Garcia.

Garry Roggenburk

Q. *How did you become a Seattle Pilot during the '69 season?*
A. Basically, I was with the Red Sox at the time and they put me on the waiver wire. The Pilots claimed me. I didn't get that much of an opportunity to pitch, though.

Q. *What was your reaction when you first heard about the switch?*
A. Well, it was kind of tough because with my family who were with me. I had started with Louisville in '69 and was called up to Boston for about one month and had to move again. But I thought it would be an opportunity. I knew some of the guys over there. The relocation was a problem, though, my wife and kids had been in Boston for only about 2–3 weeks. I had just gotten them settled. When I got traded to the Pilots they just went home to Cleveland. The season was half over already anyway.

Q. *After playing in Fenway primarily, what did you think about Sick's Stadium?*
A. It was like a AAA stadium, it wasn't really good. It needed a lot of improvement. They added some seats but they needed a different stadium. My first park in the majors was another old one, Comiskey in Chicago. It reminded me of Seattle because it was cold in the spring there too. I don't think they fulfilled their agreement with the league as far as that. Now the ballparks are a lot more nice.

Q. *You came from a team with a lot of tradition to one with perhaps the most unusual uniforms in baseball history. Any thoughts on them?*
A. I don't know, I thought they were okay. I actually had no problem with them. They were bluish on the road. I had one and lost it! I regretted that. There would be a lot of interest in it today. I had an entire road uniform, shirt, pants, hat, and socks. I went to work for the Red Sox in '78 in Winter Haven, Florida, and went down there. I had the uniform in a bag and it disappeared during the move, someone probably grabbed it. I don't even know how I got it. It must have been in my equipment bag. They didn't let you keep anything back then. We came back from a road trip to Minnesota and I must have had it with me and didn't realize it. When we got back to Seattle that's when I quit.

Q. *Do you feel the Pilots were better than their 64–98 record? Did they live up to expectations?*

A. We were an inexperienced team with veterans there too to help win our share. I think 64–98 was a pretty good record for them. We were going to lose some games as a new team, we were struggling. It's hard for an expansion team to compete right away. But I enjoyed it. Mincher wanted to win, he played the game hard. I was a teammate of his in Minnesota. He had a good sense of humor about him too. Tommy Davis was a good hitter at one time but he was hobbling with that ankle injury. He played for a lot of years but was slowed down. Barber too, he had some good years, he was a very good pitcher. Harper was an excellent player too. I played with Rich

Garry Roggenburk (Topps).

Rollins also, he was a good player but was at the end of his career in Seattle. One-hundred and sixty-two games is hard for older guys, there was not enough firepower. It's a marathon. Maybe the Pilots would have done good in a 120-game season. They tried to mix in some young guys at the end. You hate to put young guys in that environment with all that losing. That cannot be good at the start of their careers.

On the Seattle fans:
The fans were very good and supportive. They [the Pilots] tried to run promotions too. The newspapers were supportive of us too.

On manager Joe Schultz:
Everybody liked Joe. He was funny, he tried to loosen everybody up. He was a good baseball man. He knew the situation with the Pilots and didn't try to put too much pressure on you. He had the experience, he had all those years in St. Louis. I remember now that he wasn't there the following year in Milwaukee. As far as Maglie, I had him with the Red Sox one year. He was kind of laid back and just went along with the program. He instilled some of his experiences in us. He had players that were a little older and on the downside of their careers.

Q. *How well organized was the Pilots organization?*
A. Well, they were probably feeling their way too. They brought in a lot of people from different places and had no farm system to speak of. I met Milkes for the first time when I first went there. I introduced myself and signed a contract. Then I didn't see him again until I quit.

Q. *Speaking of that, you were on the Pilots starting June 23rd and on July 31st you just walked into Milkes office and quit. Why?*
A. I got to the point where I had a couple of children. I had had some elbow problems and thought it was time to move on. I got a job in the education field first since I had my degree. In today's environment with the money I may have stayed longer. I was kind of half in and half out. I was already vested in the pension system so I retired. I was out there all by myself without my family. After the trade to Seattle my wife and kids just went home to Cleveland, it was too much moving around. I probably could have stayed in the game a couple of more years, though. I was in the game a long time. I ran Winter Haven for the Red Sox for five years and then was a roving minor-league pitching instructor for them for 12 years from 1983–1994. I was glad to see the Sox finally win it!

Q. *Marvin Milkes tried to talk you out of retiring, didn't he?*
A. Yeah. Well, when I talked to him I told him that I had thought about it for a while. He didn't want to lose me that quick. He did try to talk me into staying, though. But it was something that I had been think about for months.

Q. *You walked away from every American boy's dream.*
A. [Laughs] Yeah, I know. A lot of guys have said to me, "How could you do that?"

Q. *You did pitch a few good games during your short stint with the Pilots.*
A. Oh yeah. I beat the Angels twice, once in Anaheim and once back in Seattle. I beat them in a complete game at Sick's and won 3–1.

Q. *Were you surprised when the Pilots moved to Milwaukee?*
A. I was kind of surprised because I didn't know what was going on. I read about it back in Cleveland but I wasn't in contact with anybody. They weren't too happy with the way things were going out there.

Q. *Did you think it was a good thing that the Pilots left for Milwaukee?*
A. I didn't think it was good for the game or the city. It definitely was not good for baseball what went on. The city sued the league and part of the settlement was that they got a team. So, at least they got the Mariners, that's one good thing that came out of the Pilots.

Q. *Are you glad that you were a member of the Pilots?*
A. Yes. I enjoyed the players that I played with in Seattle. It's a beautiful area

and the summer was nice. But I understand that the rest of the season was rainy.

JOHN GELNAR

On how he become a Seattle Pilot:
I had been with the Pittsburgh Pirates and was drafted by the Royals in the expansion draft. Then I was traded for Lou Piniella, of all things. I was in spring training in Ft. Myers in '69 and it was very late in the spring when it happened. Schultz didn't like Lou's attitude. He was a brash young player. You've got to remember that Schultz was from the Midwest and Piniella was from back east, they just had different ways.

Q. *What was your reaction when you first heard about the trade?*
A. You know, I had mixed emotions about it. But back in those days you went where they told you. You had no say about it. I had some emotions about leaving Pittsburgh but it was an opportunity to play. I didn't know anybody in Kansas City, we were all just thrown together. I didn't know guys in Seattle either but when I got there they had some good experienced guys.

Q. *On Sick's Stadium and the facilities in Seattle:*
A. [Laughs] They weren't very Major League. The locker rooms were rather small and condensed. The visitors' clubhouses on the road were better than our own clubhouse at home. But I wasn't in there much as a pitcher. We spent most of our time in the bullpen.

Q. *What did you think of the Pilots uniforms coming from Pittsburgh, one of the oldest and most traditional teams in baseball?*
A. They were highly unusual. There were jokes about them. Some jokes were going around the league. I wish I knew then what I know now. Back then everything was cut-and-dry. Uniforms were white for home and gray on the road. Anything with the Pilots now is highly collectible. I get collectors calling me asking for any Pilots stuff that I may have. I'd have gone throughout the ballpark collecting the ticket stubs [laughs]. Back then people didn't have any interest in that type of thing. No one knew about the worth of these items. When I was with the Pirates I was a pretty good hitter, I didn't start out as a pitcher but as an infielder. I had bats, including some that Roberto Clemente gave me. I would go with some of the players to children's hospitals and just give them away to the kids.

Q. *How well organized was the Pilots organization?*
A. Well, I wouldn't say that it was in complete disarray. But when the sale came through in 1970 it was kind of havoc. They never kept us informed of what was going on. When it finally happened some of the wives were already in

Seattle with the player's family. Then they had to move to Milwaukee. To some degree there was a failure on the part of the Pilots management. We very seldom ever saw them, it was a lackadaisical situation. It was kind of strange. In Pittsburgh you always saw the GM and even the owner. They would come around and talk to the players. In Seattle I think they just got into a situation they didn't know how to handle. However, there's no question the Sorianos made money when Selig bought the team. I think it sold for something over ten million.

Q. *There has been some question about Milkes and how he handled an expansion franchise?*
A. He had a tough position there. He had to play both sides of the fences. He may have traded and sent guys down too much. There wasn't that much camaraderie between the players because of the constant movement. We got along and there were good guys but people were always coming and going. Some guys really didn't get a chance to showcase their talents.

Q. *So, speaking about the talent, do you think they played to their abilities or should have had a better record?*
A. Well, you know I honestly think we were better than that. They were drafting older guys, they wanted to win immediately. It didn't work out that way, though. I think I started ten games for them and lost almost all of them. I got 13 runs behind me in those ten games. They just didn't give me any run support. My ERA at Sick's was a little under three. If I had had some runs I would have had a much better record like Brabender. I was taken out of the rotation and put into the bullpen. Maybe it was to help my mindset so I wouldn't get discouraged but I don't know. Back then you just did what they told you and didn't question anything. As a team, after you lose so many games you lose incentive, it just becomes natural. Harper had a great year for us, though. And Mincher didn't have a bad year either.

Q. *What did you think of your manager Joe Schultz and his being let go after the team's inaugural season?*
A. I loved the guy. He was just a nice guy. I think it was wrong that they fired him. Sal Maglie was my pitching coach there, he had been around a long time too. He was rather quiet and interesting. To *some* degree he was helpful.

On the Pilots' move to Milwaukee:
It didn't surprise me that they moved. During that second spring training we were reading about it in the papers almost every day. What surprised me was what happened after we were told we would be going to Milwaukee. I don't know if anybody told you this story but the team put us on a plane and we landed in Milwaukee at about 3:00 AM. What a surprise when we got off the plane! It was like we had won the World Series. There were hun-

dreds of people at the airport waiting for us. There were lots of police officers there and they actually had to clear a path for us. The team had buses there to take us to some hotel downtown Milwaukee. All along the route, at stop signs, there were people out there waving at us, greeting us. When we did get to the hotel there were hundreds of people there too. It was unbelievable, I will never forget that. I couldn't believe how supportive the people of Milwaukee were.

Q. *Looking back on the whole experience are you glad that you were a member of the Pilots?*

A. Well, yes, but I know for a fact that Baltimore was trying to get me in a trade. But the Pilots wouldn't let me go. Earl Weaver, their manager, had seen me in the minors and knew quite a bit about me and liked me. I had pitched against him. Honestly, I'd liked to have gone there to play. I look fondly back on my time with the Pilots now and my relationships with the other players that were there. It was unique, I'll say that.

On Jim Bouton:

I remember when *Ball Four* came out, it upset a lot of the guys. We actually didn't think he was going to write a book. After some months he would actually tell us that he was writing a book when guys asked him about the notes he was writing. Nobody thought he was serious. Some of the guys were quite angry.

BILL SCHONELY (RADIO ANNOUNCER)

Q. *You have been in radio for a long time. What were you doing professionally prior to 1969 and how did you come to be employed by the Pilots?*

A. I was a hockey announcer for the Western Hockey League Seattle Totems and was doing Seattle Angels games in the PCL for five years. When the Pilots came I was hired since I was already there and they liked me. The Sorianos hired me and Jimmy Dudley, who had done Cleveland Indians radio for a long time. They hired him, then I got the other job, we were on KVI 570. I had a Major League baseball job at a relatively young age but then lost it after just one year through no fault of my own! [laughs]

Q. *Speaking of your short Major League career, when the Pilots moved to Milwaukee was there an offer to you and Dudley to go with them?*

A. Yes and no. We were in spring training with the team [1970]. Everything happened so fast. Bud Selig was just waiting to get that team and take it back to Milwaukee. All he had was that stadium there and it was a former Major League park. He was talking to all of the owners, trying to get them to move the team. When it first happened we were going to go with them but then there was a change of direction. They wanted to go with their own people in Milwaukee and I understood that. It is the nature of this business. I had other interests in the Pacific Northwest area and went to work for the Portland Trail Blazers.

The spring training stadium in Tempe is still there, by the way, but it is much bigger now. Diablo Stadium, it has been expanded since the Pilots were there. The Angels have used it for about 12 years.

Q. *You were from the area and mentioned that you worked for the AAA Angels. So you were very familiar with Sick's Stadium. What did you think of it?*
A. I loved it. Everybody loved it as far as the players go. It was a real throwback ballpark, it was an old PCL park. The field was great, the grounds crew did a magnificent job. They did a nice job on it and the place was spotless. The team did try in that respect. But it wasn't a Major League stadium. I think it held about 12,000 max and they brought it up to 25,000. When they put those seats in the outfield they weren't very good. In essence they were planks, they were just pieces of wood that the fans had to sit on.

Ted Williams was the manager of the Senators then. He loved to come to Sick's. It was like an old Fenway-type park but without the sellouts. He really liked that ballpark, it reminded him of his early days in baseball. It was great when he came into Seattle, he really was a good guy.

Q. *How were the press boxes? I've heard stories about them.*
A. In the old PCL days they were actually on the roof behind home plate! Just a rickety wooden thing. The team installed a new one for the 1969 season. In fact, it was part of the agreement with the league in order to get the team. It wasn't modern at all but it was fine. There were steep stairs to get into it.

Q. *What did you think of the Pilots uniforms?*
A. Well, in their day and age they could have been upgraded. It was different but it wasn't very professional. The hats weren't too sharp. I don't think you'll see anything like that again.

Q. *How well organized do you think the Pilots organization was? Did you see anything that worried you right from the beginning?*
A. Well, they were just putting the franchise together. Some of us in the press saw what we believed could have been a shaky situation because of Dewey. He was a local guy and had been the president of the PCL. I don't know if they were ready for this.

Q. *What did you think of Joe Schultz and his being fired at the end of the first season?*
A. We actually had a pretty good coaching staff. Old Joe, boy, he was a character of all time. I liked him, he was an old baseball man from the old school and a fun-loving guy. He had a lot of experience from the Cardinals. It was

a fun staff. Crosetti and Maglie had come from other organizations and had a lot of years with the Yankees. For a while the team won more than they lost but after a few months the bottom just dropped out [laughs].

Q. *Lenny Anderson and Steve Farber were beat writers for the Pilots. They both said that Marvin Milkes was the weak link in the team's hierarchy (Anderson said, "Milkes couldn't have scouted Joe DiMaggio"[2]). Do you have any thoughts on that?*

A. I'll second that. I know the players hated him. Milkes didn't like Piniella and traded him away and the rest was history. Everybody was upset over that one.

Q. *The Sorianos were never able to negotiate a T.V. deal for the Pilots despite the team having the Major League's largest radio broadcast area. Do you think that a lack of a T.V. affiliate played into the team's demise?*

A. It might have, but I think the stadium had more to do with that. Had the team stayed they would have rectified that. But they were not going to televise every game anyway. Back then no team televised all of their games, it's not like today. People listened to radio more. But I still say that it was the stadium more than anything else. The owners and the city did not have enough time to get something on the drawing board to convince Major League Baseball and the American League to keep the team there. Just one year later the Kingdome was in the works. I think the fan support was there, they were very enthusiastic about the Pilots. When the team ran promotions there were a lot of fans at the games. We had a radio network that included not just Washington but Oregon, Alaska, Northern California, Idaho, Montana, Utah and as far away as North Dakota! We even had one station in Nevada. You have to remember that back then, before the Mariners and Rockies, there was no Major League team anywhere in the Northwest. And we had no problem getting sponsors.

BILL SEARS (DIRECTOR OF PUBLIC MEDIA)

Q. *How did you become a part of the Seattle Pilots?*

A. Well, I had worked in minor-league baseball with the Seattle Rainiers and then the Seattle Angels at the AAA level. I had also done professional hockey for the WHL. Dewey Soriano hired me to work for the Rainiers. He said to me one day, "We're going to get Major League Baseball here in Seattle and I want you to work for us." I had worked with him on trying to get the domed stadium passed. There was no relationship there, just that he was familiar with me.

Q. *What did you think of Sick's Stadium and its facilities and do you think it played into the team's demise?*

A. I don't think so. It might have turned away a few people but not a significant amount. It was a minor-league stadium and they didn't have another facility other than that. Dewey worked on it to increase the seating to 25,000. It had been about 14,000 tops. In terms of comfort it was not as good as the other Major League stadiums but in terms of viewing it was great. The seats were very close to the field. The box seats were excellent. The wooden seats or planks they built in the bleacher sections were not as good, though. They were a little far away. Many of the players from other teams loved to play there. They loved the field. We took very good care of it over the years. The grounds crew people at the ballpark were wonderful. They worked very hard on it. The fences were reasonable, 335 feet down the lines and about 410 to center. You could definitely hit the ball out of there. During the spring, and when it was cloudy and we had moisture, the ball wouldn't travel as far. Visiting players were complimentary of the park though. As far as the facilities, it was a minor-league ballpark. The locker rooms were not big but there wasn't anything you could do about it. We had limited room and it was impossible to expand. You really could not change it or expand in any way. But you have to remember that it wasn't meant to be a permanent stadium for the team. It was just an interim home for the Pilots.

Q. *The Pilots probably had baseball's most unusual uniform of all time. How did they come about?*

A. Well, as far as the name, I ran a contest at Dewey Soriano's instruction. The winner received a trip to spring training, I believe. Some young kid sent in the Pilots name. When I saw it I thought Dewey was going to like it. He actually had a marine captain's license. I brought it into him and said, "Here Dewey, what do you think of this?" And that was it. We tried to tie it into the marine industry and also aviation with Boeing being in the area. We threw the braids on the hats for a ship's captain and used wings on the logo. We used a combination of them. It was reflective of the community.

Q. *How were the Seattle fans? Do you feel that they supported the team?*

A. Oh, I think they did initially. You've got to remember that we were in an inferior park. But we sold all of our box seats, so there was support. We got hit with a lot of injuries in August and the losses mounted. There were a lot of people that wanted Major League Baseball in Seattle, but not enough. That was the problem. Our only knowledge of Major League Baseball was what we read in the papers. It was an old minor-league town and there was a minor-league mentality here.

Q. *How well organized was the Pilots organization?*

A. From a baseball standpoint it was organized. Dewey had been president of the Pacific Coast League and his brother Max was the treasurer. Milkes was kind of a tyrant and left a little to be desired. Schultz I thought was an excellent choice, he was a nice, funny guy. It wasn't Milkes' or Dewey Soriano's fault that the team folded. For an expansion team we were competitive but wound up out of the hunt early. We were going good until early August and then the bottom fell out. We were only six games out when that happened. We got bad publicity about ticket prices that wasn't fair. There were reports that we were the highest in the league. Boxes were $6 but they were actually $4 on the season plan. That's what everybody paid but on the ticket it said $6. That hurt. It gave everybody that wanted not to go to the games an excuse not to come.

Q. *Did you agree with the decision to fire Joe Schultz?*
A. No, I didn't think that it was the right thing to do, but Milkes liked Bristol. What it amounted to was Schultz was going to take the fall for Marvin. Bristol did have a good track record in Cincinnati and had won over there.

Q. *Were you surprised when the Pilots were finally sold and moved to Milwaukee?*
A. Well, not really. I kinda saw the handwriting on the walls. I knew that the ownership were on their heels and had no way of bailing themselves out. Dewey got really disenchanted and he took it hard. This was his town and it was like a slap in the face. He had played minor-league ball here with the Rainiers and then ran that team. He didn't say too much but I knew him and knew how upset he was. He and his brother Max decided that it was time to bail out. Selig pursued the team pretty hard. He was the driving force behind the Milwaukee effort. At a winter meeting for the A.L. owners someone who worked for Commissioner Cronin said to me, "Look over there." Selig was standing behind a big potted plant. He was hiding behind it, just watching what was going on!

Q. *The Pilots had the largest radio broadcast area in Major League Baseball. However, they were never able to negotiate a local T.V. contract. Do you think that this may have partially led to the team's demise?*
A. Well, they did televise some games. But there really wasn't any T.V. stations in town that were interested in it. It was an expensive proposition for them.

Q. *Did you think that it was a good thing that the franchise was sold and moved to Milwaukee?*
A. No, I thought it was terrible. I was broken-hearted. All of us had worked so hard with the stadium bond issue for a few years. I had a terrible time getting over it. When the Pilots pulled out we kept working on the domed stadium and we finally got the bond issue passed and got going on the Kingdome. But we had to start the process all over again to get the Mariners; going to baseball winter meetings, meeting with the owners, bringing models of the domed stadium, and so forth. But it's the old "Alls Well That Ends Well." We got the Mariners. It eventually turned out fine with a Major League team in Seattle. The attendance is fantastic here now. Some people back then said

that they will never draw there, meaning Seattle. The whole thing was a great experience that I wouldn't trade for anything but in the long run it worked out well. The city really took to this team. Danny Kaye [Mariners' original owner] was well financed and willing to spend a little money. The Kingdome made all the difference in the world. You didn't have to worry about getting rained on.

Q. *You were from the Northwest. Did you go on to the Brewers?*
A. I didn't intend to go to Milwaukee but they called me and asked me to come until things got up and running. I just thought I'd be there for a little while but I actually stayed the entire year [1970]. The following year I went to spring training and gave Selig my notice. When I told him he looked a little deflated and said, "I was afraid of this." But my family was still back in Seattle. I got a job working as the media relations person for the Seattle Convention and Visitors Bureau. It was a pretty good job too.

Q. *Marvin Milkes also stayed with the franchise the next season. What happened with him?*
A. Well, Selig and Milkes did not get along. They just didn't hit it off too well. During the winter holidays [1970] we had a Christmas party for the ballpark people. Selig told me that we were going to fire Milkes and to have a press release written up right away and get it out. I went back to my office right then and got it over to the Milwaukee Journal. I guess Bud told Marvin directly.

JACK AKER

Q. *When you got drafted by the Pilots you were already an established Major League player. What was your reaction when you heard that you were going to Seattle?*
A. I was happy to get away from Charlie Finley in Oakland. I didn't care where I went so long as it was away from him.

Q. *How was the Pilots spring training in '69?*
A. It was not particularly memorable. At that time, the stadium was way out in the dessert, away from the city. I remember one of the players used to ride his bike to the stadium every day, it had to be like five miles.

Q. *How well organized was the Pilots organization?*
A. They weren't the worst that I played with. That honor belongs to the Atlanta Braves under Eddie Mathews in the mid–'70s.

Q. *The Pilots finished in last place with a 64–98 record. Do you think they lived up to expectations or should have done better than their record?*
A. That's where they belonged.

Q. Were you surprised when you were traded in May for Talbot?
A. I had been asking for a trade, but I hadn't a clue that it was going to be to the Yankees. I had talked to both the manager and the GM about wanting to play for a better club. I was very pleased it was to the Yankees.

Q. You had a great year after leaving Seattle, this was a terrible trade for the Pilots. Do you think GM Marvin Milkes was too quick to demote and trade players?
A. I wasn't there long enough to see most of the trades and make a judgment about Milkes' judgment. I knew I could save a lot of games if I were on a team that could win any, I was in great shape and throwing well. I was pumped up by the trade to the Yankees and didn't have too many bad games that year.

Q. Even though you had moved on were you surprised by the Pilots' move to Milwaukee?
A. This isn't the kind of thing players think about, we're concentrating on what's going on on the field and not on the moves between the owners and the league.

On Sick's Stadium and its facilities:
It fit its name. They were still nailing outfield bleachers on opening day.

On the Pilots uniforms:
We all felt like we were in the Navy with all the embroidery on the caps.

On manager Joe Schultz and the coaching staff being fired:
I thought Joe Schultz was all right as a manager, the coaching staff was expendable. I can't even remember who the pitching coach was. Except for Frank Crosetti, none of them showed any signs of having had much or any pro experience, but they were sure know-it-alls.

ON RELOCATION:

At the time of the relocation the following members of the team expressed their feelings:[3]

> I'm glad they finally reached a decision. The players should be relieved. It'll be much easier to get the total concentration of the players now.
> —*Manager Dave Bristol*

> I regret that things could not have worked out better for the people of the Northwest. They were great fans last season through thick and thin. But playing in Milwaukee will be closer to home and my wife and family will like that.
> —*Gene Brabender*

Tommy Harper (National Baseball Hall of Fame Library, Cooperstown, N.Y.).

It doesn't much make a difference to me, because ballplayers go where they tell you to go. All I can do is pack my bags.

— *Greg Goossen*

I would have liked to have stayed in Seattle. I hate for this to happen to any city—to lose a team after only one year. I don't think Seattle was given enough time for a fair evaluation.

— *Tommy Harper*

Appendix B
By the Numbers

Pilots Players and Coaches by Uniform Number

1 Ray Oyler
2 Frank Crosetti
3 Joe Schultz
4 Sal Maglie
4 Dave Bristol
5 Don Mincher
6 Eddie O'Brien
7 Ron Plaza
8 Mike Hegan
9 Rich Rollins
10 John Donaldson
10 Larry Haney
11 John Kennedy
12 Tommy Davis
12 Danny Walton
13 Steve Barber
14 Jim Gosger
14 Gordy Lund
14 Miguel Fuentes
15 Gerry McNertney
16 Dick Simpson
17 Jim Pagliaroni
18 Gus Gil

19 Steve Whitaker
20 Wayne Comer
21 Tommy Harper
22 Fred Stanley
23 Jack Aker
23 Fred Talbot
24 Diego Segui
25 Jose Vidal
25 John Gelnar
26 Merritt Ranew
26 Mike Ferraro
27 Bob Locker
27 Darrell Brandon
28 Mike Marshall
28 Sandy Valdespino
30 Ron Clark
30 Federico Velazquez
31 Sibi Sisti
32 Gene Brabender
33 Marty Pattin
34 Greg Goossen
35 John Morris
36 Steve Hovley

38 Bob Meyer
38 Bill Edgerton
39 Gary Bell
39 George Brunet
39 Gary Roggenburk
40 Jerry Stephenson
41 Dooley Womack
42 Skip Lockwood
43 John O'Donoghue
45 Gary Timberlake
45 Dick Baney
46 Charles Bates
50 Gary Timberlake
51 Billy Williams
54 Greg Goossen
55 Bill Edgerton
56 Jim Bouton
57 Merritt Ranew

Honorable mention:
19 Lou Piniella
52 Tom Kelly

Game-by-Game Results, 1969

Date	W/L	Opponent	Score	Location	Record
April 8	W	Angels	4–3	Anaheim Stadium	1–0
April 9	L	Angels	7–3	Anaheim Stadium	1–1
April 11	W	White Sox	7–0	Sick's Stadium	2–1
April 12	W	White Sox	5–1	Sick's Stadium	3–1
April 13	L	White Sox	12–7	Sick's Stadium	3–2
April 14	L	Royals	2–1	Sick's Stadium	3–3

Date	W/L	Opponent	Score	Location	Record
April 16	L	Twins	6–4	Sick's Stadium	3–4
April 19	W	White Sox	5–1	Comiskey Park	4–4
April 20	L	White Sox	3–2	Comiskey Park	4–5
	L	White Sox	13–3	Comiskey Park	4–6
April 21	W	Royals	4–1	Municipal Stadium	5–6
April 22	L	Royals	2–1	Municipal Stadium	5–7
April 23	L	Royals	4–3	Municipal Stadium	5–8
April 25	L	A's	14–2	Sick's Stadium	5–9
April 26	W	A's	6–3	Sick's Stadium	6–9
April 27	L	A's	13–5	Sick's Stadium	6–10
April 29	W	Angels	1–0	Sick's Stadium	7–10
April 30	L	Twins	6–4	Metropolitan Stadium	7–11
May 1	L	Twins	4–1	Metropolitan Stadium	7–12
May 2	L	A's	8–7	Oakland-Alameda Stadium	7–13
May 3	L	A's	3–2	Oakland-Alameda Stadium	7–14
May 4	W	A's	6–2	Oakland-Alameda Stadium	8–14
	L	A's	11–7	Oakland-Alameda Stadium	8–15
May 6	L	Red Sox	12–2	Sick's Stadium	8–16
May 7	L	Red Sox	5–4	Sick's Stadium	8–17
May 9	W	Senators	2–0	Sick's Stadium	9–17
May 10	W	Senators	16–13	Sick's Stadium	10–17
May 11	W	Senators	6–5	Sick's Stadium	11–17
May 12	W	Yankees	8–4	Sick's Stadium	12–17
May 13	W	Yankees	5–3	Sick's Stadium	13–17
May 14	L	Yankees	5–4	Sick's Stadium	13–18
May 16	W	Red Sox	10–9	Fenway Park	14–18
May 17	L	Red Sox	6–1	Fenway Park	14–19
May 18	W	Red Sox	9–6	Fenway Park	15–19
May 20	L	Senators	6–5	R.F.K. Stadium	15–20
May 21	W	Senators	6–2	R.F.K. Stadium	16–20
May 22	W	Senators	7–6	R.F.K. Stadium	17–20
May 23	L	Indians	7–1	Cleveland-Municipal Stadium	17–21
May 24	W	Indians	8–2	Cleveland-Municipal Stadium	18–21
May 25	W	Indians	3–2	Cleveland-Municipal Stadium	19–21
May 27	W	Orioles	8–1	Sick's Stadium	20–21
May 28	L	Orioles	9–5	Sick's Stadium	20–22
May 30	L	Tigers	8–5	Sick's Stadium	20–23
May 31	L	Tigers	3–2	Sick's Stadium	20–24
June 1	W	Tigers	8–7	Sick's Stadium	21–24
June 2	W	Tigers	8–2	Sick's Stadium	22–24
June 3	L	Indians	3–1	Sick's Stadium	22–25
June 4	L	Indians	10–4	Sick's Stadium	22–26
June 6	L	Orioles	5–1	Memorial Stadium	22–27
June 7	L	Orioles	10–0	Memorial Stadium	22–28
June 8	W	Orioles	7–5	Memorial Stadium	23–28
June 9	W	Tigers	3–2	Tiger Stadium	24–28
June 10	L	Tigers	5–0	Tiger Stadium	24–29
June 11	L	Tigers	4–3	Tiger Stadium	24–30
June 13	W	Yankees	2–1	Yankee Stadium	25–30
June 14	W	Yankees	5–4	Yankee Stadium	26–30

Date	W/L	Opponent	Score	Location	Record
June 15	L	Yankees	4–0	Yankee Stadium	26–31
June 16	L	White Sox	8–3	Milwaukee County Stadium	26–32
June 18	L	White Sox	7–3	Comiskey Park	26–33
	W	White Sox	6–5	Comiskey Park	27–33
June 19	L	White Sox	13–10	Comiskey Park	27–34
June 20	W	Royals	5–3	Sick's Stadium	28–34
	L	Royals	6–2	Sick's Stadium	28–35
June 21	W	Royals	1–0	Sick's Stadium	29–35
June 22	W	Royals	5–1	Sick's Stadium	30–35
June 24	L	White Sox	6–4	Sick's Stadium	30–36
	L	White Sox	7–6	Sick's Stadium	30–37
June 25	W	White Sox	3–1	Sick's Stadium	31–37
June 26	W	White Sox	3–2	Sick's Stadium	32–37
June 27	L	Angels	5–3	Anaheim Stadium	32–38
	W	Angels	5–2	Anaheim Stadium	33–38
June 28	W	Angels	3–0	Anaheim Stadium	34–38
June 29	L	Angels	8–2	Anaheim Stadium	34–39
July 1	W	A's	7–1	Oakland-Alameda Stadium	35–39
July 2	L	A's	5–0	Oakland-Alameda Stadium	35–40
July 3	L	A's	6–4	Oakland-Alameda Stadium	35–41
July 4	L	Royals	13–2	Municipal Stadium	35–42
	L	Royals	3–2	Municipal Stadium	35–43
July 5	L	Royals	6–4	Municipal Stadium	35–44
July 6	W	Royals	9–3	Municipal Stadium	36–44
July 7	L	Angels	5–1	Sick's Stadium	36–45
July 8	W	Angels	3–1	Sick's Stadium	37–45
July 9	W	Angels	8–0	Sick's Stadium	38–45
	L	Angels	5–0	Sick's Stadium	38–46
July 11	L	Twins	9–3	Metropolitan Stadium	38–47
July 12	L	Twins	11–1	Metropolitan Stadium	38–48
July 13	L	Twins	5–2	Metropolitan Stadium	38–49
	L	Twins	5–4	Metropolitan Stadium	38–50
July 15	L	A's	6–2	Sick's Stadium	38–51
July 16	L	A's	6–1	Sick's Stadium	38–52
July 17	L	A's	8–2	Sick's Stadium	38–53
July 18	W	Twins	2–1	Sick's Stadium	39–53
	W	Twins	3–2	Sick's Stadium	40–53
July 19	L	Twins	11–7	Sick's Stadium	40–54
July 20	L	Twins	4–0	Sick's Stadium	40–55
July 24	W	Red Sox	8–6	Sick's Stadium	41–55
July 25	L	Red Sox	7–6	Sick's Stadium	41–56
July 26	W	Red Sox	8–5	Sick's Stadium	42–56
July 27	L	Red Sox	5–3	Sick's Stadium	42–57
July 29	L	Senators	4–2	Sick's Stadium	42–58
July 30	W	Senators	4–3	Sick's Stadium	43–58
July 31	L	Senators	7–6	Sick's Stadium	43–59
Aug. 1	L	Yankees	4–2	Sick's Stadium	43–60
Aug. 2	L	Yankees	5–4	Sick's Stadium	43–61
Aug. 3	L	Yankees	5–3	Sick's Stadium	43–62
Aug. 5	W	Red Sox	9–2	Fenway Park	44–62

Date	W/L	Opponent	Score	Location	Record
Aug. 6	W	Red Sox	6–5	Fenway Park	45–62
Aug. 7	L	Red Sox	5–4	Fenway Park	45–63
Aug. 8	L	Senators	10–3	R.F.K. Stadium	45–64
Aug. 9	W	Senators	8–6	R.F.K. Stadium	46–64
Aug. 10	L	Senators	7–5	R.F.K. Stadium	46–65
Aug. 11	W	Indians	8–2	Cleveland-Municipal Stadium	47–65
Aug. 12	L	Indians	6–5	Cleveland-Municipal Stadium	47–66
Aug. 13	W	Indians	5–3	Cleveland-Municipal Stadium	48–66
Aug. 15	L	Orioles	2–1	Sick's Stadium	48–67
Aug. 16	L	Orioles	15–3	Sick's Stadium	48–68
Aug. 17	L	Orioles	4–1	Sick's Stadium	48–69
Aug. 18	L	Orioles	12–3	Sick's Stadium	48–70
Aug. 19	L	Tigers	5–3	Sick's Stadium	48–71
Aug. 20	L	Tigers	4–3	Sick's Stadium	48–72
Aug. 21	L	Tigers	7–6	Sick's Stadium	48–73
Aug. 22	L	Indians	9–8	Sick's Stadium	48–74
Aug. 23	L	Indians	7–3	Sick's Stadium	48–75
Aug. 24	L	Indians	6–5	Sick's Stadium	48–76
Aug. 26	W	Orioles	2–1	Memorial Stadium	49–76
Aug. 27	L	Orioles	7–2	Memorial Stadium	49–77
Aug. 28	L	Orioles	4–3	Memorial Stadium	49–78
Aug. 29	L	Tigers	6–1	Tiger Stadium	49–79
Aug. 30	L	Tigers	4–3	Tiger Stadium	49–80
Aug. 31	L	Tigers	7–2	Tiger Stadium	49–81
Sept. 1	L	Yankees	6–1	Yankee Stadium	49–82
	W	Yankees	5–1	Yankee Stadium	50–82
Sept. 2	L	Yankees	5–4	Yankee Stadium	50–83
Sept. 4	L	Royals	5–3	Sick's Stadium	50–84
Sept. 5	W	Royals	5–4	Sick's Stadium	51–84
Sept. 6	L	Royals	6–2	Sick's Stadium	51–85
Sept. 7	W	Royals	7–6	Sick's Stadium	52–85
Sept. 8	W	White Sox	2–1	Sick's Stadium	53–85
	W	White Sox	5–1	Sick's Stadium	54–85
Sept. 10	W	A's	9–4	Oakland-Alameda Stadium	55–85
Sept. 11	L	A's	6–3	Oakland-Alameda Stadium	55–86
Sept. 12	W	Angels	4–1	Sick's Stadium	56–86
	Tied	Angels	1–1	Sick's Stadium	56–86
Sept. 13	W	Angels	6–4	Sick's Stadium	57–86
	L	Angels	4–2	Sick's Stadium	57–87
Sept. 14	L	Angels	4–2	Sick's Stadium	57–88
Sept. 15	W	Royals	3–2	Municipal Stadium	58–88
Sept. 16	L	Royals	2–1	Municipal Stadium	58–89
Sept. 17	L	White Sox	6–4	Comiskey Park	58–90
	L	White Sox	2–1	Comiskey Park	58–91
Sept. 19	L	Twins	2–1	Metropolitan Stadium	58–92
Sept. 20	L	Twins	3–2	Metropolitan Stadium	58–93
Sept. 21	W	Twins	4–3	Metropolitan Stadium	59–93
Sept. 22	W	Angels	5–4	Anaheim Stadium	60–93
Sept. 23	L	Angels	5–4	Anaheim Stadium	60–94
Sept. 24	L	Angels	3–1	Anaheim Stadium	60–95

Date	W/L	Opponent	Score	Location	Record
Sept. 25	W	Twins	5–1	Sick's Stadium	61–95
Sept. 26	W	Twins	4–3	Sick's Stadium	62–95
Sept. 28	L	Twins	5–2	Sick's Stadium	62–96
	W	Twins	4–1	Sick's Stadium	63–96
Sept. 30	L	A's	8–4	Sick's Stadium	63–97
Oct. 1	W	A's	4–3	Sick's Stadium	64–97
Oct. 2	L	A's	3–1	Sick's Stadium	64–98

1969 Final Standings

East			West		
Orioles	109–53	- Games back	Twins	97–65	- Games back
Tigers	90–72	19 Games back	Athletics	88–74	9 Games back
Red Sox	87–75	22 Games back	Angels	71–91	26 Games back
Senators	86–76	23 Games back	Royals	69–93	28 Games back
Yankees	80–81	28½ Games back	White Sox	68–94	29 Games back
Indians	62–99	46½ Games back	Pilots	64–98	33 Games back

Wins and losses by opponent:	W	L
Baltimore Orioles	3	9
Boston Red Sox	6	6

The one and only 1969 Seattle Pilots (Topps).

Wins and losses by opponent: W L
California Angels 9 9
Chicago White Sox 8 10
Cleveland Indians 5 7
Detroit Tigers 2 10
Kansas City Royals 8 10
Minnesota Twins 6 12
New York Yankees 5 7
Oakland A's 5 13
Washington Senators 7 5

Home/Road split:
Home   34–47   .420
Road   30–51   .370

Longest winning streak: 5 (May 9–May 13)
Longest losing streak: 10 (August 15–August 24)
Most runs allowed: 15 (August 16)
Most runs scored: 16 (May 10)
Shutout by opponent: 6
Shutouts by Pilots: 6

During the course of the 1969 season the Pilots scored 639 runs and allowed 799 runs.

Player Statistics

Name / Major League Years Played *1969 Pilots* *ML Career*	*Games* *Games*	*Hits* *Hits*	*2B* *2B*	*3B* *3B*	*HR* *HR*	*AVG* *AVG*	*RBI* *RBI*	*Runs* *Runs*
Clark, Ron / 1966–1975								
1969 Pilots	57	32	5	0	0	.196	12	9
ML Career	230	100	16	3	5	.189	43	40
Comer, Wayne / 1967–1972								
1969 Pilots	147	118	18	1	15	.245	54	88
ML Career	316	157	22	2	16	.229	67	119
Davis, Tommy / 1959–1976								
1969 Pilots	123	123	29	1	6	.271	80	52
ML Career	1999	2121	272	35	153	.294	1052	811
Donaldson, John / 1966–1970, 1974								
1969 Pilots	95	79	8	3	1	.234	19	22
ML Career	405	292	35	11	4	.238	86	96
Ferraro, Mike / 1966, 1968–69, 1972								
1969 Pilots	5	0	0	0	0	.000	0	0
ML Career	162	116	8	2	2	.232	30	28
Gil, Gus / 1967, 1969–71								
1969 Pilots	92	49	7	0	0	.222	17	20
ML Career	221	87	16	0	1	.186	37	46

Appendix B: By the Numbers

Name / Major League Years Played								
1969 Pilots	Games	Hits	2B	3B	HR	AVG	RBI	Runs
ML Career	Games	Hits	2B	3B	HR	AVG	RBI	Runs
Gosger, Jim / 1963, 1965–1971, 1973–74								
1969 Pilots	39	6	2	1	1	.109	1	4
ML Career	705	411	67	13	30	.226	177	197
Goossen, Greg / 1965–1970								
1969 Pilots	52	43	8	1	10	.309	24	19
ML Career	193	111	24	1	13	.241	44	33
Haney, Larry / 1966–1978								
1969 Pilots	22	15	3	0	2	.254	7	3
ML Career	480	198	30	1	12	.215	73	68
Harper, Tommy / 1962–1976								
1969 Pilots	148	126	10	2	9	.235	41	78
ML Career	1810	1609	256	36	146	.257	567	972
Hegan, Mike / 1964, 1966–1967, 1969–1977								
1969 Pilots	95	78	21	2	11	.292	37	54
ML Career	965	504	73	18	53	.242	229	281
Hovley, Steve / 1969–1973								
1969 Pilots	91	91	14	3	3	.277	20	41
ML Career	436	263	39	5	8	.258	88	122
Kennedy, John / 1962–1974								
1969 Pilots	61	30	3	1	4	.234	14	18
ML Career	856	475	77	17	32	.225	185	237
Lund, Gordy / 1967, 1969								
1969 Pilots	20	10	0	0	0	.263	1	4
ML Career	23	12	1	0	0	.261	1	5
McNertney, Jerry / 1964, 1966–1973								
1969 Pilots	128	99	18	1	8	.241	55	39
ML Career	590	337	51	6	27	.237	163	129
Mincher, Don / 1960–1972								
1969 Pilots	140	105	14	0	25	.246	78	53
ML Career	1400	1003	176	16	200	.249	643	530
Oyler, Ray / 1965–1970								
1969 Pilots	106	42	5	0	7	.165	22	24
ML Career	542	221	39	6	15	.175	86	110
Pagliaroni, Jim / 1955, 1960–69								
1969 Pilots	40	29	4	1	5	.264	14	10
ML Career	1160	622	98	7	90	.252	326	269
Ranew, Merritt / 1962–1965, 1969								
1969 Pilots	54	20	2	0	0	.247	4	11
ML Career	269	147	20	9	8	.247	54	68
Rollins, Rich / 1961–1970								
1969 Pilots	58	42	7	0	4	.225	21	15
ML Career	1002	887	125	20	77	.269	399	416

Name / Major League Years Played

	Games	Hits	2B	3B	HR	AVG	RBI	Runs
1969 Pilots	Games	Hits	2B	3B	HR	AVG	RBI	Runs
ML Career	Games	Hits	2B	3B	HR	AVG	RBI	Runs

Simpson, Dick / 1962, 1964–1969

1969 Pilots	26	9	2	0	2	.176	5	8
ML Career	288	107	19	2	15	.207	56	94

Stanley, Fred / 1969–1982

1969 Pilots	17	12	2	1	0	.279	4	2
ML Career	816	356	38	5	10	.216	120	197

Valdespino, Sandy / 1965–1971

1969 Pilots	20	8	1	0	0	.211	2	3
ML Career	382	176	23	3	7	.230	67	96

Velazquez, Freddie / 1969, 1973

1969 Pilots	6	2	2	0	0	.125	2	1
ML Career	21	10	3	0	0	.256	5	3

Vidal, Jose / 1966–1969

1969 Pilots	18	5	0	1	1	.192	2	7
ML Career	88	24	1	2	3	.164	10	20

Walton, Danny / 1968–1971, 1973, 1975–77, 1980

1969 Pilots	23	20	1	2	3	.217	10	12
ML Career	297	174	27	4	28	.223	107	69

Whitaker, Steve / 1966–1970

1969 Pilots	69	29	2	1	6	.250	13	15
ML Career	266	174	20	6	24	.230	85	73

Williams, Billy / 1969

1969 Pilots	4	0	0	0	0	.000	0	1
ML Career	4	0	0	0	0	.000	0	1

PITCHING STATISTICS

Name / Major League Years Played

	Games	Won	Lost	Saves	ERA	CG	SHO
1969 Pilots	Games	Won	Lost	Saves	ERA	CG	SHO
ML Totals	Games	Won	Lost	Saves	ERA	CG	SHO

Aker, Jack / 1964–1974

1969 Pilots	15	0	2	3	7.56	0	0
ML Totals	495	47	45	123	3.28	0	0

Baney, Dick / 1969, 1973–1974

1969 Pilots	9	1	0	0	3.86	0	0
ML Totals	42	4	1	3	4.28	0	0

Barber, Steve / 1960–1974

1969 Pilots	25	4	7	0	4.80	0	0
ML Totals	466	121	106	13	3.36	59	21

Bates, Dick   1969

1969 Pilots	1	0	0	0	27.00	0	0
ML Totals	1	0	0	0	27.00	0	0

Name / Major League Years Played

1969 Pilots ML Totals	Games Games	Won Won	Lost Lost	Saves Saves	ERA ERA	CG CG	SHO SHO
Bell, Gary / 1958–1969							
1969 Pilots	13	2	6	2	4.70	1	1
ML Totals	519	121	117	51	3.68	71	9
Bouton, Jim / 1962–1970, 1978							
1969 Pilots	57	2	1	1	3.91	0	0
ML Totals	304	62	63	6	3.57	34	11
Brabender, Gene / 1966–1970							
1969 Pilots	40	13	14	0	4.36	7	1
ML Totals	151	35	43	6	4.25	15	4
Brandon, Darrell / 1966–1969, 1971–1973							
1969 Pilots	8	0	1	0	8.40	0	0
ML Totals	228	28	37	13	4.04	7	2
Brunet, George / 1956–57, 1959–71							
1969 Pilots	12	2	5	0	5.37	2	0
ML Totals	324	69	93	3	3.62	39	15
Edgerton, Bill / 1966–67, 1969							
1969 Pilots	4	0	1	0	13.50	0	0
ML Totals	17	1	2	0	4.79	0	0
Fuentes, Mickey / 1969							
1969 Pilots	8	1	3	0	5.19	1	0
ML Totals	8	1	3	0	5.19	1	0
Gelnar, John / 1964, 1967, 1969–71							
1969 Pilots	39	3	10	3	3.31	0	0
ML Totals	111	7	14	7	4.19	0	0
Locker, Bob / 1965–1975							
1969 Pilots	51	3	3	6	2.18	0	0
ML Totals	576	57	39	95	2.75	0	0
Lockwood, Skip / 1969–1980							
1969 Pilots	6	0	1	0	3.52	0	0
ML Totals	420	57	97	68	3.55	16	5
Marshall, Mike / 1967, 1969–1981							
1969 Pilots	20	3	10	0	5.13	3	1
ML Totals	723	97	112	188	3.14	3	1
Meyer, Bob / 1964, 1969–70							
1969 Pilots	6	0	3	0	3.31	1	0
ML Totals	38	2	12	0	4.40	1	0
Morris, John / 1966, 1968–74							
1969 Pilots	6	0	0	0	6.39	0	0
ML Totals	132	11	7	2	3.96	2	0
O'Donoghue, John / 1963–1971							
1969 Pilots	55	2	2	6	2.96	0	0
ML Totals	257	39	55	10	4.08	13	4

Appendix B: By the Numbers

Name / Major League Years Played							
1969 Pilots	Games	Won	Lost	Saves	ERA	CG	SHO
ML Totals	Games	Won	Lost	Saves	ERA	CG	SHO
Pattin, Marty / 1968–1980							
1969 Pilots	34	7	12	0	5.62	2	1
ML Totals	475	114	109	25	3.62	64	14
Roggenburk, Gary / 1963, 1965–66, 1968–69							
1969 Pilots	7	2	2	0	4.44	1	0
ML Totals	79	6	9	7	3.64	1	0
Segui, Diego / 1962–1977							
1969 Pilots	66	12	6	12	3.35	2	0
ML Totals	639	92	111	71	3.81	28	7
Talbot, Fred / 1963–70							
1969 Pilots	25	5	8	0	4.16	1	1
ML Totals	195	38	56	1	4.12	12	4
Timberlake, Gary / 1969							
1969 Pilots	2	0	0	0	7.50	0	0
ML Totals	2	0	0	0	7.50	0	0
Womack, Dooley / 1966–1970							
1969 Pilots	9	2	1	0	2.51	0	0
ML Totals	193	19	18	24	2.95	0	0

GAMES BY POSITION

Position	Player	Games		Position	Player	Games
Catcher	McNertney	122			Kennedy	23
	Pagliaroni	29			Clark	15
	Haney	20			Donaldson	2
	Ranew	13			Comer	1
	Velazquez	5		*Shortstop*	Oyler	106
	Comer	1			Clark	38
First Base	Mincher	122			Kennedy	33
	Goossen	31			Lund	17
	Hegan	19			Stanley	15
	Pagliaroni	2			Gil	12
	Clark	1			Donaldson	1
	Davis	1			Rollins	1
Second Base	Donaldson	90		*Outfield*	Comer	139
	Harper	59			Davis	112
	Gil	18			Hovley	84
	Clark	5			Hegan	64
	Lund	1			Whitaker	39
	Stanley	1			Gosger	26
					Harper	26
Third Base	Harper	59			Walton	23
	Rollins	47			Simpson	17
	Gil	38				

Appendix B: By the Numbers

	Valdespino	7	Marshall	20
	Vidal	6	Aker	15
	Ranew	3	Bell	13
	Williams	3	Brunet	12
	Goossen	2	Baney	9
	Pagliaroni	1	Womack	9
			Brandon	8
Pitcher	Segui	66	Fuentes	8
	Bouton	57	Roggenburk	7
	O'Donoghue	55	Lockwood	7
	Locker	51	Meyer	6
	Brabender	40	Morris	6
	Gelnar	39	Edgerton	4
	Pattin	34	Stephenson	2
	Barber	25	Timberlake	1
	Talbot	25	Bates	1

Notes

Chapter 1: Early Seattle Baseball

1. David Wilma, "From Cranks to Fans: Seattle's Long Love Affair with Baseball," *HistoryLink* (10 July 2001): 1.
2. Carlson Van Lindt, *The Seattle Pilots Story* (New York: Marabou Publishing, 1993), 15.
3. Van Lindt, 16.
4. Van Lindt, 17.
5. Van Lindt, 17.
6. Kurt Schaefer, "Play Ball!," *Columbia Magazine* 2, no. 2 (2000): 2.

Chapter 2: Emil Sick and the PCL

1. Van Lindt, 20.
2. Kenneth Hogan, *America's Ballparks* (Vancouver: Pediment Publishing, 2003), 160.
3. Hogan, 161.
4. Van Lindt, 22.
5. Russ Dille, "Play Ball! A Slide Show History of Early Baseball in Washington," *HistoryLink* (2001): 8.
6. Dille, 16.
7. Dille, 25–27.
8. John Reeves, "Seattle Angels," *Seattle Mariners Dugout* (2000): 1.
9. Schaefer, 5.
10. Schaefer, 5.

Chapter 3: A New Beginning

1. Sharon Boswell and Loraine McConaghy, "Ready for the Show," *Seattle Times*, 17 November 1996, 1.
2. Boswell and McConaghy, 1.
3. Van Lindt, 29.
4. Schaefer, 5.
5. Schaefer, 5.

Chapter 4: Building a Team

1. Reeves, 1.
2. "Official Emblem with Air-Sea Theme to Dress Up Seattle Pilots," *Seattle Times,* 31 August 1968, 38.
3. Jim Bouton, *Ball Four* (New York: Wiley Publishing, Inc., 1970), 103.
4. Van Lindt, 38.
5. Van Lindt, 40.
6. Bouton, 31.

Chapter 5: Getting Ready

1. Bouton, 15.
2. Bouton, 36.
3. Van Lindt, 50.
4. Schaefer, 13.
5. Bouton, 49.
6. Gary Bell, telephone conversation, May 2004.
7. Bouton, 47.
8. Van Lindt, 51.
9. Bouton, 96.

Chapter 6: Birth of a Team

1. Van Lindt, 57.
2. Van Lindt, 57.
3. Bouton, 104.
4. Bill Sears, telephone conversation, April 2005.

Chapter 7: The Season

1. Van Lindt, 72.
2. Van Lindt, 86.

3. Van Lindt, 89.
4. Van Lindt, 90
5. Hy Zimmerman, "Exit Skipper Schultz," *Seattle Times*, 21 May 1969.
6. Bouton, 176.
7. Van Lindt, 94.
8. Van Lindt, 95.
9. Hy Zimmerman, sports column, *Seattle Times*, 25 January 1969, 28.
10. Bouton, 203.
11. Bouton, 209.
12. Bouton, 209.
13. Bouton, 216.
14. Van Lindt, 104.
15. Jim Gosger, telephone conversation, March 2004.
16. Van Lindt, 107.
17. Bouton, 17.
18. Bouton, 242.
19. Hy Zimmerman, "Pilots Fred Talbot Was Greeted Happily at Plate," *Seattle Times*, 10 July 1969, Sports 1.
20. Bouton, 246–248.
21. David W. Smith, *Retrosheet.org*, Box scores, 1969, Seattle Pilots.
22. Van Lindt, 122.

Chapter 8: The Season Continues

1. Bouton, 284.
2. Hy Zimmerman, "Exit Skipper Schultz? Rumor Annoys Pilots' Players," *Seattle Times*, 8 September 1969, Sports.
3. Garry Roggenburk, telephone conversation, April 2005.
4. Garry Roggenburk, telephone conversation, April 2005.
5. Van Lindt, 130.
6. Bouton, 284.
7. Bouton, 284.
8. Hy Zimmerman, "Will Pilots Have Place to Play: Money Crisis Looms," *Seattle Times*, 11 January 1969, Sports.
9. Van Lindt, 135.
10. Dick Baney, telephone conversation, July 2004.
11. Wayne Comer, telephone conversation, December 2004.
12. Bouton, 304.
13. Bouton, 316.
14. Bouton, 316.
15. Sandy Valdespino, telephone conversation, March 2005.
16. Bill Sears, telephone conversation, April 2005.
17. Reeves, "Pilots," 1.
18. Reeves, "Pilots," 2.
19. Frank Fleming, "Seattle Pilots," *Sportsencylopedia*, 24 March 2005.

Chapter 9: The Failure

1. Lenny Anderson, "Bristol Is Selected," *Seattle Post-Intelligencer*, 25 November 1969, Sports 1.
2. Anderson, Sports 1.
3. Hy Zimmerman, "We'll Trade, Build, and Climb, Says Bristol of Pilots," *Seattle Times*, 6 December 1969, Sports 1.
4. Van Lindt, 169.
5. Van Lindt, 96.
6. Schaefer, 17.
7. Van Lindt, 171.
8. Van Lindt, 180.
9. Reeves, "Pilots," 1.
10. "Baseball's Affluent Society?," *The Sporting News*, 28 February 1970, 16.
11. Van Lindt, 179.

Chapter 10: The End

1. Hy Zimmerman, "Cold Milwaukee Brew," *Seattle Times*, 4 April 1970, Sports.
2. "Pilots Sight Beacon, Steer Right for Milwaukee," *Seattle Times*, 11 April 1970, Sports.
3. "Pilots Sight Beacon."
4. Van Lindt, 204.
5. Schaefer, 20.
6. Van Lindt, 194–196.
7. "A Businessman's Nightmare," *The Sporting News*, 14 February 1970, 14. Reprinted with permission of TSN.
8. "Pilots Sight Beacon."
9. Hy Zimmerman, "Will Pilots Have Place to Play: Money Crisis Looms," *Seattle Times*, 11 January, 1969, Sports.
10. Hogan, 160.
11. "Clearance Sale Offers Mementoes of Pilots," *Seattle Times*, 25 April 1970, Sports.
12. Professor Andrew Zimbalist, "The Economics of Baseball," Speech at Smith College, Conway New Hampshire, 19 August 1992.
13. Ed Waldman, "Angelos, Selig meet on O's–Nationals issue," *Baltimore Sun*, 14 January 2005.
14. John Donaldson, telephone conversation, March 2004.
15. Bouton, 457.
16. Bouton, 406.

Appendix A: The Players

1. Bouton, 442.
2. Schaefer, 8.
3. "Decision on Site Relieves Players," *The Charlotte News*, 1 April 1970, 70.

Bibliography

Anderson, Lenny. "Bristol Is Selected." *Seattle Post-Intelligencer*, 25 November 1969, Sports, 1.
Baseball Encyclopedia. 10th ed. New York: Macmillion Books, 1996.
Boswell, Sharon, and Loraine McConaghy. "Ready for the Show." *Seattle Times*, 17 November 1996, 1.
Bouton, James. *Ball Four*. New York: Wiley Publishing, 1970.
The Charlotte News. "Decision on Site Relieves Players," 1 April 1970, 70.
Dille, Russ. "Play Ball! A Slide Show History of Early Baseball in Washington." *HistoryLink* 8 (2001).
Fleming, Frank. "Seattle Pilots." *Sportsencyclopedia*, 24 March 2005.
Hogan, Kenneth. *America's Ballparks*. Vancouver, WA: Pediment Publishing, 2003.
Kuhn, Bowie, and Martin Appel. *Hardball: The Education of a Baseball Commissioner*. New York: Times Books, 1987.
New York Daily News. "Yanks Win in Wet, 4-0; Pilots Protest Game," 16 June 1969.
Parrott, Harold. *The Lords of Baseball*. Westport, CT: Praeger Publishers, 1976.
Reeves, John. "Seattle Angels." *Seattle Mariners' Dugout* 2, nos. 1 & 2 (2000).
Schaefer, Kurt. "Play Ball!" *Columbia* 2, no.2 (2000).
"Seattle Pilots." *Seattle Mariners' Dugout*, vol. 1 (2000).
Seattle Times. "Clearance Sale Offers Mementoes of Pilots," 25 April 1970.
_____. "Official Emblem with Air-Sea Theme to Dress Up Seattle Pilots," 31 August 1968.
_____. "Pilots Sight Beacon, Steer Right for Milwaukee," 11 April 1970.
Shatzkin, Mike, and James Charlton. "1969 Seattle Pilots." *BaseballLibrary.com*, 1991.
Smith, David W. *Retrosheet.org*. Box scores, 1969, Seattle Pilots.
The Sporting News. "Baseball's Affluent Society?," 28 February 1970.
_____. "A Businessman's Nightmare," 14 February 1970.
United Press International. "Finley Set to Settle A's in Seattle?" 28 July 1970.
Van Lindt, Carson. *The Seattle Pilots Story*. New York: Maribu Publishing, 1993.
Waldman, Ed. "Angelos, Selig Meet on O's–Nationals Issue." *Baltimore Sun*, 14 January 2005.

Wilma, David, "From Cranks to Fans: Seattle's Long Love Affair with Baseball." *HistoryLink*, 10 July 2001.

Zimmerman, Hy. "Cold Milwaukee Brew." *The Seattle Times*, 4 April 1970.

_____. "Exit Skipper Schultz." *The Seattle Times*, 21 May 1969.

_____. "Exit Skipper Schultz? Rumor Annoys Pilots' Players." *The Seattle Times*, 8 September 1969.

_____. "Pilots Fred Talbot Was Greeted Happily at Plate." *The Seattle Times*, 10 July 1969.

_____. Sports column, *The Seattle Times*, 25 January 1969.

_____. "We'll Trade, Build, and Climb, Says Bristol of Pilots." *The Seattle Times*, 6 December 1969.

_____. "Will Pilots Have Place to Play: Money Crisis Looms." *The Seattle Times*, 11 January 1969.

Index

Aker, Jack 19, 28, 32, 34–35, 41–42, 50–52, 66, 146, 166
Allen, Bernie 54
Allison, Bob 118
American League 14, 30, 128, 133
Anaheim Stadium 27, 29
Anderson, Lenny 27, 173
Andrews, Mike 51, 96, 97
Angels, California 12, 16–17
Angels, Seattle 12, 18, 20
Aparicio, Luis 31, 74–75
Athletic Park 5
Athletics, Kansas City 13–14, 133
Averill, Earl, Jr. 11–12

Bahnsen, Stan 50, 66
Baker, Frank 99
Baldwin, Dave 43, 45
Bando, Sal 113
Baney, Dick 79, 82, 85, 118, 121, 125, 156
Barber, Steve 19, 23, 34, 36, 41, 56, 61–63, 71, 78, 94–97, 102, 105–106, 112, 115, 118, 121, 123, 130, 167
Bates, Charlie 36–37
Bell, Gary 19, 31, 33–34, 36, 40, 45, 49, 50, 55, 57, 60–61, 69, 147, 151, 160
Bellanger, Mark 62, 106
Blair, Paul 102
Boswell, Dave 86
Bouton, Jim 12, 17–18, 23, 32–33, 38, 40–42, 50, 56, 58, 61–62, 69, 72, 75, 77, 85–86, 90, 94, 97, 103–104, 140, 142, 155–156, 171
Boyd, Bob 9
Brabender, Gene 25, 29, 34, 39–40, 45, 54–55, 57, 62, 65, 68, 70, 73–74, 76, 78, 80, 82, 84–86, 89, 92–93, 95, 99, 101, 103, 107, 109, 111, 113, 115, 119, 122, 125–126, 155, 161, 170, 177
Bradford, Buddy 112
Brandon, Darrell 38, 40–43, 51, 57
Braves, Milwaukee 133
Braves, Seattle 4
Brewers, Milwaukee 133–134, 139

Bristol, Dave 127–128, 159–160, 175, 177
Brown, Randy 120
Browns, St. Louis 9, 18
Brunet, George 80, 93, 95, 97, 100, 102–103, 105, 109, 113, 120, 123
Bufford, Don 106
Bunker, Wally 116
Burbach, Bill 49, 95
Burgmeier, Tom 12, 35

Campaneris, Bert 76
Campanis, Jim 35
Cardenas, Leo 40, 83
Cardinals, St. Louis 18
Carew, Rod 33–34, 40, 83, 86, 119
Carlson, Edward 133
Cash, Norm 63
Cater, Danny 36
Chance, Dean 119
Chinooks, Seattle 5
Civic Field 6, 8
Clam Diggers, Seattle 5
Clark, Ron 82, 86, 90, 99, 109, 125, 131
Clarke, Horace 47, 96, 109
Clemente, Roberto 169
Cobb, Ty 9
Coleman, Joe 93
Colt .45s, Houston 133
Comer, Wayne 34, 41, 49, 50, 54–55, 58, 60, 62, 65, 72–73, 75, 78, 85–86, 96–97, 102–103, 105, 111–113, 115, 121, 125, 155, 158
Comiskey Park 34
Conigliaro, Tony 51, 90, 96
Cottier, Chuck 12
County Stadium 129, 139, 160
Cram, Jerry 115
Cronin, Joe, AL Pres. 15, 19, 31, 108, 129, 175
Crosetti, Frank 20, 54, 60, 126, 158, 173
Cuellar, Mike 62, 101, 105
Culp, Ray 95

Daley, William 12–15, 29, 56, 99, 108, 128, 136

Daniels, Bennie 116
Danz, Fred 129–130
Dark, Alvin 99
Davis, Tommy 19, 23–28, 34, 55, 58, 60, 62, 69, 73, 75, 78, 86, 95–96, 98, 102, 105, 107, 131, 159, 167
DiMaggio, Joe 16
Dobson, Chuck 41, 113
Dobson, Pat 63–64
Donaldson, John 65, 71, 81, 92–94, 98, 105–106, 109, 111, 115, 117, 148, 155
Downing, Al 45
Drabowski, Moe 35, 111
Drago, Dick 111
Drummund, Cal 54
Dudley, Jimmy 171
Dugdale, Daniel D.E. 4–6
Dugdale Park 5–6
Dwyer, William 133

Eckert, Commissioner William 23
Edgerton, Bill 33–37
Ellsworth, Cal 127
Epstein, Mike 54–55
Ermer, Cal 127
Expos, Montreal 18, 27, 29, 124, 139, 159

Farber, Steve 173
Fernandez, Frank 47
Ferraro, Mike 26, 36
Fingers, Rollie 41, 77
Finley, Charlie O. 13–14, 131, 145, 164, 176
Fisher, Eddie 75, 79, 11–115
Freehan, Bill 64
Fregosi, Jim 28, 38–39

Garcia, Damaso 166
Gelnar, John 25–26, 57, 62–63, 65–66, 70, 73, 76–77, 80, 84, 87, 90, 94–95, 98–99, 107, 110, 125, 169
Giants, New York 10
Giants, Seattle 5
Gibbs, Jake 65
Gibson, Russ 90
Gil, Gus 35, 50, 58, 64–65, 69–71, 73, 75, 78, 86, 104, 125
Gipson, Bob 88, 152
Gomez, Preston 126
Goossen, Greg 23, 89–90, 92–93, 98, 105, 110–112, 121–122, 125, 131, 177
Gosger, Jim 26–28, 34–35, 50, 67, 145, 155
Green, Dick 36

Hall, Jimmie 50
Hall, Tom 40, 121
Haney, Larry 38, 45, 51, 58, 60, 64, 148
Hannan, Jim 54
Hanson, Ron 34, 72
Harden, Jim 62
Hargan, Steve 100
Harper, Tommy 1, 19, 23, 27, 31, 35, 41, 50, 54–55, 57, 59–60, 62, 65, 67–71, 73, 78, 85, 92, 95–96, 98–99, 101, 103, 106, 109, 111, 113, 115, 119, 124, 136, 159, 167, 170, 177

Harrelson, Ken 99
Hedlund, Mike 35
Hegan, Mike 19, 26–28, 41, 45, 54, 57–59, 61, 65, 74, 78, 88–89, 93, 99–100, 109, 120, 124, 131, 143
Hendricks, Elrod 101, 105
Hendrix, Jimi 139
Herrmann, Ed 72
Hershberger, Mike 131
Hopkins, Gail 74
Horlen, Joel 31
Hornsby, Rogers 9
Horton, Tony 104
Horton, Willie 63
Houk, Ralph 46–47, 50, 65, 147
Hovley, Steve 12, 71, 74, 76, 78–79, 85–86, 89–90, 92, 95, 11, 113–115, 125, 155
Howard, Frank 45, 94

Indians, Cleveland 12, 14, 23
Indians, Seattle 5–6, 8

Jackson, Reggie 36–37, 76, 82, 149
Johnson, Bob 113
Johnstone, Jay 12, 28, 79
Jones, Dalton 51, 96
Joplin, Janis 139

Kaat, Jim 82, 119
Kansas City 15
Kaufman, Ewing 19
Kaye, Danny 176
Kekich, Mike 46
Kennedy, John 41, 50–51, 54, 62, 64, 69, 75, 78, 119, 125, 155
Kilkenny, Mike 103
Killebrew, Harmon 34, 40, 77, 82–84, 119, 121
Klepper, William 7
Klimchock, Lou 61
Knoop, Bobby 74–75
Knowles, Darold 94
Koegel, Pete 106
Krausse, Lew 85, 131, 135
Kubiak, Ted 130–131
Kuhn, Commissioner Bowie 23, 31
Kunkel, Bill 46

Lahoud, Joe 51, 90, 92
Lauzerique, George 130
Lelivelt, Jack 7
Lemon, Bob 13, 127
Lock, Don 97
Locker, Bob 61, 64, 69–70, 72, 76, 80 83–84, 89–90, 92–93, 97–98, 113, 125, 160
Lockwood, Skip 113, 117, 125, 143
Lolich, Mickey 63, 103, 106
Lonborg, Jim 92, 96
Los Angeles 13
Lund, Gordy 81, 84–85, 99, 100
Lyle, Sparky 96–97

Magee, Willie 166
Maglie, Sal 20, 61, 64, 68, 74, 98, 116, 126 147, 156, 167, 170, 173

Magnuson, Sen. Warren G. 15, 29, 136
Major League Baseball: expansion 15; Players Association 22
Mantle, Mickey 16, 45, 164
Manuel, Chuck 83–84, 86
Marshall, Mike 20, 29, 33, 35, 37, 41, 43, 49–51, 56, 58, 61, 64, 67, 69, 76, 78–79, 125, 130, 150, 155, 161
Martin, Billy 127, 159
Matchick, Tommy 63–64
Mathews, Eddie 176
Mattingly, Don 166
Mauch, Gene 126
May, Carlos 73
May, Rudy 120
Maye, Lee 98
Mays, Willie 157
McDowell, Sam 56, 61, 104
McGlothlin, Jim 1, 27
McGlothlin, Lynn 38
McGriff, Fred 166
McLain, Denny 64, 88, 107
McMillan, Roy 128
McMullen, Ken 54
McNally, Dave 58, 61–62, 102
McNertney, Gerry 19, 26–28, 31, 35, 40, 48–50, 54, 57–58, 60, 62, 65, 69, 71, 74–75, 81, 83, 85–86, 89–91, 94, 101, 109, 118–119, 124, 154, 160
Melton, Bill 32, 34–35, 69, 72–74, 82
Messersmith, Andy 76, 115, 135
Metropolitan Stadium 39
Meyer, Bob 106, 109, 111, 113, 116, 119, 125
Milkes, Marvin 16–18, 20, 26, 29, 33, 36, 38, 40, 52, 54–55, 58–61, 64, 66, 69–71, 76, 79, 80, 92–94, 99–100, 107, 117, 123–124, 126–127, 130–131, 143, 146, 155, 159, 165, 168, 170, 173, 175–177
Miller, Bob 85
Miller, Mayor Floyd 29, 108
Miller, Marvin 22
Mincher, Donald 19, 23, 27–28, 41, 43, 45, 50, 54, 58, 60, 63, 68, 72–73, 76, 78–79, 84–88, 91, 98–99, 102, 111, 114, 120, 124, 154, 160
Mitterwald, George 87
Modrem, Stuart 17
Moore, Jackie 128
Morris, John 26, 34, 37
Moses, Gerry 97
Motton, Curt 105–106
Municipal Stadium 56
Murcer, Bobby 46–47, 49
Murphy, Tom 114

Nagy, Mike 51
National Association of Baseball Clubs 3, 4
National League 11
Nelson, Roger 70
Nettles, Greg 34
Northrup, Jim 64
Northwestern League 4–6

Oakland 14
Oakland–Alameda County Stadium 41
O'Brien, Eddie 20, 126, 147
Odom, John 77, 84
O'Donoghue, John 36, 43, 50, 58, 61–65, 72–73, 77, 82–84, 86, 89, 97, 107, 109, 119, 121, 125
O'Doul, Lefty 10
Olerud, John Sr. 12
Oliva, Tony 34, 40, 83, 119
Oliver, Bob 116
Oliver, Gene 77
Orioles, Baltimore 10
Osteen, Claude 11
Owens, Jesse 103
Oyler, Ray 19, 27, 28, 31, 35, 38–39, 41, 46–47, 49, 51, 54, 57, 61–62, 69, 74–76, 78, 86, 97, 105, 109, 125, 130, 155

Pacific Coast League 6, 8–9, 14
Pacific Northwest League 3–5, 7, 10–11
Pacific Northwest Sports 14–15, 17, 129–130, 132–133, 135
Padres, San Diego 18, 27, 29, 124, 138, 159
Pagliaroni, Jim 55, 58, 86–87, 93, 101, 103–104, 110, 130
Palmer, Jim 58, 102
Pascual, Camilo 55
Pattin, Marty 27–29, 32, 34–36, 38–39, 41, 43, 46–47, 50, 52, 54, 57–58, 61, 63, 65, 69–70, 75, 77, 79, 82, 84–85, 92, 94, 97, 104, 116, 125, 155
Paul, Gabe, Jr. 16
Pepitone, Joe 69, 95
Perranowski, Ron 85
Perry, Jim 87, 119
Peters, Gary 68
Petrocelli, Rico 11, 50
Phillies, Philadelphia 11
Phillips, Lefty 115
Phoebus, Tom 102
Pilot Stadium *see* Tempe Spring Training Complex
Piniella, Lou 20, 24–26, 116, 151, 169, 173
Pinson, Vada 11
Plaza, Ron 126
Portland 3, 8
Powell, Boog 58, 102
Price, Bill 64
Puget Sound 4

Quilici, Frank 82

Rainier Mountains 8
Rainiers, Seattle 6, 8–9, 11, 14, 31
Ranew, Merritt 54, 58, 60
Rayor, Curt 41, 74
Red Sox, Boston 11, 12
Reds, Cincinnati 11
Reds, Seattle 3
Reese, Rich 34, 82, 86
Reichardt, Rick 12, 28
Rios, Juan 35

Robinson, Brooks 58
Robinson, Frank 58, 105–106
Rodriquez, Aurelio 81, 113, 115
Rodriguez, Ellie 35
Roggenburk, Gary 71, 76–77, 79, 82, 90, 93, 166
Rollins, Rich 26–28, 31, 41, 43, 45, 50, 60, 71, 76, 78, 124, 155, 159, 167
Romo, Vincente 97
Roof, Phil 131
Roseboro, Johnny 82, 86
Royals, Kansas City 18, 27, 29, 124, 139, 159

Salmon, Chico 25, 101, 106
Sanders, Ken 131
San Francisco 13
Santo, Ron 16
Satriano, Tom 91
Schofield, Dick 96–97
Schonely, Bill 171
Schultz, Joe 18, 20, 23, 25–26, 28–29, 31, 34–36, 44, 50, 54–55, 57–59, 61, 64, 66, 68–69, 72–76, 80, 83, 86–87, 93–94, 96–98, 101–103, 105, 107, 109, 115–116, 122, 126–127, 142, 145–146, 149, 151–153, 155–157, 159, 161–162, 165, 167, 170, 172, 175, 177
Schweppe, Alfred 132
Sealth (Indian chief) 4
Sears, Bill 173
Seattle: industry 3; population 14
Seattle Center 129
Seattle Coliseum 14
Seattles (baseball team) 3
Segui, Diego 19, 28, 32, 34–35, 42, 51, 55, 57, 60, 62–63, 68, 73, 75–76, 78, 85, 90, 95, 99, 102, 113, 115, 119, 121, 123, 125, 130–131, 152, 155, 161
Selig, Bud 67, 129–130, 133–135, 140, 171, 175–176
Senate Commerce Commission 15
Short, Ed 161
Sick, Emil 6–8, 10–11, 14
Sick's Stadium 1, 9, 12–13, 15–16, 20–21, 29–30, 33–34, 40, 44, 130, 145, 147, 149–151, 153–154, 158, 161, 164, 166, 169, 172–173
Simpson, Dick 52, 60, 62–63, 71, 78, 125
Sims, Duke 61, 104
Siwashes, Seattle 4
Smith, E.B. 130
Smith, Mayo 20, 63
Smith, Reggie 51, 92, 95–97
Soriano, Dewey 14–16, 18–19, 26, 30, 55, 99, 103, 108, 117, 128–130, 136–137, 159, 172–175
Soriano, Max 14, 16, 29, 55, 132, 136, 159, 174
Soriano, Milton 14
Space Needle 40
Spahn, Warren 127
Sparma, Joe 59–60
Spokane 3
The Sporting News 135
Stange, Lee 97
Stanley, Fred 107, 113–114, 125–126, 143

Stanley, Mickey 60
Steinbrenner, George 166
Stengel, Casey 89
Stephen, Buzz 19, 76
Stock, Wes 127
Stottlemeyer, Mel 48–49, 65, 109
Stroud, Ed 93
Supersonics, Seattle 14
Swallow, Ray 18
Symington, Sen. Stewart 15

Tacoma 3, 7
Talbot, Fred 47, 52, 56, 61, 64, 66, 70, 72, 76–77, 79, 81, 83, 86, 90, 95, 97, 99, 102, 105–106, 113, 123, 177
Tatum, Ken 76, 115
Tempe Spring Training Complex 21–22, 130, 132, 158, 172
Thomas Gorman 77, 112
Tiant, Luis 61, 99
Tigers, Detroit 8–9
Tillikums, Seattle 5
Timberlake, Gary 68, 71
Tittle, Y.A. 16
Torrance, Roscoe 7
Torres, Hector 12
Tovar, Cesar 82–84, 119
Tresh, Tom 47, 50
Turks, Seattle 5

Uhlaender, Ted 84, 119
Uhlman, Mayor Wes 130

Valdespino, Sandy 107, 164
Velez, Otto 166
Vidal, Jose 52
Volinn, Sidney 132

Walker, Harry 162
Walton, Danny 107, 109, 111–112, 114–116, 119–120, 124–125, 131, 164
Ward, Pete 32, 74
Watt, Eddie 106
Weaver, Earl 58, 62, 171
Wert, Don 107
Whitaker, Steve 25–26, 43, 45, 60–62, 69, 111, 114, 119, 122–123
White, Roy 109
White Sox, Chicago 10
Williams, Billy 101
Williams, Stan 99
Williams, Ted 160, 172
Wilson, Art 9
Wilson, Earl 58, 62, 171
Wood, Wilber 11, 72–73, 75
Woomack, Dooley 105–106, 109, 120, 162
World's Fair 14
Wynne, Billy 67, 117

Yastrzemski, Carl 16, 51, 89, 91, 97

Ziegel, Vic 65

www.ingramcontent.com/pod-product-compliance
Ingram Content Group UK Ltd.
Pitfield, Milton Keynes, MK11 3LW, UK
UKHW042009140426
5217IPUK00015B/1068